# Contents

**boundary 2**
an international journal of literature and culture

**Founding Editor**  William V. Spanos

**Editor**  Paul A. Bové

**Review Editor**  Daniel O'Hara

**Managing Editor**  Margaret A. Havran

**Editorial Collective**
Jonathan Arac, Columbia University
Paul A. Bové, University of Pittsburgh
Joseph A. Buttigieg, University of Notre Dame
Terry Cochran, University of Montreal
Michael Hays, Soka University of America
Ronald A. T. Judy, University of Pittsburgh
Marcia Landy, University of Pittsburgh
Aamir R. Mufti, University of California, Los Angeles
Daniel O'Hara, Temple University
Donald E. Pease, Dartmouth College
William V. Spanos, SUNY at Binghamton

**Editorial Board**
Charles Bernstein, University of Pennsylvania
Rey Chow, Brown University
Arif Dirlik, University of Oregon
Margaret Ferguson, University of California, Davis
Wlad Godzich, University of California, Santa Cruz
Stuart Hall, Open University, U.K.
Fredric Jameson, Duke University
Karl Kroeber, Columbia University
Masao Miyoshi, University of California, San Diego
Edward W. Said, Columbia University
Hortense Spillers, Cornell University
Gayatri Spivak, Columbia University
Cornel West, Harvard University

**Advisory Editors**
John Beverley, University of Pittsburgh
Eric Clarke, University of Pittsburgh
Christopher L. Connery, University of California, Santa Cruz
Kathryne V. Lindberg, Wayne State University
Jim Merod, BluePort Sound Archive, La Costa, Calif.
R. Radhakrishnan, University of Massachusetts, Amherst
Bruce Robbins, Columbia University
Lindsay Waters, Harvard University Press
Rob Wilson, University of California, Santa Cruz

**Corresponding Editors**
Jenaro Talens, University of Geneva, Switzerland; University of Valencia, Spain
Q. S. Tong, University of Hong Kong

# Ralph Ellison: The Next Fifty Years

*Ronald A. T. Judy*

When Jonathan Arac and I sat down in my dining room four years ago in July 1999—at his strong suggestion, I must say—we could have and perhaps dared to imagine much of what was to transpire in the imminent future of the world, particularly in the two months just prior to the November 2001 conference we were planning. That July dining room discussion was a moment in a continuing, albeit sporadic, conversation about Ralph Ellison that Jonathan and I had been having for some years since I first came to the University of Pittsburgh in 1993. Over time, the focus of our conversation became the significance of Ellison's work in the formation of American intelligence during the postwar period just after the Second World War.

"The formation of American intelligence during the postwar period." How absurd that phrase sounds today, and so appropriately American in its absurdity. An absurdity whose import is aptly articulated in the mercurial consolidation in the last five years of the past century of Ralph Ellison's stature as a novelist and essayist. Evidence of this was to be found in the 1993 *New Yorker* profile commemorating Ellison's eightieth birthday, and in the 1995 publication of the Modern Library *Collected Essays*. The cul-

*boundary 2* 30:2, 2003. Copyright © 2003 by Duke University Press.

minating event was the posthumous publication of his novel-in-progress, *Juneteenth*, in May 1999, with its attendant controversy initiated in the *New York Times Magazine* and carried on in the pages of the *New Republic* throughout that summer. In varying ways and degrees, all the spent ink and paper recalled that Ellison's thought and unwavering attention was on how expression, most pointedly for him *literary* expression, exhibited not only the history of our situation but its possibilities as well. As Ellison remarked in numerous moments in the last book of his essays to be published before his death in 1989, *Going to the Territory* (1986), expression is history. At certain points—"A Very Stern Discipline," for instance—his conception of expression is mythic. But myth is not to be understood as the antipode of truth—they are really unrelated to one another. Rather it is the marriage of the image—Ellison refers to the musical and the oral heroic image—and the novel. In this sense, the novel as myth is the antipode to the potentially fatal depictions of sociology—the too great dependence on which for presenting reality Ellison explicitly cites as a dominant factor in the demise of art's social function. In retrospect, it is now clear that Ellison was not only author of one of the most celebrated English-language North American novels of this century, *Invisible Man*, but he was also one of the major American intellectuals of the middle and later twentieth century. Indeed, his numerous essays and occasional papers exhibit a subtle and rigorous mind, whose attempts to theorize America in relation to the Negro and literary expression offer valuable insight into how we might understand the current association of "America" with what is at times now called "globality."

Among the numerous questions Ellison's work provokes is that of how to think about the historical problematics of art. A central aspect of his undertaking that task was his formation as a student of music—an area of his thinking that has yet to be adequately attended to. There are, of course, many references to Ellison's practice of "writing by riffing." Yet there is much more to learn from his exchanges with Kenneth Burke and Stanley Edgar Hyman on the issues of symbolic expression, entelechy, and the relationship between singular forms of musical expression and historical ways of thinking. Although not a systematic philosophy of music, Ellison's work with and on music exhibits the sort of seriousness and rigor commonly associated with the writings on music of Theodor Adorno and Edward Said, and has significantly informed the current received conception of the blues—a point from which Albert Murray does not shy away. And then there is the way Ellison's work engages such other questions as the nature of the connection between the novel and the democratic mind, the problematic of modernism and freedom, Vietnam and the crisis of liberal society, and even the "epistemology" of aesthetics.

These issues and more were the foci of Jonathan's and my conversation. As is the habit of scholarly minds, we suffered a bit of obsession about them, and thought what better way to blast open and so make the most of that obsession than to seek out and find those with whom we could share it. This seemed the logical thing to do. So we quickly drew up a list of likely minds, with the ambition that they be planetary in scope, for a special issue of *boundary 2* on Ellison's thinking and work. The idea was to get them to write copiously about Ellisonian speculation on America. What we sought were not essays that venerate Ellison but essays that take up any of the various issues present in his work, that think along with and/or against his work. Our wish was to treat his writing not as an object but as a resource, or catalyst, for attending to the problematics and concerns of life in the world as we know it.

Our colleagues in the editorial collective of the journal liked the idea, charging us to deliver the goods in a timely manner. What better way to get our prospective contributors to deliver a workable draft, we thought, than to have the deadline for it coincide with a conference at which they would present their work and benefit from collegial exchange on it? The event of the conference, "Ralph Ellison: The Next Fifty Years," took place 2–3 November 2001 at the University of Pittsburgh, thanks in large measure to the generous support of the dean of the Faculty of Arts and Science, N. John Cooper; the Office of the Provost, particularly the vice provost for Academic Affairs, Jack Daniel; the dean of the Honors College, Alec Stewart; and the director of the Graduate Program in Cultural Studies, Nancy Condee. The papers presented were outstanding in their thought and scholarship, as was the ensuing collective conversation, which promised to provoke some challenging ways of thinking. By that measure, the conference was as successful as we had hoped. In the end, circumstances drew out the editorial work, and the results, finished as they are, you, dear reader, presently hold in your hands. The initial plan was to publish the special issue of *boundary 2* on Ellison in the fall of 2002, coincidental with the fiftieth anniversary of the publication of *Invisible Man*. Unfortunately, production matters related to other issues of the journal required that we postpone publication until the summer of 2003. Whether the promise of the provocation to thinking has been realized in this special issue of *boundary 2*, *Ralph Ellison: The Next Fifty Years*, you will have to judge for yourself.

In closing, I wish to thank all the contributors to this issue for the care with which they prepared their conference papers and the patience with which they endured the editorial process. I also thank Margaret A. Havran (Meg), managing editor of *boundary 2*, for her characteristic professionalism and truly sterling work in bringing this and every other issue of the journal to completion.

13 February 2003
Pittsburgh, Pennsylvania

# "The Little Man at Chehaw Station" Today

*Hortense J. Spillers*

It would not be an exaggeration to say that I have known something about the "little man at Chehaw Station" virtually all my life. When I first heard Ellison's title, some years ago now, the faintest tremor of recognition came home in the sound of "Chehaw" as that of some ancient feel of a place that I could not grasp with any degree of accuracy. But the very uncanniness of it, the obscurely veiled identity that would not come clear unless dredged up from the bottom, said to me that memory might, in fact, believe before knowing. It turns out that sometime after my third birthday, my eldest sibling, my sister Theaster, went away to college at Tuskegee Institute (as it was called then), and the train she boarded—which event marks my first trauma—the "City of New Orleans" out of Memphis's Union Station, had, among its stops, Chehaw, from which terminus she would travel by car to the campus. If the loss of my sister to adulthood registers as a first memory, as the dawning consciousness of apartness, then the lesion that inscribes it will be forever linked in my mind to travel and the radical transition that sharpens the distance between "home" and "the world." Perhaps I could say, then, that Ellison's "little man," by way of Chehaw, demarcates the border between

*boundary 2* 30:2, 2003. Copyright © 2003 by Duke University Press.

the known and the unknown, the familiar and the distant, or the near and far, and, consequently, the intimate and the antipathetic. I would learn, *precisely* in *time*, that these apparent differences could not only coexist on parallel planes but belong to the at-oneness of any simultaneous contradictory moment. There is, then, a *narrative* accompaniment to my reception of Ellison's *conceptual* itinerary so powerfully pursued in "The Little Man at Chehaw Station," and whatever wisdom might be engendered by the former might help us to remap the stakes that are involved today in considerations of the latter—in other words, the work of Ellison's essay improves our understanding of what is now called the "identitarian." How it does so provides the work of this one.

· · · ·

Fittingly, this classic essay begins with its own narrative of disappointment, youth, and the riddle of the tall tale aptly put up by the mentor to an uninitiated.[1] To that extent, it is recalled, years later, on two counts—first, three years after the source event, when Ellison the youth is collecting signatures for his assignment with the Federal Writers' Project during the 1930s, then again, four decades later, when Ellison the elder is advancing a degree of possession concerning his destiny. As an icon of division between two temporal stops, one of them marked *before* Chehaw Station, the other one, *after* Chehaw, so that the telos of the latter date becomes, in fact, the 1977 essay, which I first read in the pages of the *American Scholar*, "The Little Man" participates in a degree of optimism about American democracy that is far more difficult to sustain at present. Published less than twenty years before his death in 1994, this essay may be thought of as signatural Ellison—the high moral seriousness, conceptual elegance, and, above all, the staunch conviction of American "exceptionalism." It may seem frivolous to note that Ellison uses *America* throughout the essay rather than *the United States*, but it is crucial, I believe, to the ideological context of all his essays to understand the import of *America*, because *America*, for Ellison, is quite a lot more than the nation-state entity called *the United States*. To get the right emphasis, we would need to recall the Democratic sublime of Whitman

---

1. Ralph Ellison, *The Collected Essays of Ralph Ellison*, edited and with an introduction by John F. Callahan, preface by Saul Bellow (New York: Modern Library, 1995); *Going to the Territory*, "The Little Man at Chehaw Station: The American Artist and His Audience," 489–519. Subsequent quotations come from this source; page numbers are cited parenthetically in the text.

and Emerson and the sweeping "architectonics" of Hart Crane and William Carlos Williams, for Ellison is working this awesome ground as late as 1977 and in the aftermath of the genuine crisis of leadership that breaks over the republic of the United States in the heartrending misstep of Vietnam. But from the point of view of this essay, none of that ever happened, just as, strikingly, Richard Nixon and Watergate did not, though the essay is scored by the eventualities of "Black Power," and the vision of "America" as the sublime *possibility* (a keyword in Ellison) in human becoming is as decidedly assured as it had always been for the lad in the prize writer who was born when Oklahoma was young. In other words, that *gleam* in his eye for the *idea* of America stayed steady, yet it is clear that Ralph Waldo Ellison was no naïf, nor was he blind to certain failures of the republic. If *paradox* has a term of agency—as in *paradoxicalist*—then we might as well assign Ellison to its precincts.

The paradoxicalist takes the bitter with the sweet, as we remember that invisible man "loves" and "hates" at the same time. Confronting, then, the bare blues of the American symphony, Ellison is flexed between what is and what *might* be, fundamentally wed to the notion that "one fine morning . . ."—though it will likely fructify no time soon. Before rereading the essay on the occasion of this writing, I tried to recall further what might have prompted Ellison to write "The Little Man" the way he did, when the answer is not far to seek. Poised in the midst of the essay, Ellison's report on the status of the "melting pot" assumes shape around the question of ethnicity: "So today," he begins this passage, "before the glaring inequities, unfulfilled promises and rich possibilities of democracy . . . we hear heady evocations of European, African, and Asian backgrounds accompanied by chants proclaiming the inviolability of ancestral blood" (504–5). Ellison points out that "blood magic" and "blood thinking" were at the time "rampant among us, often leading to brutal racial assaults in areas where these seldom occurred before" (505). But Ellison is also right to suggest that these "bloods" are "never really dormant in American society," so that whatever we were in 1977–78 is not so alien and unrecognizable to ourselves now. It is notable, however, that the late 1970s mark approximately the tenth anniversary of a number of Black Studies installations across the United States and might be thought of as the initial moments of maturity, expressed in the scholarship and writing devoted to a transformed curricular protocol, in the development of these regimes. Ellison's essay is written, then, against the backdrop of these changes, or we should say that this is the backdrop that he is choosing to see, and while he does not explicitly address these punctualities, they nevertheless substantially reside in the margins of this writing. And what Ellison poses as their countermand, as the counternarrative that would reprise the efficacy of the figural resources of the "melting pot," is nothing less than a pluralist democracy. As substantial as a rock, yet no more tactile than the rhetorical strategies of a Whitman or an Emerson, or the "symbolic action" of a Kenneth Burke (who emerges here and elsewhere in Ellison as a heroic intellectual figure), this Ellisonian "woe and wonder" is meant to replicate the creative intensity that shimmers across the logological project, here displaced, as American exceptionalism would have it, onto the new ground of this "nation of nations," this "culture of cultures" (512). He writes, "The rock, the terrain upon which we struggle, is itself abstract, a terrain of ideas that, although man-made, exerts the compelling force of the ideal, of the sublime: ideas that draw their power from the Declaration of Independence, the Constitution, and the Bill of Rights" (501). If we are united, as Ellison's pluralist mandate contends, then it is "in the name of these sacred principles" (501).

In the aftermath of a regnant reactionism, which would blossom over the United States following the Carter years, we could not have anticipated then what would later mature as the utterly unthinkable, and that is to say, how aspects of the very argument that Ellison deploys in relationship to his "sacred principles" would be recuperated in *opposition* to strategies of racial equality, to wit, affirmative action practices in American higher education. That the efforts put forth to redress a century of "benign neglect" and the state's outright complicity with the disciplinary regimes of violence and injustice could be turned upside down and inside out—so that the California Civil Rights Initiative of the 1990s, for example, exactly opposed what such an "initiative" might have meant in 1965—goes far to explain the considerable difference of perspective interposed between the era of "The Little Man at Chehaw Station" and that of the early twenty-first century. But we can usually count on Ellison to forestall (and surprise) the most facile of appropriative moves by weaving complications into his conceptual repertoire. In effect, Ellison is not talking about the same thing at all that a Bill Bennett or even an Arthur Schlesinger Jr. would recognize, say nothing of endorse, and it is that element of whimsical surprise, of the serendipitous twist in nuance, that would bring Ellison into communication with the current scene of theoretical debate.

Into this heady eclectic mix, Ellison's "sacred principles" have truck with the lexis of "mystery," the *democratic* "mystery," with the "rites of symbolic sacrifice" and their "cabalistic code words" in relationship to "victims" and "scapegoats," so that these ritual terms, dispersed across the terrain of

Ellison's inquiry, bring the latter in alignment with a cast of violence and the sacred, which certain critics of modernity, Freud eminent among them, have postulated as the foundation stone of human society. And to that extent, I believe, the Ellisonian version of the Democratic sublime is not simply an "Americanness" writ large but may be read as the futuristic dimension of a human order exhausted by the practices and presumptions of hierarchy, or rigid social order, and the necessity of tradition, in which case predictability and sameness yield to the death-pall of the static. We could say, then, that Ellison's democratic vistas, which give "The Little Man" its unrelenting lucidity, demarcate the future of the world, not untroubled by contention and the dark side of the paradisiacal promise, which come all the way home in the American present. This "now," because it is fluid, labile, contingent, open, improvisational, ever new, and without pause, is new time, whose representative figure, in its anonymous invisibility, cannot be represented at all; the "little man" is a type of "invisible man," unprecedented and unlocatable, though this address to "him" travels through the terminus of Chehaw: This unlikely small place on point between north- and southbound trains bears the stove warmer, who has come to symbolize nothing less, Ellison argues, "than the enigma of aesthetic communication in American democracy" (492).

The Ellisonian reflux and revision of reference, which lends *Invisible Man* its persistent citation (and subsequent siting) on an allusive plurality, create, in the essay, a layered narrative surface. Here is the source story: A young Ellison, perhaps in his sophomore year at Tuskegee, has ambitions to become a classical composer. A student of the trumpet in Tuskegee's music department, he must perform, as one of the requirements of the formation, a monthly recital before the music faculty. On the occasion that has invited the harshest of criticism from his teachers—the protagonist reports that he has "outraged" them—Ellison attempts to substitute "a certain skill of lips and fingers for the intelligent and artistic structuring of emotion that was demanded in performing the music assigned to [him]." Having fled to Hazel Harrison, the piano teacher, for "solace," he is, instead, given another lick: ". . . in this country you must always prepare yourself to play your very best wherever you are, and on all occasions" (489). It is not simply a matter of heeding the proverbial wisdom that one must do, look, and be his best, but inasmuch as Ellison is "becoming a musician, an artist," performing classical music in this country, he is enjoined to "*always* play [his] best, even if it's only in the waiting room at Chehaw Station, because in this country there'll always be a little man hidden behind the stove." And what is more, he will "know the *music*, and the *tradition*, and the standards of *musicianship* required for whatever you set out to perform" (490; Ellison's emphasis). Ellison is hardly prepared to anticipate that so "lonely a whistlestop where swift north- or southbound trains paused with haughty impatience to drop off or take on passengers" might evince so enigmatic a response, because there is nothing in itself, or its accoutrements, that would designate the investment of authority in it or lend it the least significance for anyone; we can well imagine the protagonist's sophomoric disdain. But deliberately homespun and mythically weighted at once, this droll and unseen creature will expand in Ellison's imagination into the heuristic device that comes to metaphorize what he calls the democratic "mystery"—the "little man" who draws from the "uncodified *Americanness* of his experience, whether of life or of art, as he engages in a silent dialogue with the artist's exposition of forms, offering or rejecting the work of art on the basis of what he feels to be its affirmation or distortion of American experience" (492). This "threat to social order, and a reminder of the unfinished details of this powerful nation" (493), the "little man" evidences a "'social mobility of intellect and taste,'" and while his "knowingness" is "unaccountable," the "little man" points to "our neglect of serious cultural introspection, our failure to conceive of our fractured, vernacular-weighted culture as an intricate whole" (494). This parodic farrago of image, narrative, and idea would suggest that "even the most homogeneous audiences are culturally mixed and embody, in their relative anonymity, the mystery of American cultural identity" (494–95). But it also signals that the game of culture is not "the exclusive property of a highly visible elite" (495).

Thus, the "little man" takes us back through the tortionary reflexes of paradoxical movement that so distinguishes *Invisible Man* as a black novel that speaks "on the lower frequencies" not only for the possibilities of American narrative art in a postindustrial, even computer-laden, punctuality (for this "ideal level of sensibility to which the American artist would address himself," elusively hinted in notions of a little man in a machine/instrument, works like "the memory registers of certain computer systems," insofar as "it is simultaneously accessible at any point in American society" [495]) but also for the larger critical postures that anticipate a global belonging. We should make no mistake here—Ellison viewed himself and his project as *American*, first and last, and did not flinch, either, from the conceptual and affective range of articulations that we could call the "American Negro." (I distinctly remember a student dinner, sponsored by black students at Brandeis University during the winter of 1969, when Ellison, skewered by young radicals for an insufficient demonstration of "blackness," made the table eat those words; in short, he needed no lectures—this prickly personality—from folk who had just discovered their "beauty" that morning.) But Ellison apparently believed, as his writings attest, that black culture was robust enough to be at home anywhere in the world, or, moreover, pliable and robust enough to bring the world to it. It is the latter possibility, I believe, that the latter-day revolutionaries missed, just as it is the subtle dimension of critique that the current schools of "anti-essentialism" have not fathomed.

Not unlike the moves that sustain *Invisible Man*, "The Little Man at Chehaw Station" keeps up good tension between the expository, the conceptual/theoretical, the heuristic, and the narrative elements of this articulation, proffered late in the Ellisonian repertoire; it strikes me that less than thirty years later, it is not imaginable that an essay like this one, in its liberal democratic urges, is *writable*, due in part to an intellectual infrastructure that the nation has allowed to rot and the abject failures of American democracy to move steadily along the path of progressive practice, as well as the unchallenged dominance of right-wing ideas. In effect, the reading space to which this essay is aimed—a space reserved for an urbane "common reader," as Virginia Woolf might have called her—has all but dried up, replaced by the tendentious screed, or the esoteric scrutiny, that confines the poststructuralist project to a limited, rather predictable (and narcissistic) alignment of interests. To that extent, the "little man" essay appears to belong to the tenors and tonalities of the essays in *Shadow and Act*, collected early in the previous decade, in its humanistic ambitions and its implicitly stated appeals to the most generous work and the widest possible applications of the meaning of literacy. I have no idea what appears in the pages of the *American Scholar* today (since my subscription to it lapsed some time ago), but I would not be surprised in the least if its content is never anywhere near the imaginative force, the prehensile intelligence, and the clear-eyed democratic optimism that energize "The Little Man at Chehaw Station," and I would regard such an outcome as analogous to the loss of limb. We could, in fact, gauge rather precisely what we have lost between the consequential Reagan era, instaurated three years after the publication of the essay, and the present—marked 091101. If we regard the United States as a nation called to being in the Word (which argument Ellison advances), then where is the Word, and what is it now?

In 1977, it was at play in the field of signifiers: Ellison, as we recognize from our familiarity with *Invisible Man*, proceeds through a series of dialogic initiatives to intrude the uncustomary on a scene of more familiar targets and objects—starting with Hazel Harrison herself, who poses the riddle of the "little man." The contingent and the improbable, the improvisatory and the unexpected, commingle and cavort with the seasoned facets of the vernacular in a complex Ellisonian ballet—for example, Harrison, with her autographed copy of a Prokofiev score, had been living in Berlin as a piano student of Ferrucio Busoni but was driven out of Germany with the rise of the Third Reich. Here the haunting "blues-echoing, train-whistle rhapsodies," associated with the express trains, are imagined against the canons and practices of European orchestral music, and it is proper that both idioms are accessible to Harrison's parlor, since Tuskegee itself was the locus, Ellison tells us, of a "rich musical tradition, both classical and folk" (490). This weave of styles, codes, discourses, and traditions of art is the bedrock on which Ellison's radical rehauling and rereading of a two-way ancestral imperative is predicated, for "America's social mobility, its universal education, and its relative freedom of cultural information" (493) move counter at every point to fixed notions of social hierarchy and the segregation of culture. The "random" (and therefore unpredictable) accessibility to eclectic cultural information would suggest that a Liszt rhapsody is as open to an appropriation by the citizens of Macon County, Alabama, as the vaunted harmonica and guitar of the traveling bluesman. For Ellison, this unpredictability of the random breaks through the class and economic restrictions that would place these objects of attention on either side of a *cordon sanitaire* of the arts. That these implements of pleasure and self-fashioning belong to Ellison's Everyman— the anonymous invisibility of place—conjures with power-in-dispersal, but Ellison would say that that is the democratic idea.

The dialogic culture that Ellison would evoke poses, out of its pluralness, a unity, but this "unity" is riddled with, is pocked over, by what appears to resolve the stalemate of the undecidable, and that is the "negative capability" (to borrow from an older synthesis) of a usable paradox. This "culture of cultures" is, as he describes it, "fractured and vernacular-weighted" (494). But it seems that there is a layer of complexity here beyond the logic of "e pluribus unum," insofar as the latter elides the many and the one so much so that the "many" disappears into the other of the "one" and is eventually jettisoned anyway. But Ellison's cultural identity is quite deliberately *confusing* because it is "tentative, controversial, constantly changing" (495). It is a kind of patchwork, an instantaneous bricolage, insofar as it folds "connoisseur, critic, trickster," Brer Rabbit, and the brier patch in semantic proximity; the master of cultural incongruity, this "he," "day-coach, cabin-class traveler," takes on the willfulness of the mythical rabbit in his ability to convert "even the most decorous of audiences into his own brier patch and temper the chilliest of classics to his own vernacular taste" (496). Both in and of the artist and the audience, the little man's very travel is contradictory to the degree that he moves all around—through material scenes—yet *nowhere*, having all the quotients of cultural and symbolic capital travel through him. Classics, tall tales, and jazz "without frills" all adhere, or more exactly, *converge*, and if Ellison's "little man" is no man we know, yet no matter: because this essay, in celebrating the logic of negation, banks on the future, which, of course, never quite arrives as an accomplished event. But it comes about as the thing that the culture works on; it is praxis, with all the drawbacks and regressions of the everyday, because it is the ideal. Ellison speaks of the latter as a "mystery," and the "mystery" is nothing less than the signifying element that negotiates between the real and the ideal. Ubiquitous, underground and outside, inside and outside, the "little man" takes hold of a "larger truth in which the high and the lowly, the known and the unrecognized, the comic and the tragic are woven into the American skein" (499). Ellison goes so far as to contend that the "ideal of cultivated democratic sensibility" is metaphorized in the "little man" and the unaccounted for place that he claims: As a point of arrival and departure, the Chehaw terminus might be thought of as a kind of paradigm for a global concourse, because a "wide diversity of tastes and styles of living" traverse it. If philanthropists, businessmen, sharecroppers, students, and artistic types all cross it, then Chehaw, analogously, functions like Carnegie Hall and the Metropolitan Museum, because all three loci now are "meeting places for motley mixtures of people." They are, indeed, "juncture points for random assemblies of sensibilities." Just so, American democracy, as possibility, and in its dispersion of cultural information, inscribes "a collectivity of styles, tastes, and traditions" (500). If the essay can be brought down to a fine point, then it is this broad expanse of the American cultural scene that Ellison wants to drive home in a dazzling array of referentiality.

I should like to bring this recapitulation of the essay itself to a finish by surveying a model of civic burlesque, which figuration Ellison advances in complement to the main inquiry of the essay. It is interpolated at the end of the closing segment of the essay and describes a situation that has provoked foul language, emanating from another "small, ranksmelling room" (517), where four black coal porters are debating the merits of Metropolitan Opera divas. Young Ellison is looking for signatures in this building, the work described earlier in this essay, as he finds an apt first use for Hazel Harrison's riddle in the ill fit between location and content. *How* the coal

porters are saying does not match *what* they are saying, and the protagonist, initially reluctant to even knock on the door, given what he is hearing behind it, is quite shocked to discover what is at stake in this verbal
melee. Here they were, "proclaiming an intimate familiarity with a subject
of which, by all the logic of their linguistically projected social status, they
should have been oblivious" (515–16). The subject of contention in this case
"confounded all [his] assumptions regarding the correlation between educational levels, class, race and the possession of conscious culture" (516).
After much ado, in which case Ellison must penetrate the scene—explain
his unbidden presence to a bunch of ruffians not interested in the least in
his dumb survey—he lays the "mystery" to rest: Keeping their "day jobs,"
as it were, these "Egyptians," by night, are Met supernumeraries. And so,
they "were products of both past *and* present; were both coal heavers *and*
Met extras; were both workingmen *and* opera buffs" (519; my emphasis).
What else is this *but* unexpected knowledge, materializing "at the depth of
the American social hierarchy, and, of all possible hiding places, behind a
coal pile" (519), and doesn't this scene "change the joke and slip the yoke"?[2]
The scaffolding of this many-faceted writing, then, rests on story and par-
able, always in tension here with its own theory; if, in Ellison's case, the
latter is leaving room for the grotesque and the unimaginable that surface
on the street as the smooth relay of kinetic and discursive gesture, then
so be it, because the Ellisonian theory of culture is anything but homogeneous and single layered. In fact, we might think of it as an expression of
the impure: A light-skinned, blue-eyed black man *appears* one sunny afternoon on Riverside Drive, near 51st, where he "disrupted," we are told, "the
visual peace of the promenading throng by racing up in a shiny new blue
Volkswagen Beetle decked out with a gleaming Rolls-Royce radiator" (505).
There is more to this shocking irruption, because the man himself, already
the hybridistic, cross-racial cut of an African-Americanity, proceeds to parody the notion by adding layers of visual bombardment to his own free-
wheeling, self-exacting "crisis of degree"—as tall as a professional basket-
ball player, this personality emerges from this Friedrich Porsche invention
"with something of that magical cornucopian combustion by which a dozen
circus clowns are exploded from an even more miniaturized automobile"
(505–6). His costume perfectly complements the moment, though it would
be more precise to say that the moment is conjured up in the most unlikely

2. The title of one of Ellison's essays that appears in *Shadow and Act*, the essay is incorporated in the Callahan edition, *The Collected Essays of Ralph Ellison*, 100–113.

stylistic punctuations: black riding boots, fawn-colored riding breeches "of English tailoring," leather riding crop, and a "dashy dashiki," while six feet, six inches above his heels, "a black homburg sits tilted at a jaunty angle atop a crest of [Afro-coiffed hair]" (506).

While there is in this fabula of the costume and the gesture an element of hyperbolic staging, perhaps even more than a hint of the grotesque, we should try to hold it in mind at once as an illustrative sequence whose features cannot be squared, even as we take it in. But the force of the apparition, if we could say so, is precisely its *impossibility* as a *possibility* in the comic clash of styles, but also in its formal improvisation, in its "willful juxtaposition of modes" (507).

At every turn of the essay, culture is pursued as *processual* rather than static; dynamic, even restless, over and against closed or poised. In trying to figure out how to fashion a protocol in response to recent theoretical developments in the culture field, I should like to offer the "little man" as a resource, although the very fact that Ellison was a black writer would, for some theoreticians, make an appropriation of the figure suspect. I am referring primarily to what I would call the "anti-essentialist school" of culture critique, which links what is marked as "essentialism" to the thematics of "identity." In attempting to "identify" the origins of its vocabulary—the sites of its keywords—I see the problem apparently disappearing into the dense tangle of epistemologies that converge on modern philosophy, from Hegel to Heidegger[3] to Sartre, especially the "essence/existence" debate that characterized existentialist regimes more than four decades ago, and while I can do nothing more at this juncture than sketch the directions in which this protocol might take an investigator, the outline might yield, nevertheless, useful clues for the future; these epistemic pathways, rerouted through modes of critico-theoretical inquiry since the 1960s, have led to important clarifications in the field of gender/sexuality studies (even to the subsumption of feminist critique under the latter), while they have tended to confuse the critique of "race" in ways that are not particularly helpful. To wit, instead of making a contribution to work on the ingenuities of *racism*, in its myriad of names, permutations, and configurations on both a global and local scale, the anti-essentialist school, first of all, reanimates a "raced subject," whatever that is, and quite apart from its own perceived location, and then arrogates its "find"

3. Paul A. Bové, *In the Wake of Theory* (Hanover, N.H.: University Press of New England, 1992). The opening chapter of Bové's work here is especially suggestive for the kind of protocol I am interested in pursuing.

as the leading exemplar of whatever logic set it in motion in the first place; in short, one is "raced" because he is "raced," which shows no significant gain, it seems to me, over the *objects* of racism. The anti-essentialist school, in its zeal to bring down the critique of "race," to *discipline* it (and for reasons we suspect we know all too well), which critique has been reanimated by historical events in all sectors of the globe in the aftermath of World War II, goes to work on subject matter that is evaporated and discredited, to boot, and that no one, as far as I can tell, seriously disputes today, and that is the "fact" of "race." However, I doubt that we will be able to argue now that phenotypic markers among human populations are not evident. The *only* question, now and then, that anti-essentialism can neither pose nor master is, What do they *mean*? Even if we decide that the meaning is fictional and fantastic, we will find no expulsion in the comfort of that thought from the *consequences* of it. And the question of *meaning*—an ethical one that is not put to rest by philosophical action, though it might be *informed* by it— is a *political* question, played out on the conflicted terrain of power getting and power sharing. "Anti-essentialism" is, therefore, an indictment; it is not an analysis. It is wed, however inadvertently, to the backward regimes of racialist practice that both *posit* racial difference and dare it at once. In that regard, subjects, from this vantage, are culpable rather than the systemic ascriptions that complement the orderly passage of human value. (Today's anti-essentialist school of critical practice looks rather like the Civil Rights Initiative of California Republicans that would "respect" the "intelligence" of black bachelor degree candidates, for example, by blocking their admission to Berkeley, say, since their presence there would mark an evidentiary corruption!)

How in the world did we reach this twisted course? Mimetic racism, as I would call it, repeats racism "unconsciously"—it takes over its presumptions, unexamined, whatever privileges accrue to it, "innocently," as a thing that is simply done. Less pointed than its parental ancestor, mimetic racism is no less lethal for all its kindlier countenance. If that were not so, then we would not be able to explain the actual fact that ontologies and epistemologies are still bonded in the U.S. academy, for example, and that the United States remains, perhaps, the most *intellectually* segregated site on the globe, with its lines of scholarship replicating its housing patterns and other zoning laws of sociality. While it would be inaccurate to deny that we have made considerable strides toward an integrated calculus of knowledge and culture on this site, we still live with at least the bureaucratic trappings of scientific division and, moreover, a division of intellectual labor that is demarcated by spheres of influence in "marked" and "unmarked" positions. Could we say, then, that the anti-essentialist critical move, in "identifying" with modes of authority (the supposedly anonymous cultural and racial location)—and one way we spot the authoritarian commitment is to watch it revealed in its politics of citation, for example—is the latest expression of the "identitarian"? What I expect we will discover is that the critique of "race" is misnamed as an "identity politics" and should be recognized instead as an openly assertive discursive practice with a political aim. Furthermore— and this is the real nut to be cracked—we have not exhausted the "identity" question by assigning it to an essentialist telos, because, as my hunch leads me to suspect, "identity" is not only far more complex than we are currently articulating it, but it is also partially, if not wholly, psychoanalytically staged and, as a result, "beyond" the reach of conscious mentation. Unless we are prepared to follow this hard labyrinth through its tortured course, then we will have to live with the ironic backlash of names (which the commercial sector does so well)—how, for example, a CD called the "Essential Barbra Streisand" might well end up in an anti-essentialist's den.

One of the latest systematic expressions of anti-essentialist claims is advanced in Walter Benn Michaels's *Our America*.[4] A study of contrastive racial and nationalist configurations articulate in progressive, nativist, and modernist American writers, *Our America* surveys selective instances of literary development during the 1920s, inclusive of Faulkner, Hemingway, Cather, Fitzgerald, and William Carlos Williams, among them, as well as a few practitioners of the Harlem Renaissance. But the closing segments of the work, in switching frames from imaginative writers to social theorists and anthropologists, lend the effect of sweeping up vastly divergent rhetorical and discursive aims into the same overwhelming motivation. And even though Michaels asserts that "identity" constitutes the "determining ground of action or significance" in Faulkner's *Sound and the Fury* (1), it seems that the spores of this trail of argument hound these pages from first to last, where the scene suddenly shifts to the contemporary stagings of pluralism. But we might suppose that if it is possible for Michaels to contend early on that Faulkner's "linguistic fantasy" would "naturalize" the sign, when, if anything, the linguistic element in Faulkner (of all people, I should think!) is brazenly committed to symptoms of the "non-natural" (5), then we should not be the least bit surprised that "[t]he modern concept of culture is not . . . a

4. Walter Benn Michaels, *Our America: Nativism, Modernism, and Pluralism* (Durham, N.C.: Duke University Press, 1995). Subsequent quotations come from this source; page numbers are cited parenthetically in the text.

critique of racism; it is a form of racism" (129). Furthermore, "[t]ransforming the question of whether or not there is such a thing as *individual racial identity* into the question of whether or not race is an 'essence' and thus deploying race as the grounds of the question rather than as its object, this debate reinvigorates and relegitimates race as a category of analysis" (134–35; my emphasis). As far as I can tell, African American culture critique, for example, within the American context, has not debated "race" as an "essence" of individuals or social formations in a century of discursive struggle, and from Du Bois on (with exceptions in the Afrocentric outline), the question has come to focus on culture as praxis, in which event "race" as ground is, in fact, destabilized. But this argument is interested not in distinctions but, rather, in wholesale indictments that would render any deployment of "race," even attempts to dismantle its efficacies, racist still. Even culture as praxis does not take us to new ground, Michaels goes on, since the critique of "race" (by way of Edward Sapir) is "actually the continuation of race through culture" (122). Otherwise, "cultural identity" "makes no sense" (142). By that logic, is *Our America* racist and identitarian? If the only exit strategy from "race" or "culture," or "race" *and* "culture," or even "culture" instead of "race," is not to *name* it, then I see no reason why Michaels and his project would manage an escape, because surely he cannot believe he means that his argument has achieved an Archimedean point "outside" or "beyond" the questions that he presumes to have dissolved?

What I find missing in projects like Michaels's and other manifestations of "anti-essentialism," which *mimic* deconstructive reading procedures but orchestrate the cognitive object onto the most simple-minded and reductive ground—Indian drumming, "leaving" "culture," "returning" to it, whether or not I "do" as my mother, etc.—is a dialogical dimension of cultural practice that would actually try to locate material, historical, social, discursive, and psychoanalytic facets of human activity in time and space; in other words, we attempt to understand culture in its *layered presents*, inasmuch as the speaking subjects are "caught" being born everyday, which describes the transformative project, as well as in the act of continuity, which, in its minutiae, is neither predictable nor always momentous. *Subjectness*, which emerges in culture, is the predicament of ignorance—toward the future, which I cannot yet fathom; out of the past, whose "identities" are only partially known to me, insofar as I have reinvented and "telescoped" what I know. For the anti-essentialists, culture is only a myth, a stillness of posture that indeed imagines culture as a stop sign. But it is in the play of these constantly revealed moments between the continuous and the discontinuous of social being that culture arises as a particular signature of invention: Some people live in igloos, quite a few others do not, but in any case, something is *made* with the ready-to-hand, something that is new on the landscape, or new enough. It is as though the anti-essentialist school is working with anthropomorphic dummies—like the ones used in those automobile crash tests that measure stress points and fold into the windshield of the Lexus to strains of Beethoven. These cellular units, stripped of speech and desire, of clothing, even facial features, are really like no one we know, no one we might imagine in their robotic and precise choreographies. I am suggesting that any analysis of the cultural epiphenomena, in their overlap with racial configurations, and certainly the concept of culture itself, is virtually useless unless it confronts cultural practice, and practice is not simply what my mother does and whether or not I repeat it, but how a series of subjects come upon the materials and targets at hand in any given context; in that regard, "culture," which literally started its lexical career path with reference to cultivation of the ground, as Terry Eagleton outlines the problem in *The Idea of Culture*,[5] is the modulation that goes all the way through.

The fear of what is called "essentialism," an *ascription* of traits which acts have profound consequences, as we know, starts, perhaps, from a displaced fear of contamination and a paranoid eye for the impure against a pure that is never stated these days and for the stain of the particular. We should try to discover the rise and spread of this fear—over the last decade or so—in the realm of politics (and its discourses), among political subjects, who, in the newly emergent pluralist scene of the academy, compete and contend for prizes (money, honors, et cetera) unlike never before, and on the terrain of the psychoanalytic; its tenacity signals a new, cleaned-up racism among "minoritarian" and "majoritarian" subjects in a postmodern frame. It is, for sure, the attempt at a new instrumentalization and rationalization of hierarchy in the situating speaking subjects in relationship to a false object, perhaps even a phallic object, insofar as the latter would become a source of meaning. In other words, *why* the anti-essentialist school has emerged at this time, with exactly the same target populations as its ancestral parents', is far more significant, to my mind, than *what* it is saying, for what it is saying may well recover "business as usual" in a spanking new garb.

If anything, the "little man," in his unplanned-for interstitiality, is opposed to things as they are; in creating him, Ellison was attempting a capable act of imagination for what it means to live in contemporaneity, with the threat of the contingent. I think we can do no less today.

5. Terry Eagleton, *The Idea of Culture*, Blackwell Manifestos (Oxford: Blackwell Publishers, 2000).

# The Embrace of Entropy: Ralph Ellison and the Freedom Principle of Jazz Invisible

*Kevin Bell*

*For Lee Morgan and John Gilmore*

## 1. Space Music

Thinking within what the late avant-garde trumpeter Lester Bowie once termed an "outlaw" or "daredevil" musical logic that weaves into its own written body the incessant risk, indeed the promise, of its own structural devastation, the sonorous explorations of twentieth-century composer and tone scientist Sun Ra articulate a fiercely hygienic defense system against the contaminant orthodoxies of something still calling itself American "jazz."[1] This aesthetic risk, a symphonic formalizing of abyss, an arranging of tonally incongruous information and harmonic discontinuity that courses through

1. Lester Bowie, interview with Stephen Casmier, St. Louis University, 1992. In this exchange, Bowie's likening of the improvisational musician to the anthropomorphic paradigms of "the outlaw" and "the daredevil" addresses not simply the mark of the transgressive or illicit that was for decades a stereotypical signature of the representational categories imprisoning thought surrounding this music. It also suggests the qualities of surprise, fluidity, and mutation that are foregrounded in the structure and fabric of stronger musical articulations.

*boundary 2* 30:2, 2003. Copyright © 2003 by Duke University Press.

Ra's music in the material shapes of dissonant chordal voicings, stumbling or absent time signatures, and syncopated notational accents, is a reverberation of contingency and finitude inherited from elsewhere.

The structural abyss that distinguishes the work of Ra—and many others whose musical articulations get placed within the American musical districts ironically zoned as "free"—functions paradoxically as both an aesthetic signature of conceptual/performative singularity and as a disorienting repetition of philosophical/improvisatory intensities.[2] The paradox lies in the tension between the imperative to repeat antecedent structures and the necessity to do so in a way that expresses originality. It is a tension that cannot be adequately accounted for in terms of an anxiety of influence or Oedipal struggle, as it is so often described by a reductively smug American jazz journalism. The abyssal repetition materialized by such artists as Ra, Anthony Braxton, or Lester Bowie is only another movement in a chain that extends backward and forward at once, connecting the experimentations of Duke Ellington and Charlie Parker to the very future of Louis Armstrong in a relation of adjacency. It is not foreign to, or disconnected from, the stronger practices of something that certain ancestors such as Ellington and Parker were always hesitant to reductively designate or to arrest conceptually as "jazz."[3] This critical hesitation, in the face of cultural/linguistic imperatives toward designation and transparency, is itself a form of testimony. It is a silence that enunciates for each figure a resistance to his own obsolescence, an obsolescence that would be enacted in the moment of a self-ontologizing claim to creative agency or sovereignty. A claim that would constitute a humanizing counterviolence to the improvisation of improvisation, subordinating the aggression, movement, and color of the improvisational cut to the legitimating authority of the authorial subject and the empires of category and capital embodied in its naming.

Inverting the critical obsession with the "personality" and with the name, with the "schools" and categories of improvisational music that most improvisational musicians themselves abjure, this essay investigates the theoretical challenges of the "free," sometimes called "avant-garde," and perhaps most resonantly, the "out" or "outside" movements of American

2. See James Snead's seminal essay "Repetition as a Figure of Black Culture," in *Black Literature and Literary Theory*, ed. Henry Louis Gates Jr. (London: Methuen, 1984), 59–79.
3. For further elaboration of this critical reticence on the part of many musicians before the commercial pressure to define their aesthetic practices in terms of the rubric "jazz," see Duke Ellington, "Where Is Jazz Going?" in *The Duke Ellington Reader*, ed. Mark Tucker (Oxford and New York: Oxford University Press, 1993), 324–26.

jazz. For these movements, not unlike their historical idiomatic precursors, especially bebop, think and aspire toward a certain conceptual and performative freedom that is at philosophical variance with significant Enlightenment meditations on freedom. This critical swerve sounds itself perhaps most sharply in its performance of the abandonment of mandates of "proper" musical classification and indeed of "proper" performance itself. It is born in the relinquishing of an abstracted and idealized musical "subject" always already displaced by an irruptive and fluid sound of a new questioning, a new fascination. This sound is the abandonment of every perfected musical referent, positing, or "message" that would imply the logos of a transmitting maestro. In free jazz, such implication is jettisoned in favor of the contradictory and dissonant work of sonic research pursued by musical thinkers freeing themselves of premodern imperatives of meaning, valuation, and de-notation. In so doing, they also tend to free themselves of all critical and commercial visibility. They find their work, instead, within the textural materiality and color of thought, performance, and absolute risk in sound. Fashioning a new and improvisatory agency within the voided margins outside the framing confines of "identity," "history," or "genre." Investigation of such problems in the very thinking of art, of improvisation, and of freedom, particularly where jazz is concerned, must always return to the philosophical routes opened up "on the lower frequencies" by the writings of Ralph Ellison.

Both the questions of the improvisational and the free are central to the novelistic and critical work of Ellison, his apparent disdain for the nominal conjoining of the concepts in the term and practice of "free jazz" notwithstanding. Ellison is a pivotal theorist not only of improvisational music but also of intertwined problems of subjectivity, aesthetics, and politics. His work, particularly *Invisible Man*, is concerned ultimately with how these dimensions are inflected by varying, even contradictory, modalities or notions of the philosophical, which is to say, the *material* question of freedom. Not surprisingly, he has left some very curious traces.

Perhaps foremost among these is the apparent opposition between the artistic renunciation of closure, reconciliation, and the presumptive cultural obligation to perform identity, so relentlessly deconstructed by *Invisible Man*, a textual positioning of nonpositionality—juxtaposed against an aggressively doctrinaire and conservative stance taken in Ellison's critical essays against what he viewed as "chaotic," and even pathological, developments in American improvisational music. By his estimation, these developments constituted the abjection of "form," a diminution of feeling, a mere posture of detachment and false intellectualism. It is this contradictory spirit of Ellison that his friend Albert Murray is perhaps channeling, or perhaps simply repeating, when he angrily exclaims against free jazz that "art is supposed to be a bulwark against chaos."[4]

But this channeling suffers a disruption in its communicative frequency, an irrational breaking up of the analytic by the literary—for it is at the close of *Invisible Man* that we read also, "And the mind that has conceived a plan of living must never lose sight of the chaos against which that pattern was conceived."[5] Is this an admonition of the imagining of subjectivity itself as an ongoing interstitiality and therefore anything but an autonomous agency? A paradox in which the singularity of the never distant chaos is still inhabited by the form of the reactive, oppositional pattern, and simultaneously the inhabiting of that pattern by the trace of the chaos it can never completely abandon?[6] Does the passage suggest that certain, distanced measures of chaos (an oxymoron?) can be managed, and even converted into functionality? Or does it more forcefully envision the return of this viciously repressed chaos, the resurfacing of which so completely constitutes/conditions/compromises "our certainties"? Is it, in Ellison's words, the "coming out" of Louis Armstrong and the laughing imperative to "open the window and let the foul air out" (*IM*, 581)?

In asking such questions, I am also working a philosophical consideration of the so-called musical entropy rejected so forcefully by Ellison, Murray, and others. In considering the manner in which Ellison and Murray so ardently reject what they imagine to be musical nonsense, this essay draws attention to what is at stake for the work of art in their reaction. What is troublesome for them about free jazz is its withdrawal from a nationalist American rhetoric of freedom that is structured largely by terms of subjective autonomy, tradition, and entitlement. In contrast, free jazz concentrates on a marginalized vector of thinking about freedom that unfolds independently within rituals of experimental music from Armstrong to Ellington to Charlie Mingus to Ra and beyond. That unfolding bears a certain resemblance to currents within continental philosophy over the past century or so. Which is to say that free jazz traces the question of freedom in

---

4. Albert Murray, interviewed during Ken Burns's 2001 documentary film, *Jazz*, as broadcast on PBS, 2001.
5. Ralph Ellison, *Invisible Man* (New York: Vintage International, 1980), 580. Hereafter, this work is cited parenthetically as *IM*.
6. See Maurice Merleau-Ponty, *The Visible and the Invisible*, ed. Claude Lefort, trans. Alphonso Lingis (Evanston, Ill.: Northwestern University Press, 1968), 135–36.

a way that emphasizes problems of contingency, risk, and dependency, all of which undermine the Enlightenment identification of freedom with subjective autonomy. This is the same identification that is literarily undone in *Invisible Man*—only to return in Ellison's critical writings in the form of denunciations of post-Ellington/Basie jazz. In other words, the novelistic work of Ellison can be argued to set into literary and philosophical motion some of the vital creative impulses that propel the music of free jazz. This, while much of his critical work, and that of such associates as Murray, or such self-designated "inheritors" as Stanley Crouch, generates a certain neoconservative humanist rhetoric that has helped keep free jazz publicly trivialized, indeed, all but invisible, in the United States for more than four decades now.

Impossibility is improvisation's material, as well as its conceptual point of departure, as the avant-garde pianist Andrew Hill testifies in the title of his unusually popular ensemble album of 1964, *Point of Departure*. In the liner information, Hill notes the seemingly oxymoronic necessity to his compositions of harmonic structures that enable the constant movement of chordal centers, traditionally known as "grounding," or "home," points. "The harmony is such that one scale can fit the whole tune, so each musician can pick a tonal center for his solo within that scale."[7] This particular means of materializing fluidity and futurity within practices of writing and performance is but a renewal of an anterior principle of collective improvisational music, an exploratory, nomadic principle that asserts itself and shapes its contour exactly through such writerly methods of stepping into nonpositionality. The musical articulation of multiple and, therefore, *non*positionality— a sonic homelessness or decentering that still traces its own material and philosophical specificity—still sounds a homage to an unpresentable future that withdraws from its subjection to cultural mandates of determination, valuation, and category. This "unpresentable," this rejection of accepted smooth forms in favor of those more reflective of present uncertainty and urgency, is the very future into which Armstrong sends himself more than eighty years ago. In so doing, he follows the very aesthetic principle that prompts present-day scions of this thing called jazz to suggest openly that its "free" variant is precisely "without" principle.

Such "free" practices of structural dislocation as those thought and sounded in the music of Andrew Hill and others, practices that figure uncertainty and mobility into the fabric of composition and performance, offer this

7. Andrew Hill, quoted by Nat Hentoff, in his liner notes to Hill's *Point of Departure*, Blue Note CDP 7 84167, 31 March 1964.

art its formal pivot out of the vibrational rigor mortis into which it would settle once overtaken and seduced by enveloping pressures of capital and classification. These are cultural matrices against which Ra tries to inoculate his work and his musicians by withdrawing from the public spectacle of commodified traditional "jazz" and researching the internal forces animating the music's sonic life. Organizing his groups into communal units of spiritual and musical study, Ra keeps his projects invisible before a culture industry mobilizing static, mimeticist armies of dogmatic "jazz" typologies, objectifications, and identities. Among such commercial types are the not-so-polar-opposite ocular projections of the sweating, organic, black genius of raw essence and unmediated sexuality, on the one hand,[8] and the refined, unsmiling, expensively tailored connoisseur or master of "tradition," whose facial sobriety signifies the noble attributes of quiet intensity and control, on the other. All such images are articulated to the future of an inchoate other, are re-presentations working to infect musicians yet-to-play, agents of a would-be sound with the mimetically programmed virus of simplistically egological, anthropocentric identification. Attracting them into regimes of retrohumanist, prefabricated "identity," and away from the chaos/potentiality implied by the techno-aesthetic rupture/event of sonorous air. Away from a rupture of newness, from the cut of different sound with an inscriptive/textu(r)al power of its own that goes to work at the level of the sensorium. Blunting the thinking life of sonic experience with the telic weight of marketed imagery of pre-fashioned jazz identities. Blinding the instrumentalist to be with the image of a self that is not a self, but only a new projection of the narcissism of referential institutions, whether musical, journalistic, academic, or religious. Displacing the differential sound of improvisational phrasing and its acutely particularized idioms with a returning of the culture industry to itself as it finds bodies willing to perform, that is, to mimic, the fixed phantasms projected to them as ideals. This rendering of identity into a calcified typology constitutes a violence against those notions of freedom that are not so strictly mimetic or acquisitive. The flight in afterlife of purely singular difference rejected in return for the promise of a re-presentation that will now perform the social moves of a categorical identity is the ghosting of a nonidentitarian freedom that understands itself never to be a promise, a given, or even an expectation. It is rather the imagining of movement away from each of these bounds. This "inhuman" freedom is a frame whose actual

---

8. See Graham Lock, *Forces in Motion: The Music and Thoughts of Anthony Braxton* (New York: Da Capo, 1988), 114–16, for Braxton's theories of "black exotica" and "the night of the sweating brow."

promise or potentiality inheres only in the fluid contours of its ever unfilled space. It is utterly untroubled by the burden of substantiating a typology, by the limitations of every "content" that it would bear in service to an ideal.

It is within this paradoxical zone of difference and death that both Ellison's novel and the discordant "anti-jazz" he renounces disarticulate themselves in the aesthetico-political moment of risking and becoming. Ellison gives deconstructive theater to the brutality and sheer vulgarity of linguistic interpellation's exchange of question for certitude and the narcissism motivating it on what seems every page of *Invisible Man*, animating the ideological exchange of what Werner Hamacher calls difference for position, or aporia for understanding.[9] To live in suspension of a prior notion of self may appear to counter the idea of life itself. Unless that space of aporia is viewed as a zone of potentialities that itself must be traversed or experienced in Jean-Luc Nancy's sense of this term, in which experience is constituted by the ongoing experimentality and contingency of daily life.[10] Or should I say *Ellison's* sense? It depends, as we shall see later, on what we think we say when we say "Ellison." This Ellison is from the epilogue of *Invisible Man*: "And my problem was that I always tried to go in everyone's way but my own. I have also been called one thing and then another while no one really wished to hear what I called myself. So after years of trying to adopt the opinions of others I finally rebelled. I am an *invisible* man. Thus I have come a long way and returned and boomeranged a long way from the point in society toward which I originally aspired" (*IM*, 573). The "I" to which the Invisible Man refers is a figure that is vaporized in the moment it discloses "itself," subject as that "self" has been, to the interpellative force of the social. This is a generalized pressure mandating the performance of an identity that signifies not the fluid specificity or grace of a being's singular expressionism, style, or idiom, but only one's slavelike adherence to a prefabricated register of typology, be it racialized, gendered, classed, or ordered under some other abstracted rubric of category. This pressure is manifest in the sounding of an interpellative call into "identity" that disrupts his hearing of another, of a "myself" that, if not the inhabitant of a static classification, must necessarily be a more fluid movement of being. The "I" by which the Invisible Man communicates the idea of himself is only the articulation of an anterior anxiety, a linguistic enactment of a depen-

9. Werner Hamacher, *Premises: Essays on Philosophy and Literature from Kant to Celan*, trans. Peter Fenves (Cambridge: Harvard University Press, 1996), 13.
10. Jean-Luc Nancy, *The Experience of Freedom*, trans. Bridget McDonald (Stanford, Calif.: Stanford University Press, 1993), 87.

dency on that matrix of designations and determinations to which its singularly distinct multiplicity is always radically other. The verbal "I" is a strategy of self-implication into that legislative configuration of power, whose force inheres primarily in its ability to designate and name, to determine and to place. Is only the verbal reconstitution of an idealized self-coherence that is always already shattered by the mobile experience of living thought, thought that materializes only in its transit from indecision to decision, from possibility to identity. And back again. A continual migration that, as the Invisible Man recognizes in the stolen light of his stolen cellar, can never identify any proper destination or way as being one's "own." Having "come a long way and returned and boomeranged a long way from the point in society toward which I originally aspired," he realizes that all origins and ends are strictly discursive sites, no more than verbal strategies elaborated to organize the ongoing experimentation that constitutes experience into manageable scenes of referentiality, meaning, and valuation. They are mere locales that, like the University of his youth, in the mouths of Dr. Bledsoe or Mr. Norton, or like the Brotherhood in that of Brother Jack, can be subjected to the unifying force of a mythifying narrative. Narrative that, in establishing itself as historical authority, wields the power to exclude from its self-legitimating boundaries any thinking that exceeds linguistic province. Issuing from the destituted space of his subterranean stolen hole, the very words from the cited passage are spoken from precisely such an excluded region of void, or indeed its ocular analogue, blackness—in his own words, from "outside history." This, of course, is the phrase that he uses to describe the final destiny of Tod Clifton, his former Brotherhood comrade, who, in abandoning the haven of institutional designation, plunges into what the Invisible Man can only conceive as the blackness of ontological abyss. He describes Clifton's departure from the Brotherhood as the abandonment of his own "voice," locating the agency of the would-be "subject" solely within that being's ability to be recognized and, necessarily, manipulated by a locus of social power. Which, bringing this Hegelian logic to its Fanonian conclusion, amounts only to a new incarnation of nonsubjectivity for racialized pawns of whiteness, liquidated in their very reliance on that whiteness for a sense of legitimacy.

But what is even more interesting to this investigation is the protagonist's conflation of "voice" with "identity." This move renews Ellison's rigorous and reflexive theorizing of the distinction between expressionism and signification. Or what plays out in literature and music as the distance between idiom and identity, between the incessant transmutability of style and the linguistic stasis of referentiality. The "I" that supposedly speaks or denotes a self is but a linguistic arrest of the boomeranging *flight* that is the nondevelopmental and perpetual movement of subjectivity. The "I" marks only the verbal form of a mythic agency that is necessarily absent to itself, as evinced in the moment that it is uttered. The self it signifies in the novel is absent, in the sense that it is present only in what is still silenced within the novel—this name that is never named, this nondisclosure of a selfhood that the protagonist positivizes only in forms of anonymity, experimentation, and change. Its voicing or speaking, as staged by Ellison, is never a mere vehicle by which an interiorized region of "content" or "substance" is made public, is never simply an instrument of revelatory transmission but is instead an auditory order of experience whose material reality exceeds the bounds of its coding. Not for nothing is the only "true" calling of the Invisible Man his summoning into oratory. For at no point in this purported narrative of "development" is he so naïvely bound to a particular discourse of meaning, message, or identity that he loses himself totally in the ideological imperatives of whatever institutional structure he is attached to. He admits as much in recalling his first public oration, a graduation day lecture that will later be replayed with heavily ironic reverberations after the battle royal. Of the moral content of his own paper he says, "Not that I believed this . . . I only believed that it worked." The measure of whether it "works" or not has nothing to do with the intrinsic imagination or logic of the speech but only with the extent of its public approbation. Its "success" is determined by the degree of its regurgitative force in reaffirming this culture's values to itself as well as in the execution of its style.

During his first meeting with Brother Jack, following his impromptu street speech protesting the eviction of an elderly Harlem couple, the speaker's detachment from the spoken exposes itself more baldly. He resists Jack's imposition of motive onto something that the protagonist believes is more precisely a question of performance and its improvisation: "Look, my friend, thanks for the coffee and cake. I have no more interest in those old folks than I have in your job. I wanted to make a speech. I *like* to make speeches" (*IM*, 293). The very fact of his calling into the practice of oratory itself bespeaks the totality of his envelopment not in the teleologies of signifying and signification but rather in the idiomatic movements, sounds, and textures of a singular expressionism. The distance that he remarks on repeatedly between the meaning or content of his speeches and the materiality of their utterance indicates that for him, his words "say" nothing, except in the very figurality of their *saying*, their meaning obtaining in the particularity of his verbal style or idiom. This enables him an ironic, which is to say an aesthetic, which is to say a profoundly political, line of flight beyond the narrowly telic discourses of "racial uplift" organizing and legitimating the hierarchy of the University, or of totalitarian advocacy for "the people," that justifies the Brotherhood to itself. Discovering that the particularities of style, sound, and cadence work independently of the codes of reference to which they are assigned and subordinated, he is surprised to find his deepest reality within a moment of sensorial "*non-sense*." In which the seemingly banal experimentation with a sweet potato bought on the street channels the gushing experience of liberation from every mundane logic of propriety and identity to which he has ever been compliantly "subject."

> I took a bite, finding it as sweet and hot as any I'd ever had, and was overcome with such a surge of homesickness that I turned away to keep my control. I walked along, munching the yam, just as suddenly overcome by an intense feeling of freedom—simply because I was eating while walking along the street. It was exhilarating. I no longer had to worry about who saw me or what was proper. To hell with all that. . . . If only someone who had known me at school or at home would come along and see me now. . . . I'd push them into a side street and smear their faces with the peel. . . .
>
> This is all very wild and childish, I thought, but to hell with being ashamed of what you liked. No more of that for me. I am what I am! . . .
> . . . "I yam what I am!"
> . . . What and how much had I lost by trying to do only what was expected of me instead of what I myself had wished to do? (*IM*, 264–66)

Preceding every principle of designation and identity, naming and placement, is the "wild" absence that social agents of order seek to repress through the summoning and activation of such principles. Divorcing himself from what he now sees as the policing function of prefabricated or responsibly typological selfhood, the Invisible Man embraces the irresponsible, childlike joy so long displaced by the restrictive performance of a "proper" black identity. The sweetness of the yam returns the Invisible Man to the molecular experience and engagement of his senses, to the living of a bodily selfhood that can now only feel shame for having felt shame of itself for so long. The taste and texture of the yam emancipates him from the ontological lockdown of cultural expectation attendant to his "station." Charging a self that no longer thinks in terms of its immobilized re-presentation but only in terms of reaching and surpassing its own experiential/experimental borders, of imagining and satisfying its own aesthetic contours. No longer concerned with his place *as a subject* within someone else's frame of hierarchical sociality, his exclamation "I am what I am! . . . I yam what I am!" is no claim to the clone status of mere "subject" in any slavish reproduction of ideology. It is rather the "wild and childish" precondition of his becoming. "I yam what I am" improvises the motion of idiosyncratic self-stylization and signifies nothing, repeats nothing, identifies with nothing—other than the freeing movement and tonality of its own expressionism, saying nothing except in the materiality of its own saying. Its voicing is not the externalizing of any embedded inner essence of true self but is only the sounding of *the idea* of its own sound, representative of nothing beyond the distancing it enunciates from the inhibitions that preceded it.

In this particular mode of entropic understanding, the Invisible Man anticipates the (non)figure of the Harlem hustler Rinehart. Beholden to no principle and no cause, this apotheosis of the nonidentitarian moves darkly through Harlem like an anthropomorphic unit of chaos; his look, his voice, his stride, his clothing, his "identity" absolutely improvisational and exchangeable, Rinehart embodies the thinking fugitivity of expressionism. In his inability to be identified under a stable code of referentiality, he performs the substance of movement, recognizable only by fragmentary accoutrements such as dark, green-lensed sunglasses, knob-toed shoes, and a Cadillac that rolls only by night. These, in addition to slightly more personal indicators, such as "a smooth tongue, a heartless heart," and, indeed, a readiness "to do anything" (*IM*, 493). Such attributes coalesce to form a radical singularity whose only signature is its radical *plurality*, whose differentiated modes of speaking, walking, lying, loving constitute an absolutely singular, sovereign way of being.

> Can it be, I thought, can it actually be? And I knew that it was. I had heard of it before but I'd never come so close. Still, could he be all of them: Rine the runner and Rine the gambler and Rine the briber and Rine the lover and Rinehart the Reverend? Could he himself be both rind and heart? What is real anyway? But how could I doubt it? He was a broad man, a man of parts who got around. Rinehart the rounder. It was true as I was true. His world was possibility and he knew it. . . . The world in which we lived was without boundaries. A vast seething, hot world of fluidity, and Rine the rascal was at home. . . . It was unbelievable, but perhaps only the unbelievable could be believed. Perhaps the truth was always a lie. (*IM*, 498)

Identifiable with no institutional quarter or party, Rinehart works the illicit, voided zone, or "rind," designated as "outside history" by those who claim its inside or "heart," finding himself indeed at its center. Irreducible to any single role, or to any identifiable motives such as money, power, or sex, in his embrace of multiple modes of identification, he abandons all, freeing himself to align with the fluid and shifting forces of life "underground" in plain sight. His objectives are never identified—unless they obtain, as they must, in his liquidity. Rinehart embodies multiplicity in ceaseless motion, undermining every certitude, destabilizing every authority, *concealing* the "truth" of his character *by performing* its proliferation in public.

Suspending the "subject/object" humanistic imperatives by which he would except himself from his surroundings and categorize all before him, Rinehart recognizes the fact of his always already implication in the urban landscape. At once predatory and escapist in his relation to Harlem, he embodies the hardness, the caprice, and protean becoming that constitute any urban complex of sensations and circumstances. Utterly indifferent to every question of personality, character, or "subjecthood," he is one with the movement and flux of the city, glimpsed *only* in transit, *only* as he vanishes into the terrain of Harlem night, never stopping to explain or to telegraph his destinations. His is a chaos that, like any other, is contagion, and haltingly the Invisible Man follows Rinehart's pathless lead into the voided black zone of nonhistory and nonidentity.

> . . . after first being "for" society and then "against" it, I assign myself no rank or any limit, and such an attitude is very much against the trend of the times. But my world has become one of infinite possibilities. . . . Until some gang succeeds in putting the world in a strait jacket, its definition is possibility. Step outside the narrow borders of what men call reality and you step into chaos—ask Rinehart, he's a master of it—or imagination. That too I've learned in the cellar, and not by deadening my sense of perception; I'm invisible, not blind. (*IM*, 576)

Stripped by experience of every designating and confining "rank," the Invisible Man now rejects the logic of designation as a bad faith strategy against the cultural entropy that alone lends naming its meaning, that alone enables the thinking of identity its elevation above the nothingness it combats. Suggesting instead that along the fictive "path" of linearity which has "led" the protagonist from one mask to the next in his odyssey through a taxonomic museum of institutional designations, he is accompanied by a radical alterity. It is the ironic filter by which the experience of this vast room full of socially prescribed mirrors is organized and narrated *at a critical distance*. The Invisible Man is always already exterior to a room in which all he can see is one prefigured code for one "proper" selfhood after another, without any recognition of the radical singularity that is his polyglot of aesthetico-political multiplicity and contradiction. For no single name or cultural designation can account for the always mobile reflexiveness that characterizes his thinking and speech, reflexiveness that always keeps him at a critical or ironic distance from total implication in whatever ideological imperatives supposedly provide him identity and "voice." Escaping what Amiri Baraka identifies as "an area of act that is hell . . . a place of naming."[11]

The imperative of proper naming would shield the notion of solid identity from the alterity that anticipates and demands the strategy of closure which is that name. For instance, it would keep such self-evident determinations as "jazz bassist" clean and free of such contaminants as might be added by, say, "tone scientist" or "philosopher." Ideologically instituted identity is dependent on the cleanliness of its exclusions, be they political or sensorial, and is undermined in the moment that these negativities resurface. On one of those post-University, pre-Invisible days, Ellison's protagonist is overtaken precisely by the reality of this return.

> One moment I believed, I was dedicated, willing to lie on the blazing coals, do anything to attain a position on the campus—then snap! It was done with, finished, through. Now there was only the problem of forgetting it. If only all the contradictory voices shouting inside my head would calm down and sing a song in unison, whatever it was I wouldn't care as long as they sang without dissonance; yes and avoided the uncertain extremes of the scale. But there was no relief. I was wild with resentment but too much under "self-control," that frozen virtue, that freezing vice. And the more resentful I became, the more my old urge to make speeches returned. While walking along the streets words would spill from my lips in a mumble over which I had little control. I became afraid of what I might do. All things were indeed awash in my mind. I longed for home. (*IM*, 259)

The words that issue from his lips are themselves a double reverberation, and not only of the excluded anguish of a sharply detoured desire for a sat-

---

11. Amiri Baraka, "Names and Bodies," *The Floating Bear: A Newsletter*, numbers 1–37, ed. Amiri Baraka and Diane DiPrima (La Jolla, Calif.: Laurence McGilvery, 1973), 272.

isfactory ideological destination in the lockdown of cultural identity. They are also incoherent testimony to the aporia from which language itself emerges in its urgency to reconstitute the objects for which it now substitutes. The entropy of the "discordant" material in his mind demands a solidification into an identical presence that would form the basis of a unitary and acutely visible self, excepted from the numerous undifferentiated crowds on which his subsequent career as a speaker ignites. This anxiety materializes in the protagonist/orator's frequent references to the masses before which he speaks as anonymous, collective shadows, a "blurred audience," a shape-less amalgam of "faces becom[ing] vaguer and vaguer," against which he speaks himself into what he imagines as sharply distinct presence (*IM*, 340–53). The urgency for sameness disclosed in the cited passage, the veritable mania for consistency and consonance, is only the outcome of language's metaphoric fiction revealed, in that no verbal designation of social identity can make one identical with it. The word does not ever collapse that origi-nary gap but is at best a momentary strategy against that chaotic void. A void viciously ironized throughout the body of the work, as when the paternal white benefactor of the University, Mr. Norton, traumatized by his encounter with the incestuous black sharecropper, Jim Trueblood, blurts and stam-mers his astonishment at Trueblood's "survival" of his personal horror. The shocked Norton can only shout his incredulity at Trueblood with what the Invisible Man describes as a look of both "envy and indignation," exclaiming, "You have survived . . . and are unharmed! . . . You have looked upon chaos and are not destroyed!" To which the bewildered Trueblood replies, "No suh! I feels all right" (*IM*, 51). Trueblood's complete externality to the white man's shock, and his concurrent inability to assimilate that shock, makes concrete the distance between those who would abjure chaos and those who are consigned *to live it* in the presumed void of visual and cultural blackness. This being also the distance between those who write "history" and those who are excluded from it. The fundamental incompatibility between these two levels of communication performs the social imperative toward the inver-sion of incomprehension embodied by Norton. At the same time, it localizes, in the form of Trueblood's utterance — "I feels all right" — the always already relinquishment of comprehension, the embrace of understanding's oppo-site, supposed by Enlightenment discourse from Kant to Hegel to Hume to characterize the presumed subhumanity of black existence. No rhetoric of mere marginalization, no vocabulary of simple exclusionary practice, begins to address the problematic of blackness's pure externality to the categories of modernity that Ellison theorizes in this novel. He investigates this problematic not simply as the labor of existing *within* a social void of abjection and repudiation but of *living* that experiential/experimental void of "non-knowledge" itself. Of the ongoing work and play of embodying, performing, and *improvising* life that is culturally designated as outside or beneath any self-legitimated "human" register of thought, identity, or propriety. In its utter unresponsiveness to social imperatives of identity and classification, the questioning cut of such chaos sounded by Armstrong's first experiments corresponds exactly to the discordant irruptiveness that the Invisible Man tries to repress in his head. The abdication of the idea of mastery and personal sovereignty that Armstrong performs in his identification not with any social typology but rather with sound, movement, and rhythm eviscerates the messianic impulse to reduce the sonic experimentalism of improvisational music to the willed and perfected product of any anthropomorphic "subject." The "home" for which the Invisible Man longs is a fantasy of smoothness and order that would contain and arrange the discordant voices in his head into a monadic fusion of unruly particularities, creating a sameness that elsewhere in the novel he takes pains to escape. The effacement of difference he craves in this instance counters the intensely egoistic insistence on cultural recognition of his intellectual and stylistic exceptionality that motivates the narrative.

From within the density of absolute social void, from within that black hole of stolen light, the protagonist must discern an entire negative constellation of possibility. Ellison's working of the play between the visible and the invisible resonates darkly at the differential boundary of the abject. Proceeding from the notion that the field of the visible, the legitimate world of "light," is always already governed by its other, the invisible and delegitimated, Ellison deconstructs the distance between the seer and the seen, inside and out, in a space circumscribed by transcendental imperatives of "identity" and "race." Forging a new nonspace, perhaps akin to what Ra calls "The Kingdom of Not," in which the Hegelian pressure of finding self-confirmation through the recognition of another is utterly suspended. The dialectic broken, each step further into this black hole of nonidentity is a step into the terror and ecstasy of nonrecognition. By this I mean not simply the centripetal destruction that attends any withholding of recognition of self from without; I mean the improvisational possibility of working or *playing* oneself into the semblance of a self, a self that becomes a self only in the performative materiality of its playing, not in any constative assertion of its substance. It is the improvising of what Ellison calls in the prologue of *Invisible Man* "the invisible music of my isolation." It is the experimental playing of the void, of both purely visual and culturally inscribed blackness as the embodiment of epistemological absence—as if this abyss of solid identity were a musical chord or a tone to strike.

> Before that I lived in the darkness into which I was chased, but now I see. I've illuminated the blackness of my invisibility—and vice versa. And so I play the invisible music of my isolation. The last statement doesn't seem just right does it? But it is; you hear this music simply because music is heard and seldom seen, except by musicians. Could this compulsion to put invisibility down in black and white be thus an urge to make music of invisibility? But I am an orator, a rabble rouser—Am? I *was*, and perhaps shall be again. Who knows? All sickness is not unto death, neither is invisibility. (*IM*, 14)

The pivot that Ellison puts into motion is hardly represented as a pivot, or a break of nonlinearity, at all by his narrator but is rather embedded as a purely temporal movement of development, of "straight-ahead" evolution that is easily enough self-contained. "Before that I lived in the darkness . . . but now I see" is no more than a formula for a transparent kind of redemption that stitches over the rupture or traumatic violence that any moment of correction, any conversion of nonknowledge to comprehension, necessarily constitutes. This fiction of firm channels bridging the aporetic and the comprehensible, of smooth, noncircuitous travel between blindness and insight, nonknowing and knowing, is itself a nearly indiscernible device of dislocation, programming us into a certain faith. A faith in the temporal premise of full understanding or closure that makes even the entropic point of finitude that is "playing invisibility" a reassuring notion because of its temporal status *as* an endpoint, as a destination, an outcome preceded by something else that is escaped. Invisibility, or nonidentity, is a break made soothing by the familiarity, the "good form," of the linear structure in which it reveals itself as such.

   The precise moment of transmission of transformative information is necessarily obscured. At what point is nonunderstanding converted into understanding? This is a point about which it should be impossible to generalize, and yet it can never fully be made to materialize. For Ellison, articulating the thematic of invisibility is the device of invisibility itself. He works a narrative strategy whereby the very idea of the narrator is enabled to survive only by the subtle dissembling that momentarily excludes the memory of his various traumatic shocks or rude "awakenings." These might include his expulsion from the University, the explosion at Liberty Paints, and his subsequent electric shock therapy; for his narration of these awakenings can only be a belated epistemological schema, which is to say, an absolute effect, of his devastation. This evolutionary tale at once allows the illusion of the narrator's totality and performs the self-deconstructive drive of a narrative organized by endlessly circular, self-referential principles. What is excluded, momentarily, is the event on which the system is built; but this event resurfaces later, as something like revelation or content. By the time it does return as "something" to be narrated, as an object to communicated, the solidity of the frame—this being the narrator himself—has been established, despite the crushing damage it has endured in the moments it now objectifies as the distant, survived past. The frame speaks from the presumed stability of an outside that is but a standing ruin of a never distant inside. The frame relates the interiority that would have destroyed it; the interiority conditions and traumatizes the frame that now assigns it its "proper" definition and place. For Ellison, it is precisely, indeed only, this necessary "step into chaos" that actuates the fluidity of *possibility*. It is this stripping of the reassurance of "rank," or cultural designation, that propels his protagonist into the infinite that Ra *mandates* for the musician. For as Ra says, "It didn't take a long time for me to realize that my innocence would always enable me to think of how to *do* things, while other people talked about *becoming* things. Because I'm ignorant, my mind absorbed all kinds of things, the whole cosmos, the omniverse." [12]

## 2. Playing the Invisible, Sounding the Impossible

Knowing that a "knowing subject" of jazz would be the death of a truly improvisational jazz, Ra elaborates material strategies to induce an aesthetic of profound contingency in his musicians' improvisational practice. Having studied and worked with one of the tightest bands and loosest bandleaders of all time, The Fletcher Henderson Orchestra, the former Sonny Blount, once on his own, devised countless methods of locking his musicians into their own futurity by forcing them into existential zones of pure aesthetic terror. After rehearsing freshly composed, intricately nuanced sets of arrangements repeatedly, working the same difficult charts for eight hours a day, five days a week, Ra's musicians would routinely arrive for concert, take the bandstand, and then sit in horror as their leader impetuously called

12. Jennifer Rycenga, personal interview with Sun Ra at the University of California—Berkeley, 1988; my emphasis.

out arrangements they had never seen, let alone practiced, not during the previous week, nor at any time prior. Trombonist Julian Priester describes the feeling of being called on to solo in such a context: "I'd get up, but I wouldn't know what was going on! I wouldn't know where I was in terms of a harmonic framework, I'd just have to *listen* to what was going on in back of me with the band—which was liable to be just about anything—and I'd have to work from that. I'd have to measure things instantly and start playing." [13]

The forgetting of the musical *known* in Ra's work becomes both a philosophical and aesthetic *event*.[14] His musicians perform an unscripted freedom born not merely of Ra's terroristic technique of nonpedagogy but of the musical immanence within which the experience of terror is imagined as only another particularized element of aesthetic labor. It functions as only one fast-moving necessity among others in service to an aesthetic imperative of absolute improvisation. This musical immanence is the entropic originary zone within which individual patterns, strategies, concepts, and words collide and compete endlessly. It is an improvisatory dimension in which the energies of questioning, as opposed to knowing, mobilize all local schemas and thoughts, all determinations and representations, no isolated one of which, no general set of which, can be equal in scope or intensity to the non-state or abandonment in which it is brought into always already fragmentary and alienated being. It is a dimension that Ra calls "greater infinity," a space in which "the impossible becomes the everyday." [15] It is a space in which the very idea of a subject is only momentary, significant only in its status as a figure enabled to materialize that impossibility.

> I've chosen intergalactic music; or it has chosen me . . . so it is really outside the realm of the future on the turning points of the impossible. . . . I'm actually painting pictures of infinity with my music and that's why a lot of people can't understand it. But if they'd listen to this and other types of music, they'd find that mine has something else in it, something from another world. Space music is an introductory prelude to the sound of greater infinity.[16]

13. Julian Priester, quoted in Val Wilmer, *As Serious as Your Life: John Coltrane and Beyond* (1977; reprint, New York: Serpent's Tail, 1999), 87.
14. See Fred Moten's mesmerizing "Sound in Florescence: Cecil Taylor's Floating Garden," in *Sound States: Innovative Poetics and Acoustical Technologies*, ed. Adalaide Morris (Chapel Hill: University of North Carolina Press, 1997).
15. Rycenga, personal interview with Sun Ra.
16. Sun Ra, quoted in John Litweiler, *The Freedom Principle: Jazz after 1958* (New York: Da Capo Press, 1984), 140.

In the sublime ecstasy of this public labor, such musicians as Priester are exposed to an experience of music not available within a conventional aesthetic thinking of harmony, symmetry, beauty, or continuity. They absorb in the moment of playing the import of what Ellison's protagonist means when he says in the epilogue, "I've learned to live without direction" (*IM*, 577). The productivity of the would-be musical subject's experience of nothingness, as the texture and substance of experience itself, depends on that subject's embracing the possibility of the opposite of the representations of selfhood that the musician has absorbed heretofore. The reality of its subjectivity is met at the boundary of the discovery into which it has just been forced, its truth inhering in the intensity and totality of its self-risk, in the intensity of its fearful embrace of that which is incomprehensible to it. This is why the idea of "self," or subject, is permanently disabled by the question of freedom: because freedom invites, even summons, the self into the experience of radical otherness, promising only a certain transformation— a certain death—of that self.

This auto-annihilation opens onto an aural afterlife not accessible to the logic of the properly authorial "I." The liquidation of the creative subject of composition and artistic beauty enables an accomplishing of another project altogether: a dramatic revising of improvised *sound relationships* born in the pain and ecstasy of radically shifted epistemological and emotional dynamics. Such *sound relationships* emphasize tonal singularity (which, of course, can mean ambiguity), harmonic brokenness, *and* the perpetual distance of any dream of reconciliation. Negating its own status as an object of the representational, this technique of self-abandonment converts music's sound from the "beautiful" into the chaotic and the urgent, the quavering and the tremulous into the impossible.

It is from within this auditory space of the impossible that a critical Ellison begins to long for the home he denies his abandoned protagonist in *Invisible Man*. His 1955 essay "Living with Music" recalls a pre-bop moment of his musical youth that, in his view, represents a crystallization of collective musical work in which the result is a distillation of dissonance into self-confirmation.

> The delicate balance struck between strong individual personality and the group during those early jam sessions was a marvel of social organization. I had learned too that the end of all this discipline and technical mastery was the desire to express an affirmative way of life through its musical tradition, and that this tradition insisted that each

artist achieve his creativity within its frame. He must learn the best of
the past, and add to it his personal vision. Life could be harsh, loud
and wrong if it wished, but they lived it fully, and when they expressed
their attitude toward the world it was with a fluid style that reduced
the chaos of living to form.[17]

The affirmation of which Ellison speaks is the function of an excision of self,
if, as he concludes, the chaos removed is that "of living." It is re-pressed by
collective ascesis into a particularized form that displaces the notion of artist as agent. Replacing it not with any messianic musical auteur but with a
musician who is no more than a vessel in the transmission of the art. Lester
Bowie says, "We are musical messengers. We train ourselves so that we
can receive the spirit. You just prepare yourself to be a channel . . . you don't
even know what is going to happen. You just accept it and do it."[18]

As it is at the same time a function of a series of improvisations, isn't
part of the "attitude" Ellison describes that of a certain risk? Is not confrontation with the possibility of its own catastrophe absolutely necessary to the
very thinking of a new art? Can that engagement with chaos ever be recon-
ciled into an affirmation?

Robert O'Meally makes a crucial point in noting Ellison's privileging
a certain wholeness in his negative comparison of bebop aesthetics and
even physiognomies to those of the Swing and Big Band eras. The "fullness"
of the older musicians' lives, as Ellison puts it in "Living with Music," finds
its sonic materialization in the comparative muscularity of their instrumental
tones, as well as in their substantially larger physiques. The relative thin-
ness of Charlie Parker's tone on alto, Ellison suggests in a spurt of sharply
masculinist aesthetic judgment, communicates "a sound of amateurish inef-
fectuality, as though he could never quite make it."[19]

The frenetic quality of much of the bebop period does sound a sharp,
wakeful movement along the chain out of which it forces itself in its own
agonistic birth, but again hardly a disconnection, hardly the utter chaos,
said to obtain at its narcissistic center. But the absence of what Ellison
felt to be a certain "earthiness," an absence of "feeling" signified by what
he reports as a common "rudeness" among the artists toward the pub-

17. Ralph Ellison, "Living with Music," in *Living with Music: Ralph Ellison's Jazz Writings*,
ed. Robert O' Meally (New York: The Modern Library, 2001), 6.
18. Lester Bowie, interviewed by Alain Le Roux, in *Le Jazz 9*, 1997.
19. O'Meally, *Living with Music*, 74. Thanks to Lynn Casmier-Paz for shoring up the acutely
sexist bias characterizing Ellison's statements.

lic, a tense, "studied" quality in their outward bearing, are all signatory to an even less forgivable absence. It is the absence of something he identifies passingly, in the sound of a Cannonball Adderley solo, as "human." In a private letter to Albert Murray in 1958, Ellison bemoans the disappointment of his encounter with several aging bop musicians for a magazine piece he is to write on Minton's Playhouse, the Harlem nightclub in which Parker, Gillespie, and others began developing this new musical language. He describes them in uncharacteristically harsh terms, all of which ultimately suggest the encroaching of the loathsome entropy he believed art to combat. He bitterly describes them as "lost" imitators of Parker, a sad enterprise, Ellison thought, considering how "miserable, beat and lost as *he* (Parker) sounded most of the time." He dismisses the Newport performances of "that poor, evil, *lost* Miles Davis," and the "badly executed velocity exercises" of John Coltrane. With what appears an exasperated resignation, he sums up to say, "These cats have gotten lost, man."[20]

This exasperation at loss, absence, or disjuncture is consistent with that expressed by Murray while interviewed on the topic of "free jazz," during the Ken Burns documentary series, *Jazz*. Bear in mind that free jazz is, by this point, more than forty years in the making.

> Ornette Coleman came up and said, "This is *free* jazz." But what is freer than jazz? As soon as you say jazz, you're talking about freedom, of improvisation—freedom. The whole thing is about freedom, about American freedom. So why would anybody want to free it? Because the whole idea of art is to create a *form* that is a bulwark against entropy, or chaos. You see, that is the function of jazz. It's not to be form*less*, or absolutely self-indulgent; I want to go this way, I'll go this way, I'll go that way. That's like embracing the waves in the sea. *You cannot embrace entropy.* You cannot embrace chaos.[21]

This exhortative passion for continuity, for a past coherence and unity, makes of the Armstrong/Basie/Ellington moments of pre-bop jazz a risk-free, moribund environment in which nothing was at stake. A dead space of easy listening in which improvisational thought was undertaken solely in the service of affirmation, and was therefore without any element of chance, a noncontingent effort toward reassurance. This thought echoes repeatedly during the Burns series, during which the idea that Louis Armstrong's career

20. O'Meally, *Living with Music*, 245.
21. Burns, *Jazz*, episode 9.

was predicated on the necessity of "making people feel that everything was going to be alright" becomes axiomatic. This constitutes a massive violence to the initial risk he took, in the absolute contingency of blowing into space that which he had never heard.

In its disengagement from the thinking of its boundaries, in its tonal movement beyond the historical, political, and epistemic determinations that would be its limits, a new type of music is indeed embodied in the work of Ra and other experimental musicians who appear in the late 1950s. Emerging from within and underneath the tones of bebop and hard bop soloing practice, this new music comes to be called "free" largely because it furthers the technical unhinging of sound from aesthetic laws governing totality and symmetry in the harmonic and rhythmic organizing of the styles of that sound. The supposed continuity of the earlier "straight-ahead" post-bop music of standardized chordal progression or pattern and tight rhythmic meter is itself an asymptotic process. It is not only internally differentiated by the structural tensions and dynamics circumscribing it by definition but is also amputated from the popular ideal of its totality *by its very materiality as auditory projection*. What else is multireedist Eric Dolphy addressing when he says, "When you hear music, after it's over, it's gone, in the air. You can never capture it again?"[22] if not that music is necessarily a movement of disidentification, a thinking and an enunciation of de-subjection? That in its disengagement from the language and logocentrism which would arrest it, it also discards the categorical imperatives of its cultural meaning, thereby following the call of its fluid immanence, the mutating sovereignty of its fleeting sound, texture, and imagining?

Contemporaneously with Ra, and inspired by Coltrane, such artists as Dolphy, Cecil Taylor, Ornette Coleman, Dewey Redman, Don Cherry, and, very soon thereafter, Albert Ayler, Muhal Richard Abrams, Anthony Braxton, Steve McCall, Roscoe Mitchell, and Lester Bowie permanently move into this continuity-free zone. Each instrumentalist gives sonic body to the Ra mantra, which his longtime trumpeter Michael Ray transmits to the new Arkestra and its variants today: "*You've got to play what you don't know.* Which means you're forever learning how to do something and then un-learning it. This is how *we live*."[23]

Part of what lends this urgent manifesto its resonance is the fact, at

22. Eric Dolphy, *Last Date*, Fontana Records, June 1964.
23. Michael Ray and tenor saxophonist John Gilmore, interviewed by Kevin Bell, New Orleans, August 1993.

once banal and shattering, that it is issued and absorbed within a social space of already utter marginality. The desperate and megalomanic idealism that animates the notion of radical otherness impelling racialist categorization cites as its justification an organizing absence, a defining lack, which once again functions as an articulation. The idea of the inherent absence of cognitive possibility from Hegel's African — another presumably nonthinking variant of Kant's "Negro," as explicated in Ronald Judy's incisive meditation on the collapsing of the ocular perception of blackness into the attribution of conceptual "meaning" (stupidity) thereto — is a violence of profound abstraction.[24] Whereby the singularity of the racialized figure's expressionism in boundaries of time and space is absolutely subsumed to the linguistic/ideological assessment of nonvalue or idiocy. As figures of blackness, presumably living embodiments of nothingness and nonunderstanding, surviving units of abandonment, their movement into art, particularly into a nonaffirmative, questioning modality thereof, all but negates the issue of their relative value in consumeristic, racialist, social spheres. In other words, they live the nonidentity they perform musically. This is what is meant when it is said that impossibility/abandonment is the political nongrounding of improvisational music and thought. This music gives sonically material testimony to a concentrated and violent strength in the face of hegemonic cultural mandates toward finite designation and determinism. A strength to be found in the irreducibly fluid materiality of "free" or "outside" performance, an ascetic hardness within the porous molecularity of a warlike dissonance, mobilized under a "program" of paradox that can only be articulated by the terms of its divorce from the very notion of the programmatic.

The jazz-bashing Theodor Adorno ironically allows this essay a concluding pivot into consideration of a conceptual membrane in Ellison's thought between the aesthetic force of the aporia of visual blackness and the presumptive nothingness at the foundations of anthropomorphized blackness. In so doing, Adorno also posits a critical mantra for the stronger works of free jazz, and of modernist art in general:

> To survive reality at its most extreme and grim, artworks that do not want to sell themselves as consolation must equate themselves with that reality. Radical art today is synonymous with dark art; its primary

24. See Ronald A. T. Judy's crucial essay "Kant and the Negro," in the online journal *Surfaces* 1 (1991). Concerning the question of anthropomorphic blackness as "ontological lack," see also Sylvia Wynter's brilliant article, "Beyond the Word of Man: Glissant and the New Discourse of the Antilles," *World Literature Today* 63, no. 4 (1989): 637–46.

color is black. . . . The ideal of blackness with regard to content is one of the deepest impulses of abstraction . . . ever since Baudelaire the dark has also offered sensuous enticement as the antithesis of the fraudulent sensuality of culture's facade. There is more joy in dissonance than in consonance. The caustic discordant moment, dynamically honed, is differentiated in itself as well as from the affirmative and becomes alluring; and this allure, scarcely less than revulsion for the imbecility of positive thinking draws modern art *into a no-man's land that is the plenipotentiary of a livable world.*[25]

The attitude of abyssal darkness and self-risk in this art, manifest in the spareness of the art's very fabric, is the politically discordant cut of a new sound. It is a revisionistic materialization of new tonal bodies that confront and deconstruct the anterior modes of inscription provided by Armstrong, Ellington, and Parker, *even as* these new tonal bodies helplessly perform their utter indebtedness to such ancestors. Free jazz disappears the textural density of its precursors, enacting a sounding of spatiality free of the content of telic resolutions, clearing a performative territory formerly cluttered with established patterns of rhythm and harmony. Implied is a new valence of silence, a sounding that is sometimes not actual silence but is often only the *suggestion* of such silence—it performs a *sound for silence* that offers an aural analogue to the visual experience of *blackness.* In this sonic rendering of ocular abyss, the music's foregrounding of silence and spacing by the frequent removal of supposed rhythmic and harmonic centers such as piano and bass, free jazz communicates the easy dispensability of any element, the scattering of any "home." It enunciates its utterly indifferent attitude toward its inability to be countenanced socially or assimilated epistemologically. It critiques the very will to understanding and untroubled reference that first anxiously "identifies" its discordant blackness as such, in order to legitimate casting it out as "menace," as "*other.*"

This is a rather melodic reversal, for blackness, as circulated throughout traditional Western philosophical and critical aesthetic lexicons since antiquity, is the primary conceptual metaphor for the absence of information and thusly of mental life. It is the imagistic (non)embodiment of the originary space that is filled (or obliterated) by the substitutional material of language.

Black is openly abjected by every logic and cultural practice of cer-

---

25. Theodor Adorno, "Critique of the Culture Industry," in *Aesthetic Theory*, trans. and ed. Robert Hullot-Kentor (Minneapolis: University of Minnesota Press, 1997), 40; my emphasis.

titude, the logic that lends a transcendental underwriting to the installation of the knowing "I," or the coherent subject, as the human center from which orders of understanding, classification, and subjection issue. Black, as a universalist concept and figure of nothingness, is therefore *niggered* long before it is attached to its cultural nonsubject, the Negro, the African, the non "I." Black, in other words, is radical nothingness long before it finds its anthropomorphic "referent." A "referent" whose presumable distance from legitimating Enlightenment/Idealist valuation is determined only by its surface tonality. A surface that sediments the philosophic principle of void, the abyss of un-truth or epistemological lack, within the one people on earth purported to have no access to any redemptive "truth."

This percept tends to produce *in its beholder* a shattering nonreflection of its own values. Blackness visible constitutes an absorptive withholding of the return of the gazing "I"—the desire that motivates every external gaze on the other. Blackness recognizes within itself the density of its own nothingness, feeding on the contempt in which it is held for exactly this reason—its nonrecognizing, ineluctable thwarting of social narcissism and the categories of classification erected toward this end. Blackness visible, aporia materialized and lived, is the freedom that results from relinquishment of the very imagining of subjectivity altogether, along with all of the mythifying narratives of united "positionality" that keep it propped up, such as "race," "gender," "nation," "community," and "identity." Blackness is the social void into which one drops after abandoning, like Ellison's Rinehart, like the grandfather, like Clifton, and like Louis Armstrong himself, the idea of humanist centrality; to borrow from Ellison once more with feeling, it is where one lands after falling headlong out of someone else's "History." Free jazz is a musical nomadism that reflexively meditates on the utter redundancy of this last designation, manifesting its homelessness and its immanent searching in the aural discord of its tones and rhythms, breaths, and silences. A new music, as new and mobile as the flash of Louis Armstrong, in its singing of uncertainty and the impossible, in its incantatory blowing of all air—foul, fair—far out.[26]

26. As a final note, also "far out" must go my deepest thanks to those friends and colleagues who consistently and often unwittingly inspired me in the conception and writing of this piece, namely Lynn Casmier-Paz, Stephen Casmier, Christopher Harris, Joseph C. Razza III, Kelly Regan, and Mark C. Thompson. Particular thanks go to my colleagues at Northwestern University who generously read and offered helpful advice in preparing the piece for publication. These include Brian T. Edwards, Jillana Enteen, Christine Froula, Robert Gooding-Williams, Michael G. Hanchard, Dorothy Wang, and Alex Weheliye.

# Bliss, or Blackface Sentiment

*Barry Shank*

When Senator Sunraider delivers the final speech of his career in Ralph Ellison's novel *Juneteenth*, he seems to articulate one of Ellison's most sincerely held beliefs. Urging his listeners not to "falter before our complexity," Senator Sunraider declares, "Ours is a youthful nation. . . . A marvel of purposeful political action, it was designed to solve those vast problems before which all other nations have been proved wanting. Born in diversity and fired by determination, our society was endowed with a flexibility designed to contain the most fractious contentions of an ambitious, individualistic and adventurous breed."[1] As Sunraider continues, he urges his listeners, the other members of the Senate and all auditing visitors, including his assassin, to keep in mind "the outrages committed" by black Americans. We are meant to recognize this as a common rhetorical gesture for him. Indeed, Sunraider had made his career as a race-baiting politician. But the gesture quickly takes an odd yet quite Ellisonian turn. The leaders of the nation are to keep these outrages in mind because "perhaps therein

1. Ralph Ellison, *Juneteenth: A Novel*, ed. John F. Callahan (New York: Vintage Books, 1999), 20. Hereafter, this work is cited parenthetically as *Juneteenth*.

*boundary 2* 30:2, 2003. Copyright © 2003 by Duke University Press.

lies a secret brightness, a clue. Perhaps the essence of their untamed and assertive willfulness, their crass and jazzy defiance of good taste and the harsh, immutable laws of economics, lies in their faith in the flexible soundness of the nation." For Sunraider, the flexible soundness of the nation is rooted in the ability of Americans to wear masks, "to forge a multiplicity of creative selves and styles" (*Juneteenth*, 23). Of course, Sunraider had benefited from the finest training the nation could provide in the skills necessary for the creation of these new selves. For Sunraider was born as Bliss, the literary inversion of Ellison's earlier character Bliss Proteus Rinehart and the paradoxical embodiment of the ambiguous possibilities that might be found in the practices and traditions of blackface.

Ellison's career stretched from the beginning to the end of the American Century—one might also say from the beginning to the end of "American Studies," but that is a different issue. By the time Henry Luce, the publisher of *Life*, wrote his 1941 editorial "The American Century," Ellison had been collecting black folklore for the Federal Writer's Project for three years and had written reviews and short articles for *New Masses* and other publications. In one of his earliest published pieces, "A Congress Jim Crow Didn't Attend," Ellison located "the positive forces of civilization and the best guarantee of America's future" in the faces of those in attendance at the Third National Negro Congress.[2] With the publication of *Juneteenth* in 1999, his efforts to articulate (in the fullest sense of the word) the best hopes of the nation and the cultural resourcefulness of black Americans saw their final statement. Ellison's firmly held hope was that the nation—the e pluribus unum that Sunraider tries to describe—would be conjured into existence when the special conditions that gave rise to African American culture were recognized as the generalized tragic conditions of existence and when the social and psychological inequalities that characterized those historical conditions were eliminated in the mutual recognition of a shared humanity and a national culture. Of course, Ellison was too good an artist to simply wish this mutual recognition into being. With the character of Bliss, he gave free reign to his blackface sentiment, to his longing for a national culture redeemed by black American folklore. And with the character of Senator Sunraider, Ellison illustrated the possessive investment in the mythology of whiteness that has historically prevented the materialization of this recognition. With his characteristic witty love of paradox, he made them the same person.[3]

2. Ralph Ellison, "A Congress Jim Crow Didn't Attend," in *The Collected Essays of Ralph Ellison*, ed. John Callahan (New York: Modern Library, 1995), 26.
3. Ralph Ellison, "What America Would Be Like without Blacks," in *Collected Essays*, 577–

Bliss is born into the hands of Alonzo Hickman, an itinerant gambling, drinking, and hell-raising trombone player. Hickman had returned from the road to his home in Alabama because of a family tragedy. His brother had been lynched for the rape of a white woman, a crime he did not commit. Hickman's mother had died of grief, and he wanted revenge. Instead, he is given an immense responsibility when the woman who had accused his brother and thereby caused his death delivers the baby boy—in appearance, a white boy—into Hickman's own hands in an effort to redeem herself. Hickman is a jazz man, a player in a territory band like Walter Page's Blue Devils. Ellison imagines Hickman as a natural man; his talents derive from his organic relationship to southern black culture. He has all the passions, the appetites, and drives of such a figure. He is the embodiment of the rhythms, the talent for improvisation, the hunger to experience life at its fullest, imbricated with a profound respect for life in all of its variety that Ellison identified with the core of black American folklife. But instead of achieving the longed-for, violent revenge he sought for the crime that had been committed against his family, Hickman responds to the burden of caring for this infant. After he cuts and ties off the baby's umbilical cord, Hickman holds the future of the nation in his hands.

Placed at the end of the novel, whether through the work of Callahan, the literary executor, or Ellison's own explicit designs, this is another one of those scenes where Ellison wants to make sure you don't miss his meaning. Hickman has taken on the task of training this white-looking infant in the riches of black American folklife—not the respectable, dignified culture of the black bourgeoisie but the lore of Jack-the-Bear and Brer Rabbit, the deep vocalizations of the blues singer, and the sacred histrionics of black preaching. Hickman's deeply disappointed hope is that Bliss can learn the truths embedded and reproduced in this folklife, and then go on to "speak for our condition from inside the only acceptable mask" (*Juneteenth*, 271). Hickman hopes that, by wearing the right mask—the mask of whiteness—over a soul steeped in blackness, Bliss can destroy the "white American's Manichean fascination with the symbolism of blackness and whiteness," through his simultaneous and undeniable embodiment of both.[4]

Culminating in the doubled character of Bliss/Sunraider, Ellison's blackface sentiment can be traced throughout his writings. Before I begin

---

84, esp. 582–83. See also George Lipsitz, "The Possessive Investment in Whiteness," *American Quarterly* 47, no. 3 (September 1995): 369–87.

4. Ralph Ellison, "Change the Joke and Slip the Yoke," in *Collected Essays*, 102. Hereafter, this essay is cited parenthetically as Joke.

this tracing, however, I want to explain why I am using this troubled termi-
nology. Why not simply refer to Ellison's well-known championing of black
folklore and leave it at that?

After the work of Robert O'Meally, it is incontestable that "*Invisible
Man* is built on folk foundations." Why attempt to link this with the tradition
of minstrelsy? I will argue that Ellison's ambitions for black folklore were
national in scope and integrationist in aim, reflecting his belief in the fully
saturated mixture of blackness and whiteness that characterized American culture. Despite his upbringing as Bliss, Sunraider functions as white.
Through this gesture of making Sunraider politically white, Ellison placed
the focus of this novel on the problematic condition of whiteness, a condition constituted in large part by the denial of blackness. The great American
tradition of blackface minstrelsy contained the efforts on the part of white
folk to utilize the resources of black folklore in the elaboration of the fiction of
racial difference. If Ellison's ambitions for black folklore held any possibility
of realization, characters and subjects politically and historically constituted
as whites had to be able to learn from and appreciate black folklore. The
character of Sunraider is not an experiment in passing but an experiment
in blackface—an experiment that fails in its immediate goals but not in its
fundamental recognition of the structural problem of whiteness.[5]

Ellison's efforts to place the basics of black folklore at the center of a
national culture trace a journey to an imagined place in order to bring back
a magical object that could redeem the American project of democracy in
the modern industrial age. Ellison felt that the deep wisdom, the intricately
stepped and deeply felt techniques, of black folklife was necessary equipment for living for a nation of masked jokers. This is the retrieving impulse
of a folklorist, but this longing to recover the best of the past in order to provide elements missing from the lived experience of the present is also akin
to the impulse that sparked the popularity of blackface minstrelsy a century
earlier. Like the Virginia Minstrels who journeyed throughout the South to
find the material that became the basis of their shows and legitimated their
performances as "real Negroes," Ellison had to travel imaginatively quite far
from his writing table in Harlem. These travels carried him from his position
as one of the most highly esteemed and generously rewarded writers of his
generation, back to the drugstores and shoe-shine parlors of his youth, to

5. The classic discussion of Ellison's use of folklore is Robert G. O'Meally's *The Craft of
Ralph Ellison* (Cambridge: Harvard University Press, 1980). The quote is from page 79. I
want to thank Professor O'Meally for his gracious and gently delivered advice about ways
to revise this essay.

places in his own memory, as well as to a South he had constructed out of notes taken during his work for the Federal Writers' Project, to locate the lore that could heal the nation. A fragile nostalgia, carved from the brittle idealization of unlived moments lost, shaped the recovery work of Ellison, as it had directed the research of nineteenth-century minstrels. Dan Emmett, one of the founders of the Virginia Minstrels, claimed to have grown familiar with black folkways, songs, dances, and stories during his youth in southern Ohio. Like Ellison, he studied black folklife as an adult and devoted much of his adult life to presenting that material in his own cultural production. Like Emmett, Ellison felt a simultaneous identification with and distance from those whose habits, stories, and songs he studied.[6]

In "That Same Pain, That Same Pleasure," Ellison describes the longing he felt during graduation week at Tuskegee to leave the official celebration and participate in the festival organized by the local black community: "I found their celebrations much more attractive than the official ceremonies, and I would leave my seat in the orchestra and sneak out to watch them, and while my city background had cut me off from the lives they led and I had no desire to live the life of a sharecropper, I found their unrhetorical activities on the old football field the more meaningful."[7] This sentiment is not so very distant from the longing for premodern pleasures that characterized minstrelsy. Based on a nostalgia for a form of social organization seemingly more deeply grounded in the rhythms of nature, minstrel performers projected an imaginary lost essence onto black bodies in order to momentarily recapture that loss through blackface performance. Projecting his own longing for an escape from sophistication onto the "unrhetorical" aspect of the popular celebration, Ellison was able to enjoy precisely those feelings

6. Constance Rourke, *American Humor: A Study of the National Character* (1931; reprint, New York: Doubleday, 1953), 74. In addition to Rourke, for discussions of blackface minstrelsy from its beginnings in the late eighteenth century through its transformations in the mid-twentieth, see Alexander Saxton, *The Rise and Fall of the White Republic* (New York: Verso, 1990); Robert Toll, *Blacking Up: The Minstrel Show in Nineteenth-Century America* (New York: Oxford University Press, 1974); Eric Lott, *Love and Theft: Blackface Minstrelsy and the American Working Class* (New York: Oxford University Press, 1993); Dale Cockrell, *Demons of Disorder: Early Blackface Minstrels and Their World* (New York: Cambridge University Press, 1997); William T. Lhamon, *Raising Cain: Blackface Performance from Jim Crow to Hip Hop* (Cambridge: Harvard University Press, 1998); Michael Rogin, *Blackface, White Noise: Jewish Immigrants in the Hollywood Melting Pot* (Berkeley: University of California Press, 1996); and Hans Nathan, *Dan Emmett and the Rise of Early Negro Minstrelsy* (Norman: University of Oklahoma Press, 1977).

7. Ralph Ellison, "That Same Pain, That Same Pleasure," in *Collected Essays*, 77.

and activities without threatening his own position of privilege. He had no desire to live the lives of the poor working families living near Tuskegee, but he felt a powerful desire to benefit imaginatively from their pleasures.

Ellison was not alone among black intellectuals in this struggle with folklore and minstrelsy. In his carefully detailed and wonderfully clear book *Uplifting the Race*, historian Kevin Gaines has described the tortured relationship between uplift ideology and minstrelsy found in the social prescriptions of certain members of the black elite, along with cultural producers such as Paul Laurence Dunbar and Ellison. While working to promulgate a positive understanding of black culture during the first half of the twentieth century, northern black elites regularly opposed their sense of this civilization to the minstrel stereotypes that had been firmly ensconced in the white imagination. But those stereotypes were not totally eschewed. As Gaines argues, "Uplift ideology assented to the racist formulation of the Negro problem by projecting onto other blacks dominant images of racialized pathology."[8] In fact, throughout the early twentieth century, a "confrontation with the centrality of minstrelsy" was crucial to the formation of both "black and white middle-class subjectivities" (*UR*, 207). One of the consequences of this strategy was that elite blacks "looked with disapproval . . . upon such emergent black cultural forms as ragtime, blues, jazz and the social dance styles that animated black vaudeville, minstrel troupes, traveling tent shows, and, later, musical comedy revues." As Gaines puts it, to many, "these black cultural forms were indistinguishable from minstrelsy" (*UR*, 93). Indeed, the relationship between these members of the black elite identified by Gaines and the content and form of black folklore was antifoundational. In fact, the cultural alternative laid out by the black bourgeoisie simply required the equally antifoundational adoption and mastery of European-derived artistic formulas. Understandable within the historical context of Jim Crow, "scientific racism," lynching, and the demeaning images and sounds produced by the white singers, actors, writers, and illustrators who were plundering these bountiful cultural resources, the attempted erasure of black folklife resulted in its hybrid reproduction as an alluring forbidden fruit, tantalizingly available for only the knowing few, who then made sly, if conflicted, allusions to its tastes and pleasures.

Gaines's description of Dunbar's "deep ambivalence over his own involvement" (*UR*, 190) in minstrel performances and dialect poetry illus-

---

8. Kevin Gaines, *Uplifting the Race: Black Leadership, Politics, and Culture in the Twentieth Century* (Chapel Hill: University of North Carolina Press, 1996), 75. Hereafter, this work is cited parenthetically as *UR*.

trates the difficulties of engaging with blackface's antifoundational relationship to black folklore. At the same time that Dunbar found power in these ambiguous possibilities, he was deeply hostile to "its expropriation by white popularizers" (*UR*, 191) and fearful that his own work contributed to the political project of dehumanizing blacks. Concomitantly, Zora Neale Hurston ridiculed blackface entertainers precisely for their lack of authenticity. "Without exception I wonder why the black-face comedians *are* black-face; it is a puzzle—good comedians, but poor niggers."[9] Indeed, when Hurston's book of folklore, *Mules and Men*, appeared, Franz Boas described the "great merit" of her work as a result of the way in which she "entered into the homely life of the southern Negro as one of them and was fully accepted as such."[10] In light of such concerns, it can become tempting to reproduce one form of the debate about black folklife—that it can only be a racially specific cultural resource; its complex purity prevents white interlopers from doing anything other than misunderstanding it and misusing it. For example, Henry G. Spalding remarks in the introduction to his *Encyclopedia of Black Folklore and Humor* that "an authentic black joke" must derive from "*personal involvement*; from memories of childhood's day of frolic in a black world; from a lifetime of coping with the problems unique to the black America; yes, and the exuberant joy, the zest for living even under adverse circumstances which he has expressed in song and story."[11] One might choose, then, to discriminate among Emmett's, Dunbar's, and Ellison's use of black folklore through an unambiguous appeal to racial identity. Such a move requires positing identity as a foundational category that would ground and legitimate a relatively unmediated relationship between experience and representation. But if certain subjects historically and politically constituted as black retain an antifoundational relationship to this folklore—for instance, one based more on nostalgia for an imaginary lost wholeness than on an assumed unmediated connection between life and lore—then any evaluative distinctions among their uses of the material must lie elsewhere. As with any cultural-political phenomenon, the work produced out of an antifoundational relationship to black folklore must be judged by its effects.

Regardless of who is making the claim, to posit a racially bounded

9. Zora Neale Hurston, "Characteristics of Negro Expression," in *The Jazz Cadence of American Culture*, ed. Robert G. O'Meally (New York: Columbia University Press, 1998), 308.

10. Zora Neale Hurston, *Mules and Men* (1935; reprint, New York: Harper, 1990), xiii.

11. Henry G. Spalding, *Encyclopedia of Black Folklore and Humor*, rev. ed. (Middle Village, N.Y.: Jonathan David Publishers, 1978), xiii.

culture is to appeal to standards outside of culture to arbitrate those boundaries. This position reduces in the end to an immutable biological or metaphysical definition of race. Walter Benn Michaels enjoys tracing this reduc-
tion in writers as careful as Alain Locke and W. E. B. Du Bois. He seems to
take special joy in deconstructing Hurston's attempts to discuss the fraught
connections between class and race—precisely the intersection of axes
of difference where black folklore has its strongest traction. One might be
tempted, therefore, to abandon the attempt to identify something that could
be called black folklore and describe its appropriate use. Discarding the
ontological foundational status for race, however, does not empty black folklore of its historical specificity. It is not necessary to assume the validity
of a consistent and coherent racial identity in order to make sensible use
of this genre of cultural production. An alternative approach to the same
material, one that eschews any metaphysical lures, might be traced through
the antifoundational rhetorics of blackface. Instead of pointing back toward
an authenticated folk culture, legitimated through metaphysical or biological assumptions, one might agree to encounter and confront the artificial
manipulations of blackface, the use of the historical cultural resources of
black folklore by those with an antifoundational relationship to its conditions
of production.[12]

While I do not want to say that Ellison and Emmett had identical relations to black folklore, I do want to highlight certain similarities. Emmett, the
nineteenth-century white entertainer, drew from black folklore and was able
to create through his performances an intriguing, if anxiety-producing, blend
of black and white cultures. Ellison was a twentieth-century black writer who
drew from black folklore and who based his artistry on his ability to articulate
the profound intertwining of black and white cultures. Like Emmett, Ellison
had to overcome a certain distance from black folklore. The key point I want
to make here is not one of social or political equivalence between the two
men and their work but instead the recognition of the antifoundational relationship each had to his material. To engage the strategies of blackface in
the time of Emmett or Dunbar—or even today—is to deny purity, to deny
transparent authenticity, and to recognize the proliferation and the useful-
ness of masks. If the mask cannot be judged in terms of its fit to the face
or the body beneath it, then it can be judged only in terms of the work it
performs. We now have a considerable body of scholarship that details the

12. Walter Benn Michaels, *Our America: Nativism, Modernism, and Pluralism* (Durham,
N.C.: Duke University Press, 1995), 85–93.

simultaneous investment in and disavowal of an imaginary blackness that stimulated and haunted the historical forms of blackface—the love as well as the theft it entailed. We also have the evidence of such poets as Dunbar, who attests to the ubiquity of the mask and the pain that wearing it can cause. I want to argue that one of the most important gifts Ellison has given us is his encouragement to investigate the fundamentally ambiguous realm of blackface—both its representations of premodern chaos and its articulations of black folklife. His use of black American folklore strove to aestheticize the mask and thereby to render it susceptible to meaningful standards, to cultural evaluation instead of outright condemnation, to political as well as philosophical debate, and to place it at the center of a national culture.

Gaines alludes to Ellison as one black intellectual among many others who worked to find a middle ground between the elite dismissal of black folklife and the near-minstrel celebration of it as the sole authentic blackness. Ellison was never shy to talk about the value and the danger to be found in wearing the blackface mask. In "Change the Joke and Slip the Yoke," Ellison writes that "the mask, stylized and iconic, was once required of anyone who would act the role" (Joke, 101). The role he speaks of is that of the darky entertainer, whose job it was to evoke the "fascination of blackness." However rooted in black folklore—firmly or loosely—this symbolic blackness had little to do with black people. Rather, the symbolic purging factor performed by the blackface mask was the result of the "white American's Manichean fascination with the symbolism of blackness and whiteness." As Ellison points out, "The racial identity of the performer was unimportant, the mask was the thing (the 'thing' in more ways than one), and its function was to veil the humanity of Negroes thus reduced to a sign, and to repress the white audience's awareness of its moral identification with its own acts and with the human ambiguities pushed behind the mask" (Joke, 103).

This passage is crucial in two important ways. First, it disaggregates the mask itself from "the racial identity of the performer," acknowledging the blackface performances of black artists from William Henry Lane (Juba) to Billy Kersands to Bert Williams. Secondly, this disaggregation enables the analysis of the politico-aesthetic function of the mask in specific contexts. Regardless of whether or not the face behind the mask would be recognized as white or black, the mask's function has two aspects that are intertwined with each other, yet not inextricably so. When discussing the "darky entertainer" and the most horrific of the minstrel stereotypes, it is clear that the mask's function is to reduce real black Americans to a sign, and that this sign has the further function of prophylactically protecting its wearers and the audience from full identification with the role. But the mask also enables the enactment of precisely those elements of chaotic ambiguous possibility that modern capitalism has worked so efficiently to destroy.

Eric Lott has pointed this out in remarking that blackface linked the enactment of forbidden pleasures and the embodiment of antimodern, anticapitalist desires to a strategy of simultaneous identification and displacement.[13] But the ambiguity of this strategy introduced an unpredictable level of complexity. The white performers and white audience for nineteenth-century minstrelsy were ostensibly directing the show, but they were not in control of its meanings. The psychological dissociation that the mask provided worked only when blackness was believed to be other than human. When white actors put on the mask and acted out forbidden impulses, they embodied the otherness that their racist proclamations had attempted to put beyond the pale. Ellison puts it nicely:

> When the white man steps behind the mask of the trickster his freedom is circumscribed by the fear that he is not simply miming a personification of his disorder and chaos, but that he will become in fact that which he intends only to symbolize; that he will be trapped somewhere in the mystery of hell. . . . Out of the counterfeiting of the black American's identity there arises a profound doubt in the white man's mind as to the authenticity of his own image of himself. (Joke, 107)

O'Meally has pointed out that Ellison was angered by the suggestion that his own work might be considered akin to the work of blackface entertainers. But it does seem that Ellison's desires to articulate an American culture with black folklore at its core required an engagement with that material by those who could not or would not claim to have been born to it. Ellison's own use of black folklore required the legitimation of an antifoundational relationship to the material, but this does not eradicate the responsibility for how it was used.[14]

The perhaps inescapable legacy of blackface clings to the Invisible Man throughout Ellison's great novel. One night the heat goes out in the room he rents from Mary. The pipes clang with the echoes of the neighbors pounding for the super's attention. In a furious response to the growing cacophony, the Invisible Man picks up the closest bludgeon, which hap-

---

13. Lott, *Love and Theft*, 142.
14. O'Meally, *The Craft of Ralph Ellison*, 166.

pens to be "the cast-iron figure of a very black, red-lipped and wide-mouthed Negro," a grotesque blackface bank with an outstretched arm to be used for tossing coins into the open mouth. He stops a moment to feel "hate charging" within him, wondering why Mary would keep such an image around, before smashing the bank against the pipes. As it breaks apart, coins fly out; some of Mary's savings had been stored inside the bank. He continues beating on the pipe with the shattered bank's head until Mary herself calls out to him to stop. Before the Invisible Man leaves for the day, he sweeps up the pieces of the bank along with the coins and drops them into his briefcase, hoping to smuggle all of it out of Mary's house before she notices the destruction. Safely out on the street, he tosses the entire bundle into the first trash can he sees, hoping to have dispensed with it forever. But he is called back by a woman who refuses to allow him to dump his trash in her can. Next he tries to just drop the trash in the street. This time he is chased for two blocks by a friendly man who saw the Invisible Man drop the bundle and, thinking it held something important, wants to return it to him. Finally realizing that he is not going to be able to simply get rid of the hated image, he carries it with him to his new home and his new role that the Brotherhood has created for him. However much he might want to destroy the bank, to smash it to pieces and throw it away, the blackface image sticks to him like history.[15]

The crime of minstrelsy for Ellison lay precisely in its creation of this inescapable legacy. It derived from the act of "designating another, politically weaker, less socially acceptable, people as the receptacle for one's own self-disgust, for one's own infantile rebellions, for one's own fears of, and retreats from, reality."[16] But the techniques which enabled that function—the wearing of the mask, the creative (mis)use of black folk culture that derived from the necessarily antifoundational relationship to the material, the central figure of the trickster—were fundamental American characteristics. In *Invisible Man*, Ellison gives us a picture of the playful and evasive trickster in the figure of Rinehart, "an American virtuoso of identity who thrives on chaos and swift change" (Joke, 110). Rinehart understood that "the world in which we lived was without boundaries. . . . A vast seething,

---

15. Ralph Ellison, *Invisible Man* (New York: Vintage, 1952), 318–32. Hereafter, this work is cited parenthetically as *IM*. For discussions of blackface objects, see Kenneth Goings, *Mammy and Uncle Mose: Black Collectibles and American Stereotyping* (Bloomington: Indiana University Press, 1994), and Patricia A. Turner, *Ceramic Uncles and Celluloid Mammies: Black Images and Their Influence on Culture* (New York: Anchor Books, 1994).
16. Ralph Ellison, "The World and the Jug," in *Collected Essays*, 171.

hot world of fluidity," where "perhaps the truth was always a lie" (*IM*, 498). The crime of minstrelsy for Ellison was not the enactment of this trickster figure. It was not the protean liquidity of identity that followed from donning the mask. Ellison recognized that the mask itself was born of a society that claimed to be "traditionless" and "classless," worn in aggression as well as defense. Behind that mask could stand humans of the utmost sensitivity, janitors who were opera fans as well as recent European immigrants uncertain of their identity as white Americans. Ellison understood that the mask might not be a hindrance to but a means of engaging their deepest sensibilities. The institutional crimes of minstrelsy were a matter of historical record, but the techniques of the mask and perhaps even something at the paradoxical imitative base of minstrelsy could be redeemed.[17]

One of the most stunning moments in *Invisible Man* comes when the narrator encounters Tod Clifton selling paper dolls on the street. Walking into a crowded sidewalk scene quite by accident, the Invisible Man pushes his way to the front of a "fascinated" and chuckling crowd to see "a grinning doll of orange-and-black tissue paper with thin flat cardboard disks forming its head and feet and which some mysterious mechanism was causing to move up and down in a loose-jointed, shoulder-shaking, infuriatingly sensuous motion, a dance that was completely detached from the black, mask-like face." "Throwing itself about" with "fierce defiance," "dancing as though it received a perverse pleasure from its motions," Sambo, the dancing doll, enacts some of the worst stereotypes of blackface minstrelsy, with its perverse yet detached pleasures (*IM*, 431–38). But the doll is not being sold by some slimy white hustler. The mysterious mechanism that makes the doll dance is controlled by Clifton, previously a member of the Brotherhood and a potential rival for the Invisible Man's position in that organization. When we first meet Clifton, he is described as possessing "the chiseled, black-marble features sometimes found . . . in southern towns in which the white offspring of house children and the black offspring of yard children bear names, features and character traits as identical as the rifling of bullets fired from a common barrel" (*IM*, 363–65). Perhaps it is his "Afro-Anglo-Saxon" characteristics that render Clifton particularly sensitive to Ras the Exhorter's challenges to the young man's authenticity. But Clifton is also the member confident enough and in tune enough with the people on the street to support immediately the Brotherhood's highly successful anti-eviction strategy. Soon after a fistfight with Ras, Clifton disappears, only to show up on this sidewalk, selling twenty-five-cent Sambo Boogie Woogie paper dolls.

17. Ralph Ellison, "The Little Man at Chehaw Station," in *Collected Essays*, 489–519.

*What makes him happy, what makes him dance,*
*This Sambo, this jambo, this high-stepping joy boy?*
*. . . He's . . . the twentieth-century miracle.*
*. . . he'll kill your depression*
*And your dispossession, he lives upon the sunshine of your lordly*
*smile.*
(*IM*, 432)

The Sambo dolls and the spectacle of Clifton selling the dolls fill the Invisible Man with righteous indignation. He can't bear to face Clifton for fear that he will attack him. He cannot comprehend why Clifton would drop so far out of the Brotherhood that he would be reduced to selling these abominations. Why would Clifton choose to drop out of the purposeful march of history? And why would good black Americans stand around, gawk at, be amused by, and want to purchase these symbols of degradation?

Ellison, of course, has a purpose for this scene, a point to make. But it is not a simple point. This is also the scene where Clifton is shot by a white policeman, one of the actions that changes the entire movement of the narrative. The juxtaposition is startling. Interrupted selling apparently demeaning images, Clifton dies because he won't be insulted or humiliated by the cop. His death shocks the Invisible Man, provoking an extended meditation on history, everyday life, meaning, and pleasure. It forces him to rethink his position on the doll. Indeed, what was the appeal of that paper fetish which danced so mockingly, so dangerously, on the sidewalk? How was it related to the passion and the power of Tod Clifton? How could this dancing fetish, this paper manifestation of blackface pleasure, be so powerful and yet have been left out of history? Beneath the street, waiting for a subway, the Invisible Man encounters other images, other persons who had been left out of history: sharply, perhaps overly, dressed young men, with zoot suits and pomaded hair, smelling and smiling of a kind of immediate yet perhaps cheap success, engaged in their own private battles of passion and power, fashion and style. The nuns on the subway and the blues recordings blasting onto the street at the end of the ride, the people who march in Clifton's funeral, the unseen singer who finds the perfect tune, the crowd that ceases to be a crowd and instead becomes uncountable numbers of individual men and women—all of them seem to be revolving outside the groove of history. What if the power that motivated all of these "stewards of something uncomfortable" were somehow connected to the fetish of the Sambo doll with all its unpredictable ambiguity. Or, conversely, "What if history was not a reasonable citizen, but a madman full of paranoid guile?" (*IM*, 441). What if history, like Rinehart, were not simply a boomerang but a trickster, the key to its power held by the unspeakable fetish of the Sambo doll and the smiling blackface bank? What if the antifoundational rhetorics of blackface were the key to understanding real historical racial difference?[18]

In *Juneteenth*, Bliss Proteus Rinehart is re-created as Adam Sunraider. But instead of presenting this character as a mysterious trickster who seems to know all the answers and hold all the powers, Ellison has given us Sunraider's sentimental education in blackface. Once Alonzo Hickman takes on the responsibility of educating this baby, the heavy weight of the novel's allegorical function bears down. Yet Hickman responds with grace and wisdom to the unfair burden that is placed on him. His response to the burden is to invent for himself the task of raising this child as black in the segregated South, teaching him all he knows of black folklife. With all their claims to ethnographic authenticity, Thomas Rice, Billy Whitlock, and Dan Emmett never had it so good. Bliss's blackface role, his mask, will be constructed out of the loving kindness and careful teaching of an accomplished musician and preacher—God's Trombone, Daddy Hickman. As an aside, it is tempting here to read Hickman as Ellison, and Bliss as the impossible-to-finish project of the second novel.

What sense does it make to call Bliss's education sentimental training in blackface? Does Bliss wear a mask? Or is he, by virtue of his raising, simply black? What is the source of his identity? Was it given to him at birth? Does it lie somewhere inside his person? Or is it constructed out of the daily actions that his person engages in? While Hickman sits by Senator Sunraider's hospital bed, the senator remembers his youth—the character of Bliss. He remembers being taught the intricate timing required to properly perform resurrection. He remembers clutching his Easter bunny, dressed in his best tuxedo, lying flat in the curved, carved, silk-lined coffin, waiting for his cue so that he could rise up, slowly, with his eyes closed and his Bible in his hands, and only at the right moment opening his eyes and casting his arms wide open and speaking "good" English, preaching with immaculate timing, the magic words that will save souls. What a hokey gimmick he was taught. What showbiz. A child, a "white" child, rising up out of a white coffin in a white tuxedo, with a white bunny and a Bible. What sheer overdone, absurd artificiality. The young boys from the neighborhood laugh at

18. For an eloquent discussion of Ellison's "boomerang" theory of history, see Robert O'Meally, "On Burke and the Vernacular: Ralph Ellison's Boomerang of History," in *History and Memory in African-American Culture*, ed. Genevieve Fabre and Robert O'Meally (New York: Oxford University Press, 1994), 244–60.

the theatrics of it, at its obvious links to the rhythmic signifying that is the common coin of the neighborhood. One upstart even shows off his ability to preach the alphabet, the a's, the b's, and the z's. Another responds, "Any of us can do what you're doing." But the point is that Bliss really preached salvation. His preaching worked. Its effects were felt throughout the revival tent. Hickman knew he was teaching Bliss a bag of tricks, but he also knew there was a very serious purpose behind those tricks. The techniques of play and showbiz, the white mask of the coffin, the hokey gimmickry did not demean or diminish the serious function of the preaching. It did save souls. Bliss learned how to preach. He learned the styles of Reverends Hickman, Eatmore, and Wilhite. He learned how to play the dozens. He learned how to talk. He learned all the trickster stories. He never did learn how to sing. But he did take a few lessons in how to love. Bliss grew up eating and breathing black American folklore. He learned how to wear the mask, and he never forgot the seriousness of living in the American jokeocracy (*Juneteenth*, 50).

Yet he still turned into race-baiting Senator Sunraider. How did this happen? The answer lies in the historical tradition of blackface.

A crazy white woman—perhaps his mother, perhaps not—bursts into the revival tent on Juneteenth, interrupting the service, trying to grab Bliss and claiming he was her baby. Intense emotional disruption was not unknown among the revivals, but never before had a woman brought such unexpected news. Caught by the possibility that this or some other white woman might have been his mother, the young preacher wants to know, needs to know, what's true. What is the authentic foundation of his identity? Hickman tries to calm Bliss by telling him a story about how that woman was always stealing babies. Her attempt to claim him had nothing to do with Bliss; it was simply one among many outrageous claims she made about Asian babies as well as black ones. Hickman thinks it is crazy to say that all citizens must be her children, must be white.

Later, Hickman takes Bliss to a circus where he sees a short clown wearing burned cork being chased and beaten. Something about the political-institutional reality of this performance starts to sink in for Bliss. What kind of a world is it where only the short, dark clowns get hit? Bliss wants to know if they're real people. What is their authentic nature? Hickman reassures him that the people are real, but that the circus is only a show, only an entertainment. That is no comfort for Bliss, the young preacher whose own show had such powerful effects. Outside the tent, Bliss finds the clown stripping off his costume and punches him twice.

As a creature of blackface, encountering the political articulations of blackface, Bliss starts to ask himself some crucial questions. Will Bliss be a member of the political collective who gets hit, or will he be among those who do the hitting? Bliss talks Hickman into taking him to the movies. The spectacle captures the boy, pulling him up out of his seat, onto the screen, and into the scene. For on the screen seems to be his mother—or at least the crazy woman from the revival, with her pale skin, her freckles, and her curls. Hickman warns him. They're only shadows, he says. As shadows, they are of a different form than the Word. They can't hurt you so long as you remember that they're only shadows, not acts. But it clearly doesn't feel that way to Bliss. For him, the overwhelming spectacle of show business has an undeniable intensity. Mary Pickford's white face on the screen is just as real as Bliss's white form rising out of the white coffin. This is not simply a matter of not knowing the difference between reality and illusion. No, the illusion of the whiteness of Bliss and of Pickford has powerful effects on the world, effects that are unpredictable in themselves but that take their direction from their political-institutional contexts. After a few trials of running away and getting caught, Bliss finally chases down the vision of Mary Pickford in a whites-only theater in Atlanta, and here the complex political context is fully staged.

When Bliss tries to enter the theater, the ticket taker wants to know where his mother is and asks him why he is not in school. Bliss replies that his mother is in the theater and that her name is Pickford. The young ticket taker, "as much black as he is white," laughs and warns Bliss that he had better get in there before someone big and black gets hold of her. Then with a quick dismissal, "Here Mister Bones, Mister Tambo . . . ah Rastus," the guard waves Bliss into the theater. Bliss escapes from the minstrel stage of the theater's lobby, where the young boy raised black has been engaged in dialogue with a trickster figure, fearfully passing for white in order to be allowed another ecstatic glimpse of his ideal mother, the bearer of some imagined identity, the source of Bliss's own claims to political agency, the perfect Oedipal blend of nurturing power and fearful seduction. At this moment, the premodern chaos of blackface wears the blinding mask of whiteness. And when Bliss exits the theater, he is on his way to becoming Sunraider.[19]

Ellison has a difficult time telling us much about Adam Sunraider. All we really know is that he never loses the skills Hickman taught him. Whether

19. For a discussion of the way in which the ticket taker is "as much black as he is white," see O'Meally, The Craft of Ralph Ellison, 142–43.

traveling as a filmmaking con man, preaching in a white church in Atlanta, or speaking in Congress, Sunraider continues to play the riffs he learned from God's Trombone. He can "do" his version of the Reverend Eatmore even while suffering from a gunshot wound and lying in the hospital. As Sunraider lies dying, the experience of Bliss is what he remembers. In his delirium, Sunraider seems to lament his inability to have accepted the love of the "teasing brown," a young woman he was hoping to film and with whom he did find some momentary heteronormative peace. She was the one who said, after Sunraider had been created out of the dust and shadows of old circuses and movie theaters, "You do sound like us once in a while, especially when you get that dreamy look on your face" (*Juneteenth*, 73). He remembers storytelling sessions filled with the spit and shine of rabbits, bears, and hounds. He remembers pulling a cool watermelon out of a deep well and carefully spitting the seeds far away. He also remembers planes writing warnings—stay away from the polls—in the sky. What Ellison knows of Sunraider is his inside, that inside constructed from the elements of southern black folklife. Yet Ellison cannot really tell us who this person was who could take these gifts yet attempt to avoid the obligation they carried with them. For all of his efforts to narrate the political processes of blackface, Ellison cannot imagine its psychology.

Maybe this is the novel's weakness. But it might also be its strength. When Senator Sunraider represents the black-hating factions of New England, he is no less and no more authentic, and certainly no more histrionic, than when Bliss preaches to his segregated audience on Juneteenth, for "scenes dictate masks and masks scenes" (*Juneteenth*, 328), and "America is a land of masking jokers" (Joke, 109), regardless of proclaimed racial identity. Paul Gilroy has recently argued that identity is never so much about "I" as it is about "we"; the concept is always a political consideration, primarily a means of constructing inclusions and exclusions. "[Identity] happens when political collectivities reflect on what makes their binding connections possible."[20] We encounter Bliss only through the memories of Hickman and Sunraider. Are Hickman and Sunraider members of the same political collectivity, connected through their memories of Bliss? Is it possible for memories of Bliss to function as the basis for a national culture that can embrace Asian and black babies without forcing them into the arms of a monolithic whiteness? Bliss and Sunraider can be the same

20. Paul Gilroy, *Against Race: Imagining Political Culture beyond the Color Line* (Cambridge: Harvard University Press, 2000), 99.

person insofar as that person is imagined to be both Hickman's son and Ellison's idea of this nation, worthy of loyalty and affirmation only to the extent that it remains able to think its way through its own complexity.

Sunraider exemplifies the production of whiteness through the denial of blackness. He is one of the many possible products of the antifoundational relationship to black folklore Ellison believed to be crucial for the survival of the nation. To have been raised black, in the fullness and strength of the southern black community, was no foundation for the character's identity. This is the conceptual strength of Ellison's novel: *Juneteenth* interrogates the blackface construction of whiteness as a specific political consequence of an antifoundational cultural practice. Yet culture is necessarily antifoundational, and identity is a retrospective reflection on the collective effects of cultural performance. If identity is not a thing but a continual construction out of the scenes and masks worn each day, then Bliss can become Sunraider. And, of course, if identity is not a thing but a collective constructed out of the telling of stories, the preaching of sermons and the singing of songs, then Sunraider, too, can return to Bliss.

# Ralph Ellison and Kenneth Burke:
# The Nonsymbolizable (Trans)Action

*Donald E. Pease*

## 1. Ralph Ellison Signifying on the Shadow in Kenneth Burke's Symbolic Action

Thus on the moral level I propose that we view the whole of American life as a drama acted out upon the body of a Negro giant, who, lying trussed up like Gulliver, forms the stage and the scene upon which the action unfolds. If we examine the beginnings of the Colonies the application of this view is not in its economic connotations at least too far-fetched or too difficult to see. For then the Negro's body was exploited as amorally as the soil and climate. It was later, when men drew up a plan for a democratic way of life, that the Negro began to exert an influence upon America's moral consciousness. Gradually he was recognized as the human factor placed outside the democratic master plan, a human natural resource who, so that the white man could become more human, was elected to undergo a process of institutionalized dehumanization.[1]

1. Ralph Ellison, *Shadow and Act* (New York: Random House, Vintage Books, 1972), 28–29. Hereafter, this work is cited parenthetically as *SA*.

*boundary 2* 30:2, 2003. Copyright © 2003 by Duke University Press.

Ralph Ellison first encountered Kenneth Burke on the morning of 5 June 1935, when he heard Burke direct a seminar discussion on "The Rhetoric of Hitler's Battle" at the New School for Social Research. Ellison was then a member of the wing of the Popular Front known as the League of American Writers. The evening before, Ellison had accompanied Richard Wright to Carnegie Hall, where they heard Ernest Hemingway deliver a keynote lecture encouraging members of the league to join the Abraham Lincoln Brigade in the war against Spanish fascism. That Ellison was in the company of Wright when they heard Hemingway and Burke speak on consecutive days was a coincidence which would soon acquire the significance of a decisive turning point in Ellison's career. Burke's theory of symbolic action would subsequently become the framework for analyzing the social problems that Ellison would address in his fiction and essays. The fact that the theoretical structure in which Burke posed these problems seemed better attuned to social conditons than the Marxian orientation of the Popular Front would lead Ellison to disassociate from that group. Moreover, after it was mediated through the fictional techniques Ellison learned from Hemingway, Burke's theoretical perspective would also provide Ellison with the imaginative resources to distinguish his literary practices from Wright's.

During his seminar at the New School, Burke discussed Hitler's rhetorical strategies within the context of his analysis of scapegoat rituals. Burke described these rituals as comprised of three separate phases: merger, division, and reunification. The merger phase described a situation in which recalcitrant economic and political dilemmas were shared by all the members of a social order. When its members selected a person who was made to represent their irresolvable problems, a principle of division was introduced within the merged society that became the basis for a different social order. As the representative of the merged society's ineradicable tensions, the scapegoat performed the role of vicarious atonement for those who believed themselves purified through the scapegoat's expulsion. After the chosen recipient of the iniquities was thus ritualistically alienated, a principle of unification was created for the members of a new social order, who defined their newly purified identity as structured in their "dialectical opposition to the sacrificial offering."[2]

Ellison had already been struggling for some time to understand the

---

2. Kenneth Burke, *"A Grammar of Motives" and "A Rhetoric of Motives"* (New York: Meridian Books, 1962), 406.

mentality of lynch mobs when he heard "The Rhetoric of Hitler's Battle." He found in Burke's explanation of the dynamics of repression and the transference of complex emotions onto scapegoat groups an analytic framework that was better suited to this pursuit than the Marxian dialectic. Burke's Freudian reading of German anti-Semitism exposed the limitations of Marxian analyses, which had explained Nazism in strictly economic terms.

Ellison found the Marxian theory of class exploitation especially deficient for its failure to explain the surplus psychological benefits that economically deprived Southern whites seemed to acquire when they organized into lynch mobs. After analyzing the dynamics of the lynch mob within the Burkean framework, he concluded that these collective acts of ritualistic violence produced a symbolic compensation for poor Southern whites who "lynched as one of the leading symbolic and ritualistic means of asserting their dominance."[3]

With Burke's discussion of the scapegoat mechanism in mind, Ellison undertook a comparable analysis of the "Negro complex" underpinning the psychology of white Americans. From 1937 to 1940, he composed narratives, review articles, and essays on the topic of lynching that incorporated Burke's insights. The short stories "Boy on a Train," "I Did Not Know Their Names," and "The Birthmark" situated Burke's explanatory model within a narrative framework Ellison organized out of the fictional techniques he learned from a careful reading of Hemingway's *In Our Time*.

Ellison did not limit the psychological complex that undergirded the scapegoat ritual to the geographical borders of the American South. Although his editors refused to publish it on the grounds that it would produce dissension within the ranks of the Popular Front, the original manuscript of his 1939 *New Masses* article, "Judge Lynch in New York," concluded with one of Ellison's interviewees opining that the only difference between the North and South is that in the former geographical region "they're beating the Jews as well as the Negroes."[4]

Burke's analysis of the scapegoat mechanism comprised but one facet of his more encompassing study of the dialectical relations in which symbols and actions were inextricably embroiled. According to Burke, a symbolic action did not merely take place within a particular situation; it also took place as a response to a situation. Burke defined symbolic action as

3. Lawrence Jackson, *Ralph Ellison: Emergence of Genius* (New York: John Wiley and Sons, 2002), 196.
4. Ralph Ellison, "Judge Lynch in New York," Literary and Scholarly Manuscript Collection, quoted in Jackson, *Ralph Ellison: Emergence of Genius*, 219.

"the interrelation and transformation of active and passive principles."[5] If a *symbolic* action involved the linguistic unfolding of an intellectual aim, a symbolic *action* could be understood contrarily as the condensation of the symbolic forms that motivated it. Insofar as a symbolic action named a state of affairs, it also implicitly prescribed an attitude toward the state of affairs so named. And insofar as it prescribed an attitude, a symbolic action contained the recipe for a potential change in attitude.

*Motive* was the keyword in the Burke lexicon. A Burkean motive named the active principle within the dialectical process that transformed a symbolic form's resistant factors into the incitement to act. When considered from the standpoint of the motives that informed them, symbolic actions involved their social agents in a "dramatistic pentad" "of act (what was done) and agent (who did the act and under what subjective conditions), scene (the environment in which the act took place, the extrinsic causal factors that determined it), agency (how the act was done, what instruments were used) and purpose (why the act was done, its ultimate motive or final cause)."[6]

With observations such as these, Burke endowed seemingly every verbal transaction with the potential for verbal inventiveness and rhetorical improvisation that Ellison associated with the Negro folk tradition of "signifying." Burke's characteristic excess of interpretive response—his use of puns, his deployment of paradox, his introduction of multiple and often incongruous perspectives—seemed to Ellison to share the traits of hyperbole and understatement that characterized "signifying" at its best.

But Burke's speculations were not, for Ellison, merely an alternative way to describe the social order; his theory also produced the technology Ellison required for imagining its transformation. Symbolic actions animated discourse in general with socially transformative resources that Ellison's Marxist orientation had previously restricted to historical processes. As symbolic "equipment for living," verbal and visual art posed symbolic solutions for recurring human problems. Moreover, in their status as charted behaviors, these symbolic actions provided instructions to readers in how they might transform these into symbolic solutions.

Ellison isolated Burke's analysis of the socially transformative potential latent within the motives that animated symbolic actions as the single most valuable aspect of his theory. As extrapolations of his critique of the

5. Burke, *"A Grammar of Motives" and "A Rhetoric of Motives,"* 263.
6. Greig E. Henderson, *Kenneth Burke: Literature and Language as Symbolic Action* (Athens: University of Georgia Press, 1988), 32.

scapegoat ritual, Burke's theory described how social discord might be confronted and addressed without the need for scapegoats. More specifically, Burke supplied Ellison with a rhetoric of motives with which he might transform the racist attitude of the social order.

But before he could formulate this change in attitude, Ellison found it necessary to adapt Burke's theory of scapegoating to the psychological dynamics underpinning American racism. American racism differed from German anti-Semitism in that American racist practices entailed the segregation rather than the complete expulsion of American Negroes. The Negro scapegoat was deployed on two separate but inextricably connected levels: At the social level, the Negro scapegoat introduced a principle of racialized division into the social order that the social policy of segregation consolidated; at the psychological level, the Negro scapegoat facilitated collective processes of disavowal and projection which buttressed that social policy.

The social policy of segregation inevitably resulted in perceptible contradictions between Americans' professed democratic ideals and the oppressive social and economic conditions under which Negroes were compelled to live. But the psychology that motivated the scapegoating of Negroes emptied the social field of its reality and transformed the American Negroes whose lives were in fact threatened by social conditions into representations of a Negro stereotype that was described as posing a threat to the social order. In the era of Jim Crow, the Negro stereotype constituted the limit to the norm of similitude that regulated cultural assimilation. The psychological properties that were ascribed to the Negro stereotype transformed American Negroes into the representatives of social behavior that could not be integrated within the social order.

According to Ellison, white Americans' perception of the Negro's diminished social freedoms resulted in symbolic solutions to actual social inequalities, which required a more complex understanding of white Americans' motives than the model Burke had proposed in *A Grammar of Motives*. According to Burke, it was their need to avert recognition of their guilt over actual social inequalities that compelled white Americans, figuratively, "to force the Negro down into the deeper level of his consciousness, into the inner world" (*SA*, 100). This collective act of repression replaced American Negroes with stereotypes.

The Negro stereotype was Ellison's name for the psychological double white Americans invented so that they might split the agency responsible for this oppressive social order away from the policies of Jim Crow and project the specter of threatening oppression onto the Negro community victimized by those policies. Negro stereotypes did not merely repress white Americans' guilt over perceived social injustices; they transformed American Negroes into representations of socially prohibited behavior. These Negro stereotypes instrumentalized the symbolic action through which white Americans supplanted their actual perception of social inequalities with images of the antisocial urges that Negroes were compelled to represent. The latter substitution changed the object cause of white Americans' guilt from perceptible social inequalities to the desire to emulate the Negro's socially tabooed behavior. Rather than acting on the motive to change unequal social conditions, white Americans associated the motive for social change with the socially tabooed behavior of the "subhuman" Negro stereotype. After thus transforming actual American Negroes into "subhuman" agents inhabiting an other-than-human netherworld, the Negro stereotype also justified segregation of this realm as the foundational act of the social order of white Americans.

With Burke's theory of symbolic action as warrant, Ellison augmented his explanation of the role Negro stereotypes played in the reproduction of racist hierarchies with an account of the symbolic forms that gratified the need of white Americans to believe in them. When psychological guilt displaced social guilt, the Negro problem mutated into what Ellison called the "Negro complex." The "complex" here should be understood in the Freudian sense as the interpenetration of noncomparable forms of guilt that did not confront one another and hence could not be simultaneously negotiated. Because they were fashioned out of the anxiogenic complex onto which white Americans projected disavowed perceptions and disallowed behaviors, Negro stereotypes functioned as socially regulative objects. The Negro stereotype regulated the social order of white Americans by associating the desire to change it with the "subhumans" who had already been segregated from the social order. According to Ellison, the ritualistic use to which Negro stereotypes were put had reorganized this ambivalent attitude into a complex that set the need of white Americans to believe and to repress into a relationship of "cooperative antagonism." Their need to believe was partially gratified by the representation of their prohibited drives as having been acted on by the "subhuman" stereotypes. But their need to repress these drives was gratified by their isolation within a "natural" realm that was segregated from normal American culture.

Ellison portrayed the Hollywood film industry and the U.S. literary tradition as the cultural agencies responsible for the production and distribution of the will to believe in these stereotypes. He called this will to believe a cultural "superstition." He named the forms that were constructed out of these structures of superstition "shadows," and he represented the activities responsible for the shadows' production as "illusions." Ellison elaborated on this extraordinary mode of cultural production:

> In the beginnning was not the shadow, but the act, and the province of Hollywood is not action but illusion. Actually, the anti-Negro images of Hollywood films were (and are) acceptable because of the existence throughout the United States of an audience obsessed with an inner psychological need to view Negroes as less than men. Thus psychologically and ethically, these negative images constitute justifications for all these acts, legal, emotional, economic and political, which we label Jim Crow. The anti-Negro image is thus a ritual object of which Hollywood is not the creator but the manipulator. Its role has been that of justifying the widely held myth of Negro inhumanness and inferiority by offering entertaining rituals through which that myth could be reaffirmed. (*SA*, 276–77)

Shadows were the imaginary effects of the Jim Crow legislation that contradicted Americans' stated beliefs in freedom and equality. These shadows emerged in a realm that lay between what Burke called a socially sanctioned motive and a socially symbolic action. As the effects of acts that could not be symbolized in the terms of the nation's foundational beliefs, these shadows inhabited an interstitial realm between the democratic motives that white Americans assigned to their actions and the unacknowledged superstitions through which white Americans justified policies of racial segregation. The need to believe in this nonintegratable realm produced the shadows who were imagined to dwell within it. Insofar as the shadows were imagined to conform to the "subhumans" over which Jim Crow exercised jurisdiction, these shadows accomplished the imaginary justification of this legislation.

Ellison found a literary source for these shady figures in the following lines from T.S. Eliot's "The Hollow Men": "Between the Idea and the Reality / Between the Motion and the Act falls the Shadow." Interpreted from within the context of "The Hollow Men," Ellison's shadows named the motives that remained nonsymbolizable within the social order, but they also described the acts that were the outcome of these socially extraneous beliefs. Ellison's shadows designated the agents and the effects of the acts of hollow men (like Jim Crow) whose legislation was incommensurable with the beliefs and principles out of which the social order was officially constituted. Because they could not be symbolized in the terms of the nation-constituting actions, the acts responsible for social segregation were represented as taking place within the nonsymbolizable terrain between socially symbolic motives and these unspeakable psychosocial needs.

In "Twentieth-Century Fiction and the Black Mask of Humanity," Ellison described blackface minstrelsy as a representative instance of the shadow act through which white Americans acted on their nonsymbolizable needs. According to Ellison, whites who performed in blackface acted out the terms of a racially exclusionary model of American nationalism that insisted on the racial difference between those it awarded full citizenship and those it did not. Ellison believed that blackface performance participated in a social dynamic that undergirded the entire history of American literature. Blackface minstrelsy constituted a collective ritual which produced a national self-consciousness that gave white Americans "an ironic awareness of the joke that always lies between appearance (of freedom) and reality (of racial inequality) . . . the darky act makes brothers of us all." "For a nation of former colonials and immigrants," as Ellison explained this joke, "the Declaration of Independence meant taking on a mask" (*SA*, 49).

By putting on this black mask, the colonials achieved a kind of psychological catharsis of the guilt they experienced for breaking with the institutions and authority of the past. The black mask allowed the citizens of the newly declared American nation to project their guilt over rebelling against authority and breaking with their "old world" pasts onto Negro Americans. When white Americans put on the mask of blackface, they did so in an effort to disidentify themselves from their own actions and from the moral quandaries they pushed behind this mask. The Negro stereotype constructed out of this projection was made to symbolize the rebellious underground side of the white American citizenry. Insofar as it was indelibly associated with the rebellious activities the white citizenry wished to put behind them, the Negro stereotype was symbolic of the white colonial's guilt over rebellion and of the repression of that guilt.

Cultural historian Michael Paul Rogin links Ellison's insight with the influence on American literature of his namesake, Ralph Waldo Emerson, when he observes that blackface minstrelsy and the Emersonian belief in the self-made man were historically contemporaneous events. But in Ellison's account of this history, it was blackface minstrelsy rather than Emersonian self-reliance that was the cultural agency responsible for a white

American's acquisition of a new self.[7] White Americans' assumption of the blackface mask permitted Emerson's self-made man to construct their open futures as the other to the Negro past. When they donned this mask, these self-reliant Americans dissociated from the previous identities they projected onto the nonidentity of the black mask.

Although Ellison believed them crucial to the reproduction of the discourses of American literature and American racism, however, such shadow acts remained curiously unthematized within the Burkean theory of symbolic action. There was a very good reason why the Ellisonian shadow could not become an analytical category within Burke's theory of symbolic action. Burke founded his theory of symbolic action by way of an act of symbolic violence, which articulated a distinction between the symbolic and the nonsymbolic. He grounded this distinction on the conviction that a symbolic action could only properly originate with the motive to break free of the hold of animal immediacy, which he described as the realm of "nonsymbolic motion."[8] This decisive distinction enabled Burke to differentiate symbolic actions from the senseless motions of bestial nature. But this very same distinction made it impossible for him to render the Ellisonian shadow an object of theoretical reflection—the figures Ellison called shadows were constructed at the very site on which Burke erected the distinction between the symbolic and the nonsymbolic.

Whereas Burke's symbolic actions took place in the realm of the symbolizable, the shadows Ellison understood to be the primary integers of the American racist order populated a nonsymbolizable terrain that lay outside the realm of symbolic action about which Burke theorized. As placeholders for the socially unacknowledged activities that took the place of officially motivated symbolic actions, Ellison's shadows nevertheless haunted Burke's theory of symbolic actions with representations of beliefs and enactments Burke could neither fully analyze nor adequately describe.

But the fact that Ellison's shadows had added this extraneous factor to Burke's theory of symbolic action should not obscure the extent of Burke's influence on Ellison's project. Ellison adopted key terms from Burke—*representative anecdote*, *psychology of form*, *perspective by incongruity*, *dramatistic pentad*, *symbolic action*—to describe his own artistic performance. Throughout most of his literary career, Ellison was involved in a dialogue

7. Michael Rogin, *Blackface, White Noise: Jewish Immigrants in the Hollywood Melting Pot* (Berkeley: University of California Press, 1996), 36–40.

8. Burke elaborates on this distinction in "Non-Symbolic Motion/Symbolic Action," *Critical Inquiry* 4 (summer 1978): 809–83.

with Burke that emulated the structure of call and response of the Negro spiritual. In the preface to *Shadow and Act*, he acknowledged Burke as "the stimulating source" of the essays, which were dialectically constituted out of their interlocution. In 1971, Ellison explained to interviewers that Burke had provided him with a "Gestalt through which I could apply intellectual insights back into my materials and my own life."[9]

When Ellison began sketching out the contours of *Invisible Man* in 1945, Burke's literary theory had become such an intimate aspect of his imagination that, as Lawrence Jackson observes, Burke's formulations played an indispensable role in the manuscript's composition. Ellison's method, as Jackson explains it, "was to outline the movement of each chapter using the Burkean schemata, then to write a textured summary."[10] The part Burke's theory was made to play in Ellison's creative processes would attest to the fact that, in addition to a mentor and an ideal interlocutor, Ellison discovered in Burke's philosophy an alternative social order. Ellison found in Burke's vision the symbolic resources he needed for the creation of his own art form. As he transformed Burke's schemata into *Invisible Man*, Ellison resituated himself within a social order that was grounded in the critique rather than the repetition of scapegoat rituals.

Despite these observations concerning Burke's influence, however, I do not intend, in what follows, to read Ellison's project in terms of Burke's theory. I wish to track, and thereafter to elucidate, a transaction between Ellison and Burke that, in disclosing what could not be accommodated within Burke's theory of symbolic action, effected a profound transformation in the basis of their relationship. The transaction to which I refer took place over a forty-year period. It began in 1945, when Ellison constructed "Richard Wright's Blues" out of Burke's theory of symbolic action. Then, in his 1950 edition of *Rhetoric of Motives*, Burke focused on a passage from Booker T. Washington that Ellison had quoted in "Richard Wright's Blues" so as to disagree publicly with Ellison's interpretation of Wright. Ellison indirectly responded to Burke in a scene within *Invisible Man*, and, in 1985, Burke published a private letter to Ellison in which he retracted the terms through which he articulated his disagreement.

---

9. "The Essential Ellison, an Interview," with Ishmael Reed, Quincy Troupe, and Steve Cannon, *Y-Bird Reader* 1 (fall 1977): 127.
10. Jackson, *Ralph Ellison: Emergence of Genius*, 357.

## 2. Ralph Ellison's Crisis of Nomination

I did not destroy that troublesome middle name of mine, I only suppressed it. Sometimes it reminds me of my obligations to the man who named me. (*SA*, 166)

Ellison experienced a lifelong crisis of symbolic investiture that had originated with the naming ritual that took place at his birth. The crisis involved a breakdown in the transfer of the symbolic empowerment that would have allowed him to take up a socially mandated position as an authorized identity within the social order. Burke shed light on Ellison's crisis when he explained that naming was not reducible to the purely nominalistic procedure whereby an empty signifier was attached to a subject whom it was made to designate. In its capacity to shape perceptions concerning a child's destiny as well as the significance attributed to them, naming was responsible for the discursive construction of the child's fate. The first way to come to terms with one's fate, as Ellison explained this symbolic power in the essay "Hidden Name, Complex Fate," involved dealing with the name as a conferral of destiny: "For it is through our names that we first place ourselves in the world. Our names being the gifts of others, must be made our own" (*SA*, 147).

Ellison's father made it extremely difficult for his son to take ownership of his birth name when he named the boy after the "writer and philosopher" Ralph Waldo Emerson. In endowing his son with this literary name, Ellison's father positioned his son within the lineage of a writer whose recognition of African Americans was restricted to their deployment as metaphors for a condition of embodiment he wished to transcend. Having been ushered into life by a name that presupposed the absence of blacks from the symbolic order, Ellison felt expelled from the symbolic universe by the very same name that positioned him within it.

When he was a child in rural Oklahoma, each time Ralph Waldo Ellison was hailed by his birth name, the experience severely interfered with his powers of symbolic identification: "Emerson's name was quite familiar to Negroes in Oklahoma during those days," Ellison recalled, "when World War I was brewing and adults, eager to show off their knowledge of literary figures, and obviously amused by the joke implicit in such a small brown nubbin of a boy carrying around such a heavy moniker would invariably repeat my first two names and then to my great annoyance, they'd add 'Emerson'" (*SA*, 152).

To remind ourselves of the relationship between the name *Ralph Waldo Emerson* and the literary history of racialized exclusions the name *Emerson* authorized, we need only recall the passage from "Self-Reliance" in which Emerson represented what summoned him to his literary signature:

> If an angry bigot assumes the bountiful cause of Abolition and comes to me with his last news from Barbados, why should I not say to him, "Go love thy infant, love thy wood-chopper, be good-natured and modest. Have that grace, and never tarnish your hard uncharitable ambition with this incredible tenderness for black folk a thousand miles off. Thy love afar is spite at home." Rough and graceless would be such a greeting; but Truth is handsomer than the affectation of love. Your goodness must have some edge to it else it is none. The doctrine of hatred must be preached as the counteraction of the doctrine of love, when that pules and whines. I shun father and mother and wife and brother. When my genius calls me, I would write in the lintels of the door-post, "Whim." I hope it is better than whim at last, but we cannot spend the day in explanation.[11]

This passage is marked throughout by anxieties of address: how to address the truth to an abolitionist, how properly to respond to genius when it calls. The slaves on Barbados were made to occupy the position of strangers, which was then defined against the status of kin. But in addition to their geographical distance, the black slaves of Barbados represented for Emerson the barriers to sympathetic identification native to the social formation Orlando Patterson has described as the natally alienated. Natal alienation, or the social condition of radical kinlessness, constituted, as Patterson has explained, the communal fiction through which slave societies rationalized slavery as a form of social death.

The extraordinary emotional contradictions in this passage are evident in Emerson's assertion that he wished to be liberated from the affective alliances which organized the structure of feeling undergirding the abolitionist movement so that he might reinvest those emotions within the family. But the images of the woodchopper and the infant recall scenes of forcible separation and the violence of the auction block that they are supposed to supplant. Moreover, the shift from the family man to the public man with which the passage ends turns on a complex figure that retrieves images of the

11. Ralph Waldo Emerson, "Self-Reliance," in *The Selected Writings of Ralph Waldo Emerson* (New York: The Modern Library, 1968), 148–49.

slave experience—in the citation from Passover—but is void of the slave's African embodiment.

In the journal entries Emerson subsequently drew on when composing his address celebrating the anniversary of the successful slave revolt in the West Indies, he endorsed this correlation of African slavery with social death when he wrote, "It is plain that so inferior a race must perish shortly"; blacks are destined "to serve & be sold & exterminated."[12]

But if Emerson produced an equivalence between the abolitionist's cause and his alienation of domestic affection, the call of genius, insofar as it effects the shunning of two generations of kin, would appear to have intensified that disaffection. Indeed, the single trait that distinguished Emerson's domestic instabilities from the abolitionist's is the fact that while the latter would appear to be an unconscious displacement of affection, the former effect is the outcome of Emerson's conscious decision.

In postwar American literary culture, the name *Ralph Waldo Ellison* went unspoken because the field of American literature had totalized around the name *Ralph Waldo Emerson*, which arrogated the power to represent the universality of the American experience. Emerson believed he occupied the nation at the level of its constitutive norms and grounding assumptions, and that he was the enactor and agent of the national will. In order to become Ralph Waldo *Ellison*, Ellison had to decisively pass through the name of the American writer who had described blacks as the residua he sloughed off so that he might better represent universal man.

Overall, the name his father had conferred on him rendered Ellison unnameable within the social order for which Emerson supplied the overname.[13] At the time he heard Burke deliver his analysis of Hitler's *Mein Kampf*, Ellison had aligned his own work with the literary project of Wright, who accompanied him to hear Burke lecture. Wright's repudiation of the world from which Emersonism excluded him seemed to furnish Ellison with a symbolic solution to his crisis of nomination. This rejection of the Emersonian order inspired Ellison to transform Wright into a countername for Ralph Waldo Emerson. Thereafter, Ralph Ellison situated his literary project

12. Ralph Waldo Emerson, *The Journals and Miscellaneous Notebooks of Ralph Waldo Emerson*, ed. William H. Gailman et al., 16 vols. (Cambridge: Harvard University Press, 1960–1982), 7:393; 9:125.
13. I am indebted to Kimberly W. Benston for the notion of "unnaming" and for the framework for much of my thinking about Ellison's crisis of nomination. See "I Yam What I Am: The Topos of (Un)Naming in Afro-American Literature," in *Black Literature and Literary Theory*, ed. Henry Louis Gates Jr. (New York: Methuen, 1984), 151–72.

between Ralph Waldo Emerson's essays, whose capacity to uplift his white readers derived in part from the exclusion of blacks from their symbolic field, and from Wright's fiction, which violently protested against the injustice of such exclusions. As the literary embodiment of the social forms Emerson wished to transcend, Wright became the Other of the name *Ralph Waldo Emerson*, with Wright's powers of de-nomination becoming most efficacious at the crossroads where the declaration "You are a disciple of Richard Wright" contradicted the accusation "You are Ralph Waldo Ellison."

While Wright's calls for the complete overthrow of the racist social order may have gratified Ellison's retaliatory instincts against his patronymic, however, they did not satisfy his desire to position himself within a viable social alternative. Consequently, after reflecting on Burke's analysis of the dynamics of the scapegoat mechanism, Ellison interpreted Wright's enthusiastic embrace of a space cut off from the U.S. symbolic order as an alternative enactment of the scapegoat ritual. Unlike others who had been selected to take up this mantle, however, Wright performed the work of social excision on himself.

But after Ellison represented Wright's protest in Burkean terms as a form of self-scapegoating, he also began to construe Burke's theoretical system as a symbolic substitute for the U.S. social order. Becoming proficient in explaining the world in Burkean terms, Ellison felt as if he had undergone an initiation into the world of symbolic forms and functions that had been denied him at birth. Instead of merely providing an explanatory framework with which to understand the world of symbolic functions, Burke's logology now seemed to offer Ellison a mandated identity within an alternative symbolic world. Insofar as Burke's world was grounded in a critique of the scapegoat mechanisms at work within the order that excluded Ellison, it seemed to convoke a social order that did not require scapegoats.

Burke's heterocosm also appeared to resolve Ellison's uncertainty about what the symbolic order wanted from him. Throughout his literary career, Ellison would construe himself as constituted at the crossroads of contradictory addressees—where the "you" Wright feared was missing from the realm of Negro culture intersected with the Negro "you" Emerson excluded from the symbolic order. The fact that Burke described his project as a continuation of Emerson's seemed to open up a place for Ellison that was missing from the realm of their common ancestor.[14]

14. Burke acknowledges his place in the Emersonian tradition in Kenneth Burke, *A Grammar of Motives* (Berkeley: University of California Press, 1969), 277–79.

In the following letter, which Ellison addressed to Burke in 1945, we discover that one of the material effects resulting from their interaction entailed Ellison's use of Burke's system to undermine the powerful effect that Wright's ideology of protest then had over his writing and thinking: "The one stable thing I have in this sea of uncertainty is the raft of [Burke's] concepts on which I lie as I paddle my way towards the shore."[15]

Ellison initially found in Wright's fiction the resources with which to reject the Emersonian universe from which he felt natally alienated. But Ellison then turned to Burke, who named Emerson as one of his literary ancestors, to assist the change in his attitude toward Wright, from that of a literary disciple overshadowed by his influence to that of an artist with an alternative vision.

### 3. "The Blues . . . Provide No Scapegoat but the Self"

Western culture must be won, confronted like the animal in a Spanish bullfight, dominated by the red shawl of codified experience and brought heaving to its knees. (*SA*, 93)

Ellison articulated the grounds for the turning point in his relationship with Wright in an essay that the *Antioch Review* published in 1945 under the title "Richard Wright's Blues" and that Ellison republished in *Shadow and Act* in 1963. The blues supplied Ellison with the cultural and emotional means to accomplish his dissociation from Wright. The essay is divided into two parts. In the first part, Ellison produces a knowledge about the blues; in the second part, he deploys the blues as an alternative form of knowledge. Both knowledges are coordinated around the relationship that obtains between the blues and the scapegoating of the Negro. Wright's autobiography, *Black Boy*, provided a representative case study of that relationship.

The essay's symbolic action involves removing Wright from the position of the scapegoat and repositioning him within the tradition of the blues. At a key moment in the essay, Ellison quotes the following passage, from *Black Boy*, as evidence of the difference between Wright's representations of black life in America and the blues: "Whenever I thought of the essential bleakness of black life in America, I knew that Negroes had never been allowed to catch the full spirit of Western civilization, that they lived somehow in it but not of it. And when I brooded upon the cultural barrenness of

---

15. Ralph Ellison to Kenneth Burke, 29 November 1945, cited in Jackson, *Ralph Ellison: Emergence of Genius*, 316.

black life I wondered if clean positive tenderness, love, honor, loyalty and the capacity to remember were native to man. I asked myself if these qualities were not fostered, won, struggled and suffered for, preserved in ritual from one generation to another" (*SA*, 93).

Ellison cites this passage from *Black Boy* because it revealed the cultural limitations of Wright's protest discourse, in which Negro life was portrayed as essentially bleak and culturally barren, replicating the image of the netherworld out of which white Americans constructed the Negro stereotypes and which had relegated Wright himself to the position of a cultural scapegoat. The passage recounted Wright's suspicion that his alienation from American life was compounded by the absence within the black community of interlocutors capable of hearing his protest. Indeed, the despair that had overtaken Wright seemed augmented by the impossibility of addressing a black readership that could comprehend him.

In responding to this passage, Ellison personifies the qualities of "positive tenderness, love, honor, loyalty and the capacity to remember" that Wright believed were missing from black culture. However, when Ellison takes up this position as the listener over whose absence Wright has complained, he does so as the member of a blues audience. "Richard Wright's Blues" decisively undermines Wright's suspicions as well as the Negro stereotypes they corroborated. The essay accomplishes this subversion by distinguishing the Negro life world from the nightmare realm white Americans projected in its place and by demonstrating how the blues facilitated collective resistance to the stereotypes white Americans imposed.

When Wright cried out against the racial injustice of the social order as if he had undergone this experience alone, he ignored the organized resistance of the blues, which redescribed the mundane objects of everyday life as signifiers of resistance. Wright's expression of despair empowered Ellison to represent the community, which was mobilized to carry the individual through this desolation. In responding to Wright's outcry as a participant within a vital blues life world, Ellison contradicts Wright's depiction of "the cultural barrenness of black life." Ellison then correlates Wright's autobiography with the signature formula used by Negro blues artists whose lyrics had trained Wright's readers in how to listen: "If anybody ask you who sings this song / Say it was ole (Black Boy) done been here and gone" (*SA*, 77).

The blues are a verbal art form in which African oral traditions are combined with Western literate forms to foster a communal taste for irreconcilable complexities. The call and response structure underpinning the blues effect a nonhierarchical equivalence between the individual performer's interior expression and the response of the blues community, which fosters the consciousness of dependence on the blues community for a sense of belonging. Indeed, there is a sense in which the "I" does not exist except in its function as a participant in this dialogic musical structure. Because the subject of the blues is constituted through the dialogue between the blues performer and the blues community, this subject does not exist unless it is understood as somehow in expectation of a response.

Irreducibly intersubjective, the blues are socially rather than individually oriented. As a consequence of their orientation, the blues do not bolster the individual performer's ego. They instead associate the fantasy of the individual's self-sufficiency with the scapegoating mechanism constitutive of the oppressive social order. The blues comprise the medium through which the figures the social order has identified as scapegoats return in the transposed form of the nonidentificatory movement in between the interlocutory position of the "you" calling and the "you" responding. In the blues, the scapegoated "I" becomes part of a collective blue "you," whose identity oscillates between comic and tragic identifications. "The blues fall short of tragedy," Ellison explains apropos of this movement, only "in that . . . they provide no resolution, provide no scapegoat but the self" (*SA*, 77).

It was because Ellison considered the blues a way to cultivate a sensibility which flourished within the social formation Burke described as the state of merger that Ellison assigned the blues a foundational role in black culture. The blues convoked a society whose members did not depend on the scapegoat mechanism to sustain social order. In place of the ritual alienation of iniquities from the self to the scapegoat, disturbing social problems were shared by all members of the social order. Without a scapegoat onto whom to project it, social discord was confronted, acted out, and worked through within the parameters of the blues community.[16]

Ellison's repositioning of Wright's autobiography as a lyric performance within the blues tradition undermines the scapegoat mechanism Wright internalized. Wright may have considered black folk art a damaged form of civilization. But in his response to *Black Boy*, Ellison discerns traces of the blues tradition within Wright's cultural genealogy: "The immediate folk culture into which (Wright) was born . . . the specific folk art-form which helped shape the writer's attitude toward his life and which embodied the impulse that contributes much to the quality and tone of his autobiogra-

16. This discussion of the blues draws on Albert Murray's discussion of their relation to the protest genre in *The Omni-Americans: Black Experience and American Culture* (New York: Vintage Books, 1983), 13–69, 142–71.

phy was the Negro Blues" (*SA*, 78). "Richard Wright's Blues" brought *Black Boy*'s emotional content into relief as an object of communal deliberation. The blues community revalued Wright's anguished outcry as a virtuoso performance that contributed to the development of the blues as a form of knowledge and as an alternative to the symbolic order.

The relationship Ellison constructs between Wright's autobiography and the blues lyric facilitates the following definition: "The blues is an impulse to keep the painful details and episodes of a brutal experience alive in one's aching consciousness, to finger its jagged grain, and to transcend it, not by the consolations of philosophy but by squeezing from it a near-tragic, near-comic lyricism" (*SA*, 78). According to Ellison, the blues supplied the subterranean connections between Negro writing and the rituals and symbols of Negro folklore, as well as instructions on how to cope with and how to survive the deep problems arising out of the oppressive structures of American racism. When reinterpreted from the perspective of the blues, even Wright's representation of the cultural barrenness of black life was transformed into an affirmation. "He has converted the Negro impulse toward self-annihilation and 'going-underground' into a will to confront the world, to evaluate his experiences honestly and to throw his findings unashamedly into the guilty conscience of America" (*SA*, 94). If, however, the blues comprise the cultural unconscious of Wright's protests, what motivated his suppression of this vital folk art form "into which he was born"?

Although Ellison never explicitly asks this question, his essay might be described as an effort to formulate an adequate response. Ellison's answer requires that he shift the focus of his essayistic attention from the blues as a social formation that requires explanation to the blues as the epistemological basis for an alternative explanation of U.S. society. In elaborating on the sociological and anthropological significance of Wright's autobiography within the cognitive framework supplied by the blues, Ellison places the knowledges the blues produced on equal footing with these more specialized knowledges, thereby constructing for himself a social position that differed from preexisting social categorizations.

Ellison explains Wright's distrust of the forms of collective sociability produced within the blues community as resulting in large part from the traumatic memories attending his experience of growing up in the "pre-individualist" Southern black community (*SA*, 83). In the Jim Crow South, a Southern black male did not exist in his own right but "only to the extent that others hope to make the race suffer vicariously through him" (*SA*, 84). The member of a Southern black community was compelled to favor the group over the individual because each member was singled out by the racist majority "not as a person but as the specimen of an ostracized group" (*SA*, 84).

Ellison's blues account links the preindividualist ethos that predominated in Southern black communities with Southern scapegoating rituals. Unlike the sociologists who represented Southern blacks' "docility" and "conformity" as qualities inherent to the Negro sensibility, Ellison describes these traits as the effects of a racist scapegoating that recalled Burke's 1937 discussion of Nazi anti-Semitism. "Like the regression to primitive states noted among the cultured inmates of Nazi prisons . . . socially [this preindividualist ethos] is effected through an elaborate scheme of taboos supported by a ruthless physical violence which strikes not only the offender but the entire black community" (*SA*, 84).

As Ellison describes it, the preindividualist sensibility undergirding Southern black communities served two interrelated social functions: It protected Negro children from the terrifying violence of the lynch mob; and it suppressed the individual Negro's expression of the desire for the civic freedom that would incite the lynch mob's reaction. Because these communities struggled to protect their children from the terrifying violence of the lynch mob, the otherwise opposed emotions of kindness and cruelty were "as quickly set off against the member who gestured towards individuality as a lynch mob forms at the cry of rape" (*SA*, 90).

Ellison's designation of the Southern lynch mob as the phantom mediator between Southern blacks and their preindividualist ethos comprises a counterstatement to the sociologists who had complained that *Black Boy* failed to represent the attractive dimensions of life in the South. In failing to recognize the role that these scapegoat rituals played in the construction of the members of black communities throughout the Jim Crow South, these sociologists were complicit in the production of Negro stereotypes. Whatever else the Southern community may have contained, as Ellison writes in response to the sociologists, "it had as little chance of prevailing against the overwhelming weight of the child's unpleasant experiences as Beethoven's Quartets would have of destroying the stench of a Nazi prison" (*SA*, 82).

When he invokes the Nazi concentration camps as the historical analogue for the preindividualist ethos of Southern black communities in which Wright had grown up, Ellison suggests that Wright's need to isolate himself from the entirety of black cultural life should be understood as a symptomatic remainder of this concentration camp mentality. Ellison recalls a metaphor coined by Booker T. Washington to provide the mentality that Wright disavowed with an apt objective correlative:

> *Black Boy*, however, illustrates that this personal quality, shaped by outer violence and inner fear, is ambivalent. Personal warmth is accompanied by an equally personal coldness, kindliness by cruelty, regard by malice. And these opposites are as quickly set off against the member who gestures towards individuality as a lynch mob forms at the cry of rape. Negro leaders have often been exasperated by this phenomenon, and Booker T. Washington (who demanded far less of Negro humanity than Richard Wright) described the Negro Community as a basket of crabs, wherein should one attempt to climb out, the others immediately pull him back. (*SA*, 90–91)

Wright had Booker T. Washington's crab basket in mind when he complained of the "essential bleakness" and "cultural barrenness" of black life. Since the crab basket ethos represented the form of Negro sociability with which Wright was most familiar—the world of blocked mobility in which blacks remained imprisoned so that white Americans could imagine themselves as running free—he could not distinguish its preindividualism from the blues. But Ellison invokes the image of the crab basket to contrast the crabs' immobility to the blues' mobilization.

The members of the blues community differed from Washington's detainees in that they found their way out of this imprisoning metaphor. And the blues were unlike Wright's protest fiction in that the blues organized resistance into a collective movement rather than individualist expression. As a highly volatile field of transposition, the blues empowered performers within its venue to juxtapose words of place and words of movement so as to work through the pain of displacement.

"Richard Wright's Blues" might itself be described as having effected a comparable transposition—from Wright's protestations to Ellison's blues. In effecting this transition, Ellison reenacts the investiture ceremony surrounding the aforementioned crisis of nomination. On the authority of Burke's theory, that is to say, Ellison exercises the symbolic power to change the name of the genre under which Wright produced his work so as to effect a change in Wright's mandated literary identity, from that of a protest novelist to a blues performer. After he positions Wright's protest fiction within a blues context, however, Ellison does not merely add another interpretive perspective. By reclassifying Wright's protest fiction as a blues performance, he, more importantly, charts a literary territory of his own.

"Richard Wright's Blues" transformed the scene within which Ellison accomplished and reflected on his own future work. And this change of scene brought with it a change in all the other factors making up what Burke called the "dramatistic pentad." The new field transformed the agency Ellison understood to inform his project, the actions he undertook there, the motives for performing them, as well as the agent through whom they were accomplished.

Burke's theory of symbolic action supplied Ellison with the linguistic resources with which to differentiate his project from Wright's. But instead of acknowledging Ellison's transformed literary identity, Burke reenacted the very scapegoat ritual he had formerly criticized.

### 4. Kenneth Burke's Shadow Act

Rather than affirming this change in Ellison's identity, that is to say, Burke reduced Ellison's entire essay to the passage in which he quoted Washington so as to interrogate Ellison's motives for undertaking it:

> Ellison says that Booker T. Washington "described the Negro community as a basket of crabs wherein should one attempt to climb out the others should pull him back." Is there not an internal compulsion of the same sort as the individual Negro visits the same judgment on himself? For he may also take the position of what Mead would call the "generalized other": he may visit upon himself the antagonistic attitude of the whites; or, he may feel as "conscience" the judgment of his own class, since he would in a sense be "disloyal" to his class, in transcending the limitations traditionally imposed upon him as a member of that class. Striving for freedom as a human being generically, he may do so as a Negro specifically. But to do so as a Negro is, by the same token to prevent oneself from doing so in the generic sense; for a Negro could not be free generically except in a situation where the color of the skin has no more meaning than the color of the eyes.[17]

Burke published this gloss on "Richard Wright's Blues" during the heyday of McCarthyism and the Communist witch hunts in 1950, when Wright's continued affiliation with the American Communist Party led to the branding of him as a national security risk. When Burke invoked Ellison's

17. Burke, *"A Grammar of Motives" and "A Rhetoric of Motives,"* 193.

class "conscience" as one of the referents for the "generalized other" over-seeing the upper reaches of the crab basket, he revealed his own anxi-eties over the political implications of Ellison's turning from Richard Wright's communism to Richard Wright's blues. It was ostensibly because Ellison deployed his theory of symbolic action in undertaking this change in his artistic loyalties that Burke retrieved Washington's crab basket.

As we have seen, "Richard Wright's Blues" enabled Ellison to trans-form the motives and vocabulary that had previously informed his project— from the Popular Front's Marxian focus on class struggle to the blues tra-dition's opposition to American racism. Burke ventriloquized the voice of George Herbert Mead's "generalized other" in an effort to recover the class consciousness that "Richard Wright's Blues" supplanted. In so doing, he revealed his own anxieties over Ellison's substitution of race matters for the class struggle. In wondering whether Ellison's individual successes would lead him to feel "disloyal" to his class, Burke silently put Ellison's actual dis-loyalty to the party in place of this imagined disloyalty to the Negro race. At the conclusion of these reflections, Burke declared his own continued loyalty to the category of class when he asserted that it is only as a member of the proletariat class that a Negro can transcend particularisms and participate in the universal "unfolding of history as a whole." [18]

When Burke then shifted attention from the question of Ellison's disloyalty to members of his class to disloyalty to members of the Negro race, he articulated the latter disloyalty in terms of the irresolvable tension between universal humanity and Negro specificity. "Striving for freedom as a human being generically, he must do so as a Negro specifically. But to do so as a Negro is, by the same token, to prevent oneself from doing so in a generic sense." But in shifting the pronominal referent of the enunciator of this dilemma from a third person ("*he* must do so as a Negro specifically") to a stand-in for himself (to prevent *oneself* from doing so in a generic sense), Burke impersonated the voice of the Negro conscience to enunciate the dilemmas of a white liberal.

But the dilemmas articulated here do not in fact represent the Negro conscience; they describe instead the founding paradox of white Americans' liberal humanism. When restated within the context of the social policy of Jim Crow, the white liberal's dilemmas give expression to the reverse side of the white racist's particularism. Whereas the racist denies that the black is a human being, the white liberal refuses to recognize the black in the

18. Burke, *"A Grammar of Motives" and "A Rhetoric of Motives,"* 195.

human being. The former wants to discredit the representation of the black as human so that only the image of the black outcast will remain; the latter wants to dissociate blackness from the representation of the human being in order to preserve the representation of the disembodied, unmarked subject of white liberalism.[19]

After the recitation of this apparently irresolvable quandary, Burke would appear to have moved from a simple account of the dilemma to a validation of the racist premises that imposed the dilemma. Burke enacted his own political right to represent human freedom in general through the very act of differentiating his unlimited power from the restriction he imposed on Negro freedom. He impersonated Washington's conscience so that he could retrieve the crab basket as the objective correlative for the restrictions white liberalism had imposed on Negro freedom. When Burke then positioned Ellison within the contours of these seemingly irresolvable dilemmas, he did so on the grounds that Ellison's refusal of the metaphor constituted a disavowal of a painful truth. But Burke had not merely repositioned Ellison within the rejected scene. He ventriloquized the voice of Washington so as to extend the metaphor's powers of containment to encompass the entire black community. Burke's criterion for this expansion of the basket's inclusionary prerogatives apparently derived from the belief that Washington's signification enjoyed a referential relation to the experience of blacks in the world.

For Ellison, Washington's metaphor had only a negative value: It failed to refer to black experience, and it was a false representation of actual black experience. Burke interrupted Ellison's essay at the moment in which Ellison denied the referential accuracy of Washington's crab basket metaphor so as to represent himself as empowered to adjudicate between Washington's representation and Ellison's delegitimation. In thus positioning himself as the empowered arbiter, Burke presumed the correctness of his perspective on Washington's judgment of the black's experience. How could Burke claim the power to correlate Washington's cognitive structure in language with black experience without claiming the power to determine what does and does not constitute authentic black experience? Does Burke's power to adjudicate between these contestatory accounts of the black experience presuppose his knowledge of black experience, or does

19. For a more fully elaborated account of this dilemma, see Magobo P. More, "Outlawing Racism in Philosophy: On Race and Philosophy," in *The African Philosophy Reader*, ed. P. H. Coetzee and A. P. J. Roux (New York: Routledge, 1998), 365.

it disclose his will to believe in constructions of black experience that are necessarily external to the blacks who are represented in these terms?

Burke established a hierarchy in the relations of representation in which he designated himself as the representer of black experience and included Ellison among the represented. Burke apparently exercised these representational powers on the grounds that Ellison could not occupy the position of the universal, which constitutes the precondition for arriving at a verdictive judgment. Before he could become the universal representative of black experience, Ellison would have been required to remove himself from the crab basket, an act that Washington's metaphor declared impossible.

If Burke disallowed Ellison the position of the universal, hadn't he also thereby necessarily denied Ellison the possibility of successfully referring to or even representing reality? But why should Burke have then taken Washington's historically specific act of signification as a true representation of black reality? If it was impossible for Ellison to occupy the position of the universal subject, how could Washington have arrived at the representation of the black experience without occupying this universal position that Burke disallowed Ellison? Moreover, if Washington's account did not represent Ellison's experience within the black community (as Ellison stated that it did not), and if it did not represent the black community, for whom did this metaphor count as a universalizable truth?

Burke apparently felt evoked into the scene by way of Ellison's refusal of Washington's account. Burke's occupation of the position of the metaphor's addressee—the subject before whom the representation is intended to count as an accurate representation of the black experience—would suggest that the metaphor of the crab basket represented black experience for a subject before whom that image corroborated a preexisting image of the black community.

But precisely what subject position did Burke occupy when he verified Washington's description? Did Burke speak as a black? Did he speak as the secondary addressee of Washington's metaphor? Burke's arrogation of the power to describe the conditions which pertain within the crab basket presupposed that he occupied a position which is external to the crab basket and hence unrepresentable within its terms. His representation of this scene could not take place within the crab basket but lay outside its frame. But if this is the case, had Burke taken up the position of the bearer of the crab basket that Washington's metaphor tacitly projected?

While nothing in Washington's metaphor allowed for any representation of the act responsible for the continued uptake of this metaphor, that act was founded on the distinction between the universalizable subject position which interprets the goings-on from a space external to the crab basket and the nonsubjectivizable particularisms which are perforce confined within the basket. Stated somewhat differently, the condition of universalizability with which Burke aligned his representation is produced out of this differentiation from the nonuniversalizable particularity of the crabs—and, by extension, Ellison's blues culture.

I previously described Burke's theory of symbolic action as grounded in its differentiation from the realm of "non-symbolic motion." In the passage I have been discussing, Burke found his way back to that theory in the distinction he adduced between agents who can perform a universalizable symbolic action (members of the proletariat class) and those figures who are consigned to the realm of nonsymbolic motion ("Negro" crabs). At the outset, I also noted Burke's difficulty in rendering what Ellison called a shadow act into an object of theoretical reflection. The previously cited passage from *A Rhetoric of Motives* clarifies the grounds for this difficulty. Burke could not reflect on the shadow acts responsible for the reproduction of the Negro stereotype because his theory was founded on the performance of such an act.

But after he reestablished the distinction on which his theory of symbolic action was founded, Burke also uncovered the dialectical limit of the realm of symbolic action. In placing Ellison's transformed identity within the crab basket, Burke positioned it within the realm of nonsymbolic motion, which cannot be assimilated to the realm of symbolic action. At the very moment in which Burke reconstituted his realm of symbolic action out of the exclusion of the immobilized crabs, however, the scapegoat mechanism underwent a change of position within Burke's system. Burke's exclusion of the crabs from the order of the symbolizable transposed the scapegoat mechanism into a structural cause of Burke's theorization of symbolic action rather than an object of theoretical reflection within it.

Before he could reperform this representative act that was foundational to his symbolic order, was not Burke required to perform the additional shadow act of pulling Ellison into the confines of Washington's metaphor? Or was it the much lengthier shadow of Burke's ancestor, Ralph Waldo Emerson, that fell across Washington's crab basket at the instant Burke reinstated the foundational distinction between the individual's universalizable human actions and the preindividual crab's fractious motions? In this reinstatement of the distinction between agents who are empowered to perform symbolic actions and cultural figures who are consigned to the realm

of nonsymbolic motion, had not Burke simply reenacted Emerson's exter-
nalization of the Negro from the symbolic order?

I have proposed that the ghost of Emerson supplemented Burke's
theory of symbolic action so as to draw out an event that is implicit in Burke's
interpretation. In removing the quality of generalizability from the Negro,
Burke's reading repeated the constitutive exclusion of Negroes that Ellison
associated with Jim Crow in the political sphere and with Emersonism in
the cultural sphere. Burke performed this reinterpretation, moreover, as a
blackface minstrel whose possessive investments in Washington's image of
black culture supplanted "Richard Wright's Blues." Burke's minstrel remarks
effectively removed Ellison's symbolic transformation from the social realm
organized out of Burke's theory of symbolic actions. Burke's derecognition
of the action's symbolic efficacy has the effect of reactivating the crisis in
symbolic investiture that, as we have seen, initially motivated Ellison to write
"Richard Wright's Blues." Burke reanimated this crisis, that is to say, within
the very Burkean symbolic order that Ellison previously believed to be an
alternative to the Emersonian order.

### 5. How Ralph Waldo Ellison Changed His Name;
### or, Kenneth Burke's Blues

I reduced the "Waldo" to a simple and I hoped mysterious W . . .
(SA, 153)

This discussion began with a consideration of the use to which Ellison put Burke's theory of symbolic action in his effort to imagine a world that
did not depend on the support of scapegoat rituals. It moved to an analysis
of Burke's need to exclude Ellison's envisioned alternative in order to sustain
the coherence of the realm of symbolic action. Following his 1950 discussion
of Ellison, Burke's theory underwent a dramatic transformation in its relation
to Ellison's art—it moved from the position of creative inspiration and source
of support of Ellison's craft to a representation of the scapegoat mechanism
Ellison wanted to change. Having discerned the equivalence between the
scapegoat mechanism and the act that founded Burke's symbolic order, I
wish to conclude this discussion with a brief analysis of a scene in which
Ellison's former mentor and ideal interlocutor attempted to explain Ellison's
project in the terms of his own theory of symbolic action.

To draw out the significance of this encounter between Ellison and
Burke, I shall interpret it as Burke's failed effort to reverse the procedure

through which Burke's (and Ellison's) literary ancestor, Ralph Waldo Emerson, had constituted the symbolic order out of the exclusion of the Negro. Burke's reversal of Emerson's act of exclusion assumed the form of a celebratory acknowledgment of Ellison's literary achievements. As a consequence of Burke's efforts at reversal, the symbolization crisis that had severely compromised their relationship was transposed into the occasion for a second investiture ritual in which Ellison would come into his own name by changing the way in which this descendant of Emerson now acknowledged him.

Before turning to that task, however, I want to emphasize the reciprocal benefits of the dialogue Burke and Ellison sustained throughout their friendship. Through the call and response relationship he sustained with Burke, Ellison amplified the "you" that was lacking in Wright, and he reanimated the "you" he was denied in Emerson. And Ellison disclosed to Burke the limitations to the field of symbolic expression that the theory of symbolic action ratified. In an open letter to Ellison, Burke recapitulated the significance of their relationship to himself, and to American literature more generally, when he repositioned Ellison as an addressee within the field from which Emerson removed Negroes as competent interlocutors. But, as we shall see, once Ellison was resituated as a respondent within the field of American literary studies, his modes of interlocution radically disrupted that field's categorizations as well as its terms of acknowledgment.

The transaction between Burke and Ellison to which I refer took place within "Ralph Ellison's Trueblooded *Bildungsroman*." In this essay, which was published in 1985 in a collection of essays edited by Kimberley W. Benston entitled *Speaking for You: The Vision of Ralph Ellison*, Burke formally retracted his previous reading of Ellison's project and struggled to find the terms with which to represent Ellison's literary achievement. Burke cast his retraction in the form of a revision of a letter that had previously been addressed to Ellison but was expanded to include a much wider audience.

"Ralph Ellison's Trueblooded *Bildungsroman*" opens with Burke in the midst of a parapraxis: He cannot find the letter he claims he began to write to Ellison some time ago. After this false start, Burke describes the loss of the original to be a stroke of good luck, because in the interval he has changed his mind about Ellison's project. As an indication of the significance of this change of mind, Burke begins his formal account of Ellison's project with the repudiation of the passage previously quoted from the *Rhetoric of Motives* in which he consigned Ellison's project to Washington's crab basket. Burke describes the retraction as a symbolic compensation for failing to respond adequately to "Richard Wright's Blues": "Those remarks I wrote in connection with your literary situation then were done, of course, when I had not the slightest idea of what you were to unfold in your (literally) epoch-making novel."[20]

Rather than remaining within the epistolary mode of the mislaid letter, Burke stages his revision as if it were a continuation of the scene from Ellison's *Invisible Man* in which the protagonist is made to carry a letter that, unbeknownst to the Invisible Man, contains sentiments which are prejudicial to the letter's bearer. The agency of the letter is decisive here. Ellison's Invisible Man quite literally becomes a man of letters by bearing the letter Dr. Bledsoe addressed to Mr. Emerson. The difference between the letter Burke mislaid and the lettter he has revised turns on Burke's interpretation of his earlier view of Ellison's project within the context of the letter Dr. Bledsoe sent to Mr. Emerson in *Invisible Man*. In reducing the entirety of "Richard Wright's Blues" to the message he gleaned from the crab basket metaphor, Burke has, in effect, turned Ellison's essay into a carrier of the letter the founder of the Tuskegee Institute addressed to Burke. Washington's letter restated Dr. Bledsoe's directive to Keep This Nigger Boy Running—within the immobilizing motion of the crab basket.

The revised letter is intended to represent the rationale for Burke's change of mind. In placing the former passage within the mislaid letter, Burke would have this parapraxis perform the symbolic work of disowning responsibility for the authorship of the earlier passage. But the open letter bears a closer resemblance to a parapraxis than a symbolic action. For despite Burke's efforts to reformulate Ellison's projects in terms that are compatible with his theory, Burke's change of mind becomes indistinguishable from his inability to make up his mind about how exactly to describe Ellison's literary achievement. Indeed, the composition of the revised essay can be described as a series of false starts.

Burke assigns the proximate cause for his change of mind to the experience of having reread *Invisible Man*: "Recently, on re-reading the book I begin to see it differently. As I see it now retrospectively, and in the light of your own development since it was first published, despite its (we might say 'resonant') involvement with the cultural problems of the Negro in the United States, its fixation on that theme, I would choose to class it pri-

20. Kenneth Burke, "Ralph Ellison's Trueblooded *Bildungsroman*," in *Speaking for You: The Vision of Ralph Ellison*, ed. Kimberly W. Benston (Washington, D.C.: Howard University Press, 1987), 350.

marily as an example of what the Germans call a Bildungsroman."[21] Burke
intends this comparison with Goethe's *Wilhelm Meister* as a way to describe
the development of Ellison's art as a bildungsroman. But this model has
instead disclosed his will to master *Invisible Man* by subordinating its singularities to the universalizable model of the bildungsroman. The comparison with *Wilhelm Meister* effects a scapegoating through exclusionary idealization rather than demonization. Ellison's *Invisible Man* does not develop
within the terms of the German bildungsroman; it artfully disrupts this hier-
archized progression as the delusions of the master race.

Burke's own observation of the negative connotations sedimented
within the word *meister* leads him to abandon the bildungsroman as an interpretive framework. He then turns to an elaboration of the claim that *Invisible
Man* is "quite literally epoch-making" as a more satisfactory rationale for his
change of mind. Burke understands *Invisible Man* as epoch making in the
sense that its exposure of the breaches of the nation's democratic ideals
refounds the promise of the U.S. Constitution. But after noting the incom-
mensurability between the universality of the constituent people and the particularity of Ellison's constituency, Burke then gives up on that description
as well. Here and elsewhere in the essay, Burke's wish to acclaim the "universality" of Ellison's poetic project founders on Burke's recognition of the
particularity of Ellison's ideological intentions. These contradictory descrip-
tions are evident in almost every paragraph of Burke's open letter and are
fully on display in passages like the following: "All told, I take it that the
motivational design of the book is in its essence thus: Though ideological
'prejudices' (and I would call the black-white issue a branch of such) make
humans 'apart from' one another, we are all for better or worse, 'part of' one
humankind—and at least on paper, an amended U.S. Constitution holds out
the same promise to us all."[22]

Overall, Burke's letter consists of a series of unsuccessful attempts
to find the terms that would assimilate Ellison's project to his preexisting
categories. But Burke cannot explain Ellison's project for the very good reason that it represents what Burke's theory of symbolic action must exclude
in order to constitute itself as a coherent body of knowledge.

Burke's dialectic reinforced the logic of assimilation that regulated
the social order: It subsumed differences within the symbols through which
they become meaningful. But Ellison's project artfully interfered with the act

21. Burke, *Speaking for You*, 350.
22. Burke, *Speaking for You*, 353.

of distinguishing between the nonsymbolizable and the symbolic through which Burke set his project of symbolic action into motion. Ellison's extraneous figures of thought added what Burke's order was required to lack in order to sustain its coherence. Because Ellison's *Invisible Man* bore the traces of the nonsymbolizable violence on whose exclusion the realm of symbolic action was founded, his project could not be included within the realm of symbolic action organized out of this logic.

Had he successfully assimilated Ellison's project to his categories, Burke would have neutralized Ellison's intervention by representing it as a harmless addition to the canon of American literature, a symbolic compensation for what the American literary canon structurally lacks. Neither assimilable within the categories of Jim Crow nor symbolizable within the Burkean model of symbolic action, Ellison's *Invisible Man* effected an undermining of both forms of cultural categorization. Ronald Judy has described the effect of Ellison's project as the "(dis)forming of the American canon."[23] Burke's inability to situate Ellison's project within the literary categories organized out of the theory of symbolic action provides evidence of the effects of this disforming. Burke's interpretive misfirings also would endorse Ellison's revaluation of the field of American literature as corroborative of a "tradition of intellectual evasion for which Thoreau criticized Emerson with regard to the Fugitive Slave Law, and which had been growing swiftly since the failure of the ideals in whose name the Civil War was fought."

Burke's acknowledgment of Ellison's literary achievement thereby assumed the displaced form of acting out the impossibility of placing this extraneous figure within the realm of symbolic action. Instead of reperforming his ancestor's act of exclusion, Burke discovered what could not be accommodated either by the symbolic order or by the theory of symbolic action through which it was regulated. Unable to perform the distinction that differentiated it from nonsymbolic motion, Burke's letter went through the motions of a symbolic action but without moving from the site of the initial retraction. It is because he could not subsume it within his symbolic actions that Burke never stopped returning to the site at which he recognized the difference between his order and Ellison's disruptions.

But insofar as the field of American literature depended for its coherence on the foreclosure of this scene, this event cannot be said to have

23. My indebtedness to Judy's thinking about the nonrecuperable negativity of Ellison's signifying practices is evident throughout this essay. See Ronald A. T. Judy, *(Dis)Forming the American Canon: African-Arabic Slave Narratives and the Vernacular* (Minneapolis: University of Minnesota Press, 1993).

taken place within the field of American literature. As the event out of whose evasion and foreclosure the field of American literature has been organized, Burke's and Ellison's encounter took place at the site of the limits of the realm organized out of the socially regulative distinction between the symbolic and the nonsymbolic. This event took place instead within the aforementioned interstitial realm in which Ellison hollowed out a different space between the American literary tradition and an emergent formation. Because those exercises were grounded in Ellison's vision of a social order without scapegoats, they perforce took place at the limits of U.S. social order. As they encountered one another within this space, they produced a social relationship without scapegoats, which Ellison apsired to materialize.

In the earlier discussion of Ellison's investiture crisis, I described Ellison's literary identity as constituted at the crossroads of contradictory addressees—where the "you" Wright feared was missing from the realm of Negro culture intersected with the Negro "you" Emerson excluded from the symbolic order. I also described the role that Burke played in calling forth each of these otherwise invisible "you's" in the passage previously quoted from *Rhetoric of Motives*. Throughout "Richard Wright's Blues," Ellison's complex literary fate involved his discovery of the practices through which he would produce nonexclusionary exchanges between a Negro interlocutor lacking a world and a symbolic world without Negro interlocutors. Ellison discovered his hidden name through the deployment of this doubling of "you" into the figures of thought out of which he constructed the essay, coming into a name of his own—that is to say, by learning how to transform the two literary figures who unnamed him into the agents who called forth interimplicated "you's" that lacked existing identifications within the already symbolized world. Instead of feeling derecognized by either Emerson, who had excluded Negro interlocutors, or Wright, who did not believe a Negro was competent to be his interlocutor, Ellison turned the "you" who was excluded in Emerson, toward the "you" who was lacking in Wright, into his hidden literary name. The literary form this name practiced involved transposing these contradictory "you's" into forms of address to the as yet immaterial "you's" within his readers. It is plain to see in the passage quoted from *Rhetoric of Motives* that Burke, who had been Ellison's ideal interlocutor, reanimated Ellison's investiture crisis when he failed to discover the doubled "you's" within himself capable of responding to these passages of thought.

By way of a conclusion, I want to describe this final public transaction between Burke and Ellison as one in which Ellison recovered his proper name through Burke's discovery of the doubled "you" through which to respond to Ellison. For that description permits the observation that Burke's very inability to position Ellison's figures within his symbolic order led Burke to think against the Emersonian identity that his theory of symbolic action otherwise continued. As he failed to subsume Ellison's "you" within his categories, Burke encountered the "you" that Ellison addressed outside the conditions of Emersonian identification through which Burke had otherwise recognized himself. In responding to Ellison's call, Burke happened on a crossroads of contradictory addressees wherein the Emersonian "you" who felt empowered to subsume Ellison's figures within his preexisting categories was interrupted by a "you" within Burke who could not be secured within any of the preexisting categorizations of identity. In the following passage from the essay "Hidden Name, Complex Fate," Ellison demetaphorized the doubling of these "you's" to inscribe the hyponym *W*, which is his hidden name—"I reduced Waldo to a simple and I hope mysterious W." In place of a symbolic action, Burke's parapraxis in his open letter to Ellison might be described as his acting out an unidentifiable "you" that Ralph *Waldo* Emerson could not cross out.

# "I Am I Be": The Subject of Sonic Afro-modernity

*Alexander G. Weheliye*

We clamor for the right to opacity for everyone.
—Edouard Glissant, *Poetics of Relation*

And let us not insist upon the optic metaphor which opens up every
theoretical view under the sun.
—Jacques Derrida, *White Mythology*

Sounds go through the muscles
these abstract wordless movements
they start off cells that haven't been touched before
. . . waking up slowly.
—Björk Gudmundsdóttir, "Headphones," from *Post*

This essay forms part of a book-length manuscript in progress entitled *Phonographies: Grooves in Sonic Afro-modernity*. Earlier versions were presented in the context of "Ralph Ellison: The Next Fifty Years," a *boundary 2* conference at the University of Pittsburgh, and the Fellows' Workshop of the Alice Berline Kaplan Center for the Humanities at Northwestern University. I extend gratitude to Kevin Bell, Jennifer DeVere Brody, Jillana Enteen, Ronald Judy, and Michael Hanchard for comments on earlier drafts of this essay.

*boundary 2* 30:2, 2003. Copyright © 2003 by Duke University Press.

Surely "the subject" represents one of the more embattled concepts in the recent history of the Anglo-American humanities; structuralist and poststructuralist discourses were almost singularly concerned with dissolving and/or resituating the self-same subject (in some cases putting it under erasure) as it appeared in Western thinking, idealist philosophy in particular. The main thrust of these debates troubled the coherence and unmediated presence of this subject, seeking to displace the subject as the uncontested center in a variety of thought systems, with varying structures (linguistic, anthropological, political, psychic, economic, and so forth), or, in the post-structuralist case, rendered visible the fissures, traces, and ruptures contained within and undermining these very structures that enabled the subject's intelligibility, and, therefore, constrained its ability to appear as the center from which all movements flow. If the advent of structuralism and its ensuing postformations provide one of the crucial reformulations of the humanities project since the 1960s, then the coming to the fore of "minority discourses" stands as the other major shift in this context. Although some scholars, for example, Hortense J. Spillers and Sylvia Wynter, have thought these two developments together fruitfully, usually they are perceived as mutually exclusive, at least contradictory. In most instances, however—and this bears stressing—the two processes are not thought related at all.[1] One version of this argument discerns the irony in the dissolution, and perhaps even abandonment, of the subject as a category of critical thinking, just as "minority" subjects are being recognized as subjects within academic discourse; in fact, the uttering of minority and subject in the same breath seems counterintuitive, if not paradoxical.[2] While this essay surely does not seek to undermine this particular claim here, or reinstate an earlier and more innocent version of the subject, I would like to take the occasion to think about the subject from the perspective of the "minoritarian" with this particular critique in mind. In that vein, I refer to "black studies" as opposed to

1. Any debate about the recent history of the U.S. academic humanities might benefit from consulting Hortense Spillers's magisterial "The Crisis of the Negro Intellectual: A Post-date," *boundary 2* 21, no. 3 (1994): 65–116. For Sylvia Wynter's arguments, see "Columbus, the Ocean Blue, and Fables That Stir the Mind: To Reinvent the Study of Letters," in *Poetics of the Americas: Race, Founding, and Textuality*, ed. Bianard Cowan and Jefferson Humphries (Baton Rouge: Louisiana State University Press, 1997), 141–202; and "On Disenchanting Discourse: 'Minority' Literary Criticism and Beyond," in *The Nature and Context of Minority Discourse*, ed. Abdul JanMohamed and David Lloyd (New York: Oxford University Press, 1990), 432–69.
2. See Barbara Christian, "The Race for Theory," in *The Nature and Context of Minority Discourse*, 37–49.

more specified forms of Afro-diasporic thought to keep concerns of institutionality in mind, since neither of these forces can be disarticulated from the other. Furthermore, while I focus primarily on black studies for the purposes of this argument, many of these points pertain to other forms of racialized minority discourse in the U.S. academy as well. These reflections will be preceded by a discussion of how sound recording and reproduction figure in twentieth-century black culture, followed by an analysis of the prologue of Ralph Ellison's *Invisible Man*, in which I examine the way he imagines a subject of "sonic Afro-modernity." Ellison constructs a model of subjectivity in relation to sound technologies, which bears witness to specificities of black life while also gesturing toward a more general condition of Western modernity. I use the playful yet germane phrase "I am I be" as a shorthand that garners its argumentative and evocative force via juxtaposition and facilitates both the magnification of the putative gulf that divides "subjectivity" and "identity" within current academic discursive formations as well as their suggested compatibility within the context of my own argument.[3] In other words, by linking "I be" as a linguistic instantiation of Afro-diasporic particularity (identity) and the normative declaration "I am" (subjectivity) without the interruption of punctuation worries the manner in which these two modalities are routinely construed as mutual exclusives rather than as coeval.

### Sonic Afro-modernity

The invention of technological sound recording in the form of the phonograph at the end of the nineteenth century offered the ability to split sounds from the sources that produced them, thus generating a "post-technological" orality and musicality in twentieth-century black culture. Since the space and time of audition were separated from the contexts of reception, orality and musicality were no longer reliant on the immediate presence of human subjects. Two results of this development, the technological recording and mass distribution of music, are often construed as lacking the authenticity and immediacy of live performances and/or as the wholesale appropriation of musical cultures by various capitalist formations in current critical discourses. Although these interpretations surely possess some form of value, they tend to neglect the possibilities occasioned by this audiovisual disjuncture for black cultural production, or any form of cultural production for that matter. The complex interfacing of mod-

3. De La Soul, "I Am I Be," *Buhloone Mind State* (New York: Tommy Boy Records, 1993).

ern black culture and sound technologies grants the venue for imagining and producing a variety of cultural practices, constituting a domain I call sonic Afro-modernity. While the literature on black musics comprises an expansive archive, encompassing numerous disciplinary approaches and spanning various historical periods, work that considers the technological mediation of these sounds occurs less frequently. However, if we are to analyze a sounding black modernity, we should strive to understand how technologies have affected the production, consumption, and dissemination of black popular music, and vice versa, an endeavor that is even more pertinent today due to the increasing globality of black musical practices. In other words, we need to probe the conditions for the possibility of "modern black sounds"; what makes these perceptible in the modern era are sonic technologies.

Not too long ago, both Paul Gilroy and Houston Baker attempted in their work to account for the crucial place of sound within modern black culture. Like many other critics, however, they largely glossed over the technological aspects (which are never simply reducible to technology) of black popular music.[4] Carefully assessing the effects of the recording, reproduction, and international distribution of black popular music, Gilroy and Baker stopped short of reflecting on these factors as such. Nonetheless, they were right to think together black popular music and modernity, since black musical practices are routinely described as pristine and untouched forms of "vernacular" expression. Any consideration of black music might do well to surmise the ramifications of this particular culture qua information imbrication without succumbing to the pitfalls of technological determinism or celebrating the vernacular authenticity of black popular music.

When phonographs began to augment and replace live performances and/or musical scores at the end of the nineteenth century, they created a glaring rupture between sound and vision. Both performer and score clearly provided some discernible human origin for sounds, where the phonograph gave the listener only "a voice without a face," to use David Laing's phrase.[5] Now this newly invented technological apparatus stood as the main visual counterpoint to the sounds emanating from its horn, ostensibly reproducing sonic data without the intervention of human subjects.

4. Paul Gilroy, The Black Atlantic: Modernity and Double Consciousness (Cambridge: Harvard University Press, 1993), especially chaps. 1 and 3; Houston Baker, Modernism and the Harlem Renaissance (Chicago: University of Chicago Press, 1987).
5. David Laing, "A Voice without a Face: Popular Music and the Phonograph in the 1890's," Popular Music 10, no. 1 (1991): 1–9.

Even the telephone, although similarly disrupting the spatial configuration of linguistic communication, offered a clearly palpable human source for its sounds at the other end of the line. As a direct reaction to this gash between sound and visual source, a profusion of cultural maneuvers has sought to yoke the two back together; the iconography of record covers and music videos are some obvious examples. Before these developments, however, records were produced without much graphic and/or visual accompaniment. In this particular framework, written notation suggested the most "natural" material grounding of the "ephemerality" of music, since this particular way of writing sound represented the phonograph's immediate historical precedent in the West. The phonograph suggested a machinic materiality, one that acutely destabilized any notion of an "absolute music" and called attention to other forms of aural embodiment, whether a concert stage, a musical score, or a human body. It is precisely this conflict between the phonograph's material and ephemeral dimensions, as well as the machine's worrying of the immediate connection between sound and writing, that makes it such a crucial site for the articulation of black cultural practices in the twentieth century.

Because the technology of the phonograph seemingly heightened the nonrepresentational, disembodied, ephemeral qualities of music, almost from its very inception various discourses—more specifically those revolving around questions of copyright—attempted to capture fleeting sounds in writing, extending the linkage between writing and sound already embedded in the very designation *phonograph*. Several critics concerned with the wider social and epistemological implications of the technology of the phonograph have stressed the way in which it refigured the connection between sound and writing.[6] In a discussion about musical copyright and the Copyright Act of 1909, the first to include recorded music, Lisa Gitelman holds that the central debate concerned the split between sound and vision, especially writing, in the technology of the phonograph.[7] Since musical copyright law was hitherto based on sheet music, in order for recorded music to function as intellectual property, composers had to prove that the phonograph "read" their music in the same or a similar way as consumers who played the music from printed scores. The dispute over the Copyright Act revolved

6. See Thomas Y. Levin, "For the Record: Adorno on Music in the Age of Its Technological Reproducibility" *October* 55 (1990): 38, 40–41; Theodor W. Adorno, "The Form of the Phonograph Record," trans. Thomas Y. Levin, *October* 55 (1990): 60.
7. Lisa Gitelman, *Scripts, Grooves, and Writing Machines: Representing Technology in the Edison Era* (Stanford, Calif.: Stanford University Press, 1999), 97–147.

around whether recordings based on copyrighted sheet music merely represented the use of the score or a particular performance of a composition
as opposed to an altogether different material manifestation of music. In
these debates, the sounds contained on phonograph records were fixable
as objects only under the purview of copyright law if they were proven to
be the mechanical equivalent of written notation and/or alphabetic script.
Record companies, in particular, argued that phonograph records did not
represent written embodiments of the composer's score, since they were
not legible to humans, in order to claim all the profits from record sales. Conversely, composers and publishers, defending their own economic interests,
attempted to establish that recordings could, indeed, be read by the phonograph. This new technology also magnified the embodiment of music per se,
because it queried the naturalization of musical notation as the most faithful
record of sonic information. Since the phonograph possessed the ability to
make sounds audible, even though these noises could hardly be heard as
mimetic due to technological limitations in this particular situation, marks on
a page now seemed glaringly mute in comparison.

Surely, the conjoining of writing and sound has particular ramifications for black cultural production given the importance of orality as the
major mode of cultural transmission in this temporal setting. Because alphabetic script was such an embattled terrain for black subjects in nineteenth-
century America, the phonograph did not cause as many anxieties in black
cultural discourses, and thus musical notation and writing were not necessarily apprehended as the most "natural" way of recording music. Much has
been written about the fraught status of writing in Afro-diasporic configurations, particularly in regard to nineteenth-century African American literary
history, but rather than redacting these arguments here, suffice it to say that
black subjects did not have the same access to alphabetic script as white
subjects and therefore were also barred, both discursively and materially,
by a variety of repressive, and at times violent, mechanisms, from writing's
attendant qualities of reason, disembodiment, and full humanity. This is not
to argue that orality and music were the only channels for black culture in this
period, but that the relationship between sound and writing imploded by the
discourses around the phonograph in mainstream American culture carried
different cadences in relation to black culture. Thus, we need to account for
how orality and music, the two main techniques of cultural communication
in African America, were transformed by the technology of the phonograph.
In what sense does the decoupling of sound and source shift the central
place of orality and music in the production, transmission, and reception of
black culture? How do these modes of cultural transfer change at the end

of the nineteenth century through the incorporation of orality and music into written texts and the technological recording of sound and speech?

In the literary domain, writers such as Pauline Hopkins, W. E. B. Du Bois, Zora Neale Hurston, Ralph Ellison, James Baldwin, and Toni Morrison, to name only a few, have "sounded" modern African American culture, utilizing aspects from the varied histories of black music in their writings. In addition, black literature has also produced a multitude of "speakerly texts" by stressing the oral performative dimensions of written language.[8] Understood as sound recordings, then, these texts suggest a different way of merging the *phono* and *graph* than the technology of the phonograph, underscoring how sound and writing meet and inform each other in the written annals of twentieth-century African American literature. Subsequently, black performers, not always under the most advantageous economic and political circumstances, have been leading actors in the national and international dissemination and immense prominence of U.S. popular music. Examples are too numerous to list here, but the obvious point remains that modern black cultural production is intimately tied to sound as it is embodied by a variety of technologies, such as literary texts, films, records, tapes, and CDs. Not only did these technologies modify the ways in which cultural artifacts were produced, but, and perhaps more importantly, by virtue of radically altering how music was consumed, they enabled new modalities of existence for black subjects within and against Western modernity: sonic Afro-modernity. Given the brief gloss on sonic Afro-modernity, how might we ascertain its subject? Can it even suggest a subject given the nominal prefix *Afro*?

Contemporary critical idioms often take the linguistic sphere as their axiomatic horizon when theorizing the subject. Judith Butler, for instance, offers one of the more succinct recitals of this trend: "The subject is the linguistic occasion for the individual to achieve and reproduce intelligibility."[9] For my purposes, the sonic in its nonlinguistic musical form provides one of the best examples of what Edouard Glissant has called "opacity." By opacity, he means that "which is not obscure, though it is possible to be so and accepted as such. It is that which cannot be reduced, which is the perennial guarantee of participation and confluence."[10] Rather than apprehending

8. See Henry Louis Gates Jr., *The Signifying Monkey* (New York: Oxford University Press, 1986), xxv–xxvi and passim.
9. Judith Butler, *The Psychic Life of Power: Theories in Subjection* (Stanford, Calif.: Stanford University Press, 1997), 11.
10. Edouard Glissant, *Poetics of Relation*, trans. Betsy Wing (Ann Arbor: University of Michigan Press, 1997), 191.

opacity in terms of deficiency or lack, Glissant accentuates how "opacity . . . is not enclosure within an impenetrable autarchy but subsistence within an irreducible singularity."[11] In this sense, the sonic is an instance of opacity because it fails to cast either intelligibility or transparency in the role of its logos, which enables us to, paraphrasing the prologue from *Invisible Man*, "listen around corners."[12] Focusing on the sonic does not intimate privileging another mode of discursivity as the preferred figure for the articulation of subjectivity over the linguistic. Instead, it opens up possibilities for thinking, hearing, seeing, apprehending the subject in a number of different arenas that do not insist on monocausality. Still, we should not hastily rush to the sonic as a preconscious, open, fragmented, and fluid sphere that sounds in strict opposition to the visual and/or language, because music does not rely on meaning making in the same way as language.[13] Put crassly, humans do not use music as their main mode of communication—it calls attention to its texture and confluence rather than striving for intelligibility, networking it squarely within the charged currents of opacity. I hope it is sufficiently clear that I am in no way suggesting an uncomplicated contrast between language and the sonic; rather, I am simply highlighting their different properties. Locating the subject in the sonic grants a quite different notion of this concept—which does not mean that the subject as a linguistic category is rendered null and void; it just relocates it to a new analytic neighborhood without losing its ties to old friends—one that does not posit meaning and/or intelligibility as its teleological end point but enables "[o]pacities [to] coexist and converge, weaving fabrics. To understand these truly one must focus on the texture of the weave and not on the nature of its components."[14] By concentrating on texture and not meaning, as effervescent as it may be, "thinking sonically" adduces a mode of divining the world that sounds

---

11. Glissant, *Poetics of Relation*, 190.

12. Ralph Ellison, *Invisible Man* (New York: Random House, 1952), 13: "[T]o *see* around corners is enough (that is not that unusual when you are invisible). But to hear around them is too much; it inhibits action." While hearing around corners might mitigate activity, certainly it does not prohibit critical thinking. Subsequent quotations from this work are cited parenthetically as *IM*.

13. See the arguments on behalf of the fluidity of the sonic in Steven Connor, "The Modern Auditory I," in *Rewriting the Self: Histories from the Renaissance to the Present*, ed. Roy Porter (New York: Routledge, 1997), 203–23. For a psychoanalytic version of this argument, which interprets all listening practices as harking back to a presymbolic oceanic mirror stage, see David Schwarz, *Listening Subjects: Music, Psychoanalysis, Culture* (Durham, N.C.: Duke University Press, 1997).

14. Glissant, *Poetics of Relation*, 190.

its multitude of opacities without drowning their singularities in the noise of transparency.[15] Similarly, the subject that emerges from Ellison's ruminations on the intersectionality of sound and technology remains a contingent opacity that never quite achieves any determinate form of intelligibility.

### Listening around Corners

Ralph Ellison's poetics, situated at the interstices of music and technology, bridge the putative divide between black cultural production and modern informational technologies, probing the textural and overdetermined interdependence rather than their opposing "natures." In *Invisible Man*, his essays (particularly "Living with Music"), and in numerous interviews, he has consistently turned to questions of sound recording and reproduction.[16] At several key points in "That Same Pain, That Same Pleasure: An Interview," Ellison mentions his early enthusiasm for building radios. When asked by his interviewer, Richard J. Stern, how he managed to encounter the world beyond the black community, Ellison responds, "Ironically, I would have to start with some of the features of American life which it has become quite fashionable to criticize in a most unthinking way—the mass media. Like so many kids of the twenties, I played around with radio—building crystal sets and circuits consisting of a few tubes, which I found published in radio magazines."[17] As opposed to proving that "[w]ithin the safety of one's own home, and out of public view, one's masculinity could be tested and reaffirmed," Ellison describes the sociality building radios granted him, utilizing his radio hobby not to cut himself off from the world around him but to connect to communities and discourses beyond immediate physical reach, redacting on a biographical scale the possibilities occasioned by sound technologies in general.[18] In this way, he not only insists on the sociality of sonic technologies but also bears witness to the plethora of ways in which

15. Glissant's differentiation between *nature* and *texture* will have to be complicated in an expanded version of the current argument. Although this distinction is crucial, it should occasion only a first step in the exhuming of "nature" within "texture," and vice versa.
16. Ralph Ellison, "Living with Music," in *Shadow and Act* (1955; reprint, New York: Vintage, 1995), 187–89.
17. Ralph Ellison, "That Same Pain, That Same Pleasure: An Interview," in *Shadow and Act*, 4. Ellison also evokes his radio hobby when pontificating on the role of music in his life, linking both his status as a musician and radio hobbyist with his proclivity for creating things.
18. Kier Keightley, "'Turn It Down!' She Shrieked: Gender, Domestic Space, and High Fidelity, 1948–59," *Popular Music* 15, no. 2 (1996): 160.

they structure modern life worlds, heaving black life out of a mythic, Luddite, unusable past and into the center of Western modernity. Sadly, critics have paid scant attention to Ellison's engagement with sonic technologies, zeroing in only on his thoughts about jazz and the blues rather than the interplay of content *and* transmission so crucial to the Ellison oeuvre. We might even say, *pace* Walter Benjamin, that Ellison locates the aura not in the original musical utterance but in the mode of mechanical reproduction itself, which makes him one of the foremost theorists of sonic Afro-modernity.

*Invisible Man* is framed by the protagonist's consumption of and engagement with Louis Armstrong's recording of the Andy Razaf and Fats Waller tune "(What Did I Do to Be So) Black and Blue." Armstrong recorded several versions of this piece after he encountered it as part of the stage musical *Hot Chocolates* in 1929, where it was performed by a very light-skinned chanteuse, and legend has it that the song was composed because the financier of the show, Mafioso Dutch Schulz, demanded a humorous musical rendering of the black experience. While Ellison's protagonist draws on "Black and Blue" as "one of the first instances of racial protest in American popular music," he emphasizes the quality of Armstrong's voice embodied in the particular performance rendered on record and not primarily the signification of the song's lyrics.[19] The prologue establishes the protagonist's social invisibility, the major theme of the novel, by depicting his hibernation in a hole, the basement of a "whites only" building, and describing his condition in the following fashion: "I am a man of substance, of flesh and bone, fiber and liquids—and I might even be said to possess a mind. I am invisible, understand, simply because people refuse to see me. . . . When they approach me they see only my surroundings, themselves, or figments of their imagination—indeed, everything and anything except me" (*IM*, 3). By way of explicating how he is refused representation in the field of vision, the protagonist also insists on the intersubjective workings of his invisibility rather than construing it as an ontological absolute. This is crucial since, according to Sylvia Wynter, the prologue as a whole performs "the possibility of their/our recognition of this imposed 'invisibility,' which leads to a new demand for another concept of freedom, another possibility of a livable being that culminates in [the protagonist's] recognition of his alterity."[20] Wynter's invocation of the protagonist's "alterity" appears at

19. Eric Sundquist, ed., *Cultural Contexts for Ralph Ellison's "Invisible Man": A Bedford Documentary Companion* (Boston: Bedford Books, 1995), 115.
20. Wynter, "On Disenchanting Discourse," 452.

the interstice of self and other, which is to say that the protagonist remains "foreign" to himself as much as he does to others, although evidently not in the same way.

While the racial metaphorics of this predicament—white subjects' inability and/or outright refusal to recognize black people's subjectivity— appear abundantly clear, the question of visuality merits more than a brief glance here, since Ellison explicitly situates the protagonist's "non-subjectivity" in the ocular domain.[21] Recently, the hegemony of vision in Western modernity, what Martin Jay has referred to as its ocularcentric discourse, has been scrutinized for a variety of reasons.[22] Afro-diasporic thinkers, in particular, have stressed the centrality of the ocular in Western constructions of race and racism, wherein the look of white subjects deduces supposed inferior racial characteristics from the surface of black subjects' skin—what Frantz Fanon terms "the racial epidermal schema." Fanon shows the slippage from racial identity, as it is grafted on and therefore legible from the epidermis, to assumed inferiority as synonymous in the scopic regime of racialization.[23] Likewise, W. E. B. Du Bois explicitly implicates ocular mechanisms and ideologies in the workings of "double-consciousness," as in the following famous passage from *The Souls of Black Folk*: "It is a peculiar sensation, this double-consciousness, this sense of always *looking* at one's self through the *eyes* of others, of measuring one's *soul* by the tape of the world that *looks on* in amused contempt and pity."[24] If looking at oneself through the eyes of others squarely locates the subject of double-consciousness in the visual field, then for Du Bois the sonic, linked throughout *Souls* to the Sorrow Songs, and at times taking on the form of

21. Perhaps the protagonist's invisibility can be described, in Hortense Spillers's formulation, as both "a signifying property *plus* [and *minus*]." Hortense Spillers, "Mama's Baby, Papa's Maybe: An American Grammar Book," *Diacritics* 17, no. 2 (1987): 65.

22. Martin Jay, *Downcast Eyes: The Denigration of Vision in Twentieth-Century French Thought* (Berkeley: University of California Press, 1993). See also David Michael Levin, ed., *Modernity and the Hegemony of Vision* (Berkeley: University of California Press, 1993). For a discussion of visual modernity that takes in questions of race, consult Robyn Wiegman, *American Anatomies: Theorizing Race and Gender* (Durham, N.C.: Duke University Press, 1995), 21–42.

23. Frantz Fanon, *Black Skin, White Masks*, trans. Charles Lam Markman (1952; reprint, New York: Grove Press, 1967), 112.

24. W. E. B. Du Bois, *The Souls of Black Folk* (1903; reprint, New York: Penguin, 1989), 5; my emphasis. For a more detailed consideration of Du Bois's ruminations on racialization as it cuts across vision and sound, see Alexander Weheliye, "In the Mix: Hearing the Souls of Black Folks," *Amerikastudien/American Studies* 45, no. 4 (fall 2000): 535–54.

Wagner's *Lohengrin*, provides an altogether different realm for the articulation of black subjectivity. Surely, Ellison's utilization of invisibility takes into account the vexed vicissitudes of race and visuality in Western modernity as well, while also insisting on a sonic-cum-technological formulation of the black subject.

The problematic of visuality is picked up again later in the prologue, when the protagonist reflects on his desire for brightness: "My hole is warm and full of light. Yes, *full* of light. I doubt if there is a brighter spot in all New York than this hole of mine. . . . Perhaps you'll think it strange that an invisible man should need light, desire light, love light" (*IM*, 6). However, the desire for light seems noteworthy only in a world where social visibility is a given. As an a priori, social visibility already functions as light, legislating the boundary between the visible and invisible, and therefore does not necessitate any further illumination. The text proceeds: "But maybe it is exactly because I am invisible. Light confirms my reality, gives birth to my form. . . . Without light I am not only invisible, but formless as well; and to be unaware of one's form is to live a death. I myself, after existing some twenty years, did not become alive until I discovered my invisibility" (*IM*, 6–7). This contradictory insight underscores the protagonist's urgency to comprehend his invisibility while simultaneously reformulating this very predicament by consuming light, since he needs to "look at himself through the eyes of others" in order to not disappear from his own line of sight. Illuminated by the 1,369 lightbulbs covering the ceiling of his hibernating hole, the protagonist pilfers the electricity from the Monopolated Light & Power, which ensures, both literally and metaphorically, that his illumination cannot be disentangled from his invisibility. In this scene, Monopolated Light & Power, as the modernized and electrified capitalist reformulation of Western-style heliocentrism, caustically encodes the structures at the root of the protagonist's invisibility. The electricity rechanneled from the company is turned against itself, because instead of presenting his visual nonpresence as an ontological and political fait accompli, it allows him to illuminate, and thus verify, the fact of his invisibility, which disenchants the truth-value of light as such. In other words, if the protagonist's invisibility can be set alight, then maybe seeing the light does not always already imply luminosity as self-evidence, or, in Ellison's formulation, "Truth is the light and light is the truth" (*IM*, 7). Hence, the ideological and material currents of subordination electrically cross the protagonist's inscription as lack in the field of vision, in the meantime giving birth to his sonic interpellation, a movement further evident in his identification with Thomas Edison, the "father" of both the lightbulb and the phonograph (*IM*, 7).

The electricity the protagonist reroutes from the large company also powers his radio-phonograph, assuring that the aural component of the protagonist's subjectivity and his scopic invisibility are fully interfaced. A single radio-phonograph, however, does not do the job; the protagonist yearns for five machines: "I'd like to hear five recordings of Louis Armstrong playing and singing '(What Did I Do to Be So) Black and Blue'—all at the same time." The reason, he claims, stems from the sonic characteristics of the basement: "There is a certain acoustical deadness in my hole, and when I have music I want to feel its vibration with my whole body" (*IM*, 8). If the multiplicity of lights reflects the protagonist's craving to understand his social invisibility, then the corporeal viscerality of the protagonist's ideal listening scenario manifests an intense longing to experience his body in sound in ways that he cannot do visually. Wanting to embody and be embodied by sound, the protagonist imagines his flesh as an eardrum, transforming his corporeal schema into a channel for his sonic subjectivity, which, in turn, emerges only in relation to his scopic interpellation. Thus, the sonic and the scopic, far from being diametrically opposed, provide occasion for one another; visual subjection begets sonic subjectivation.

In this way, formlessness elides the protagonist only insofar as the music sounds his invisibility, particularly Armstrong's voice: "Perhaps I like Louis Armstrong because he's made poetry out of being invisible. I think it must be because he's unaware that he *is* invisible. And my own grasp of invisibility aids me to understand his music" (*IM*, 8). On the surface, the protagonist detects similar qualities of invisibility in Armstrong's recorded voice, so that it presumably serves as an aural mirror of his own predicament. Yet, despite this strong identification, there exists a crucial difference between them: Armstrong has no conception of his invisibility, at least in the eyes and ears of the protagonist, which powers the poetic motor of his music. In the earlier, visually mediated passages, the protagonist's condition was predicated on others' negation of his optic presence; in this case, however, he can embody his own invisibility via the sounds of another invisible subject. Consequently, sound, particularly recorded and mechanically reproduced sound, grants the protagonist access to his invisibility in a different fashion than the not-so-soft glow afforded by the 1,369 lightbulbs. Even though this aspect of the protagonist's being is staged intersubjectively—his invisibility is amplified by the effect of Armstrong's voice on the phonograph—it differs quite significantly from the visual one because it relies not on negation and abjection but on recognition, or rather on the protagonist's recognition of Armstrong's supposed misrecognition. More than a simple identification, the protagonist recasts Armstrong as his former self, the self not able to ascertain its own invisibility.

Apart from filling the dead air in the basement with music, the phonograph stages Armstrong's nonpresence just as much as it allows the protagonist to reside within the contours of his invisibility. Armstrong's invisibility manifests itself in several ways: the manner in which his racial identity figures in the musical text, both in terms of lyrical content and vocal delivery, in addition to Armstrong's literal invisibility to the protagonist, since he cannot see Armstrong but only hears the specific way in which the phonograph represents his voice. The protagonist's emphasis shifts from the visual to the aural because being unable to visually face Armstrong makes him more susceptible to the quality of invisibility transacted by Armstrong's voice. As a result, this visual lack becomes even more indicative of the social invisibility faced by black subjects due to its phonographic transmission. Since there are no visual cues—only Armstrong's phantomlike voice accompanied by instrumentation on the recording—the protagonist projects his own invisibility onto Armstrong's vocal apparatus. Recently, Lindon Barrett has argued that the black voice functions as a figure of value within African American culture, particularly as it is contrasted with the lack of value ascribed to blackness in American mainstream culture. He distinguishes *the singing voice* from the *signing voice* of Euramerican alphabetical literacy. He contends that "the African American singing voice emphasizes—rather than merely glances at—the spatial, material, dative, or enunciative action of voice. Singing voices undo voice as speech per se."[25] Barrett offers a model that reformulates the writing-as-freedom problematic in black literary studies by allotting the voice a central role in the shaping of black subjectivity, even if at times it risks ontologizing the corporeal provenances of the black voice by not stressing enough questions of skill and technique, especially those of the black female voices so central to his argument. Focusing on how the black voice is worked on like an instrument refashions the voice as a cultural technology with specific meanings in black cultural contexts rather than as a side effect of epidermal melanation. Moreover, the characteristics Barrett ascribes to the black voice are magnified in the phonographic listening sce-

25. Lindon Barrett, *Blackness and Value: Seeing Double* (New York: Cambridge University Press, 1999), 84.

nario, when the singer's embodiment rests chiefly in his or her voice. When the visual bolsters disappear, the ghostlike ruminations of the voice stand as the last and only vestiges of the corporeal, sonically folding the body into the voice, and vice versa. In the process of this folding, the ear is directed toward the sound process itself—the ways in which the black voice performs and constructs its corporeality.

The phonograph's ability to disconnect the singing voice from its face further heightens its materiality, which impels the protagonist to imbue Armstrong's voice with a surplus of signification; in order to achieve this feat, however, light cannot function as the sole source of illumination: "It was a strangely satisfying experience for an invisible man to hear the silence of sound. . . . I've illuminated the blackness of my invisibility—and vice versa. And so I play the invisible music of my isolation. The last statement doesn't seem just right, does it?" (*IM*, 13). Taken literally, the statement does seem just right though, for the phonograph represents, if anything, invisible music, since it denies the listener visual access to the performer. What initially seems oxymoronic actually provides the most succinct description of the protagonist's invisibility in relation to Armstrong's voice flowing from the phonograph's speaker. The protagonist and Armstrong are joined not only by their social invisibility as black subjects but also by their reliance on sound to transmit their invisibility—Armstrong, by singing his invisibility; and the protagonist, by listening to Armstrong. What is called for is an ear that recognizes the value of the African American singing voice. The protagonist has just such an ear, or, in the extreme, is the ear that sonically "illuminates the blackness of [his] invisibility—and *vice versa*" (*IM*, 13). As a consequence, the value of Armstrong's voice lies in his skill at sonically representing his invisibility. Nevertheless, in a moment of disavowal, the protagonist casts Armstrong in the role of the naïf, rather than skilled performer, in order to better understand the parameters of his own invisibility. For the protagonist hears not an eternal spring of blackness welling from Armstrong's throat but the deftness and grace with which Armstrong manipulates his voice in relation to the sonic apparatus.

Still, Armstrong's voice should not be understood as the only form of embodiment in this scene. At the most basic level, the sonic apparatus itself provides a material grounding for the ephemeral "voice without a face" inasmuch as it replaces Armstrong's appearance as the visual counterpoint to his voice, substituting a machinic for a human presence and inducing the protagonist's urge to hear and feel Armstrong's voice more ardently in an effort to counterbalance the paucity of visual stimuli. Because Armstrong remains invisible to the protagonist, he imagines being both assailed and enveloped by the sound of Armstrong's voice from five directions. The protagonist realizes that there is no chance for visual accompaniment to the sonic in his situation, so his desire is displaced onto the apparatus itself. Yet the machine, even if multiplied by five, supplies principally aural information, which explains why his fantasy involves hearing Armstrong's voice further amplified and not looking at five phonographs. Hearing Armstrong intonate from so many different machines at once, even if only in the realm of the phantasmatic, produces an aural materiality. As opposed to grounding sound in writing, the protagonist acutely positions the palpable dimensions of sound within the phonographic voice. Accordingly, he does not suggest hearing five different singers, or even five different Armstrong recordings, but the same five Armstrong recordings simultaneously. Possibly, more than Armstrong's voice itself, it is the "voice without a face"—the voice of the phonograph—that grounds and transacts both Armstrong's and the protagonist's invisibility. Rather than dissipating into thin air, as early discourse on the phonograph suggested, the disembodied voice is precisely what frames the social invisibility of the black subject in this scene. As a consequence, the phonograph does not so much occasion a faceless voice as it transforms the voice into a face. In this particular instance, the phonograph reconfigures the protagonist's invisibility via sonic envisage; denied representation in the field of vision, Armstrong's phonographic voice facilitates the protagonist in recognizing the mechanics of his invisibility—his aural face, as it were. Overall, light projects the silhouette of his invisibility, where Armstrong's voice fills the visual contours with sound, or to put it crudely, where light confirms invisibility as fact—choosing either *I am* or *I be*—the phonographic voice sonically reticulates invisibility as process, enabling a two-way sonic flow between *I am I be*; taken together they provide the contingency for the subject of sonic Afro-modernity.

Throughout his work, Ellison listens carefully not only to the complexities and subtleties of black musical expression but also, and this distinguishes him from other writers, to the intricate manner in which these sounds are intertwined with informational technologies in the modern era. This sensibility enables Ellison to suggest a grammar for thinking, if not hearing, the subject of sonic Afro-modernity located in that explosive audiovisual disjuncture engendered by the phonograph. This subject appears at the spatiotemporal crossroads, where the performer's ghostly sounds merge with the ear of the listener on those lower frequencies, which resituate, reframe, and resound the black subject's visual invisibility, producing a flash point of subjectivity gleaned in and through sound. In the force field of sonic Afro-modernity, sound technologies, as opposed to being exclusively determined or determining, form a relay point in the orbit between the apparatus and a plethora of cultural, economic, and political discourses. Insisting on the central place of technology in this formation goes a long way toward conjecturing how musical production and structures of listening have shifted over the course of the last century. At the very least, this might move us away from the zero-sum game of authenticity versus commodification, which will surely entail letting out some of the old Bad Air without losing all of its funk. At most, we could fire up the old phonograph and open our ears to those instances in which, according to Ellison, "instead of the swift and imperceptible flowing of time, you are aware of its nodes, those points where time stands still or from which it leaps ahead. And you slip into the breaks and look around" (*IM*, 8).

Emmanuel Levinas describes and links these nodal moments to the general provenances of the sonic as follows:

> In sound, and in the consciousness termed hearing, there is in fact a break with the self-complete world of vision. . . . In its entirety, sound is a ringing, clanging scandal. Whereas, in vision, form is wedded to content in such a way as to appease it, in sound the perceptible quality overflows so that form can no longer contain its content. A real rent is produced, through which the world that is *here* prolongs a dimension that cannot be converted into vision.[26]

Levinas underscores one of the reasons sound retains such a crucial place within black cultural formations: openness, particularly when contrasted to the way vision has been codified in Western modernity. Over the course of the twentieth century, this openness has been boosted by sound technologies such as the phonograph, which, by disturbing any seemingly predetermined symbiosis between the aural and the visual, have allowed for a multiplication of practices and contexts for both the production and reception of black musical cultures. Rather than suggest that this dimension (subjectivity) can be converted into or represented in sound, I would like to retain its "scandalous" qualities, since the sonic realm grants aural "opacities" qua subjectivity: pathways to moments of subjectivity set off against subjectivity per se; a sonic subjectivity that does not lose sight of the black subject's

---

26. Emmanuel Levinas, "The Transcendence of Words," in *The Emmanuel Levinas Reader*, ed. Sean Hand (London: Blackwell, 1989), 147.

visual interpellation but noisily "rings" and "clangs" beyond, above, below, and beside the optic nonetheless.

This modality of subjectivity might explain the immense global popularity—without inescapably succumbing to the tenacious lure of the empirical—of black popular music over the course of the last century. In other words, rather than exclusively presenting a racially particular identity, black music, in the form of the varying technological structures of sonic Afro-modernity, advances and constructs a subject, at once more and less than its attendant minor identity without which it cannot be thought or perceived. Just as this subject occupies the nether regions between the sonic and the scopic, it correspondingly dislodges the subject/identity bifurcation running amok in current debates within the Anglo-American humanities by refusing to separate *I am I be*, while filling the space and time between these phrases with sonic technicity. The interface of black music and sound technologies yields a rich, varied, and complex field, which amplifies the opacities included therein; as in the words of Levinas, "Form can no longer contain its content," converging the textures of the technosonic weave rather than the nature of its components (Glissant). Even if this constellation could just as easily walk the dark corners of the earth in the cloak of identity, there is a climacteric methodological and theoretical point to be made about wielding the category of the subject from the standpoint of black studies in order to dispel "the pervasive operative presumption that general theory or conceptual reflection is formulated elsewhere than in African Diasporic (American) Studies, and that it is only applied here," since this frees black life from the conceptual chains of radical particularity and embarks on a global journey to ascertain how black cultural practices do not merely mimic or recast those of Western modernity "proper" but are constitutive of this modernity sui generis.[27] This will not entail abandoning the particularities of black life in favor of a color-blind, can't-we-all-just-get-along critical theory and practice as much as reconstructing black life and Western modernity in their mobile relationality, so as not to construe them as mutually exclusive, or even all that different. More succinctly: *I be* (sojourning—both leisurely and contentiously—in the spaces and times between) *I am*.

27. Nahum Dimitri Chandler, "Originary Displacement," *boundary 2* 27, no. 3 (fall 2000): 250.

## Checking Our Balances: Ellison on Armstrong's Humor

*Robert G. O'Meally*

What the black actor has managed to give are moments—indelible moments, created, miraculously, beyond the confines of the script: hints of reality, smuggled like contraband into a maudlin tale, and with enough force, if unleashed, to shatter the tale to fragments.
—James Baldwin, *The Devil Finds Work*

But if all this seems too pessimistic, remember that the antidote to *hubris*, to overweening pride, is irony, that capacity to discover and systematize clear ideas. Or, as Emerson insisted, the development of consciousness, consciousness, consciousness, a more refined conscientiousness, and most of all, that tolerance which takes the form of humor, for when Americans can no longer laugh at each other, they have to fight one another.
—Ralph Ellison, "American Humor"

Louis Armstrong is one of the inventors of jazz, a true revolutionary in art. He is the key figure in the invention of the instrumental jazz solo, of the quality of inevitable-seeming momentum that the world calls swing, of

*boundary 2* 30:2, 2003. Copyright © 2003 by Duke University Press.

the relaxed, and of the playful impulse to reinvent a song that is called jazz singing. Harder to evaluate with certainty are Armstrong's cultural politics, the varied offerings and takings of his image and music, his significance as an American icon. Here I refer to "Ambassador Satch," the tireless worker for the State Department and the one who stood up to Dwight Eisenhower at Little Rock, the man who surprised his white agent by saying angrily that Eisenhower, waffling in sync with Governor Faubus, had two faces and *no heart*. At the same time, I refer to the familiar comic image Armstrong began to offer the public as early as the 1930s. What do we make of Armstrong's semicircular, shining smile? His signature flourish of a blazing white hand-kerchief? If in these familiar scenes what he wears is a comic *mask*, then what does it conceal? And how do we understand the meaning of the mask (or as Constance Rourke might say, the "double-mask"[1]) itself? What can Louis's smiling face tell us about the man who took his stand against a U.S. president? How, if at all, does this face affect the way we hear his music? Is the comic act something he transcends (Figures 1 and 2) in his creation of high art music, or is the comedy part and parcel of an evidently contradictory artistic whole?[2]

I want to explore such questions with Ralph Ellison's theories of comedy as a guide. In so doing, I also hope to see how understanding Armstrong's manifold art can shed light on the world according to Ellison's own art as a writer. How can Louis's sound and smile make us see and perhaps hear Ellison's writing more clearly? (Invisible Man asks, "Could this compulsion to put invisibility down in black and white be thus an urge to make music of invisibility?")[3] I choose Ellison as a critical guide because before becoming a writer, and indeed even in his first years of trying to write fiction, the future author of *Invisible Man* defined himself, in his "heart of hearts," as a musician. He was a trumpet player who, by day, paid his dues to Bach and Sousa (as a college boy, one of his jobs every morning was to wake the campus with reveille, after which he would blow sustained tones to increase

1. See Constance Rourke, *American Humor: A Study of the American Character* (Boston: Harcourt, Brace, 1959).
2. For superb discussions of Armstrong and stereotypical racial humor, see Krin Gabbard, "Actor and Musician: Louis Armstrong and His Films," in *Jammin' at the Margins: Jazz and the American Cinema* (Chicago: University of Chicago Press, 1996), 204–38, 310–28; and Brent Hayes Edwards, "Louis Armstrong and the Syntax of Scat," *Critical Inquiry* (spring 2002): 618–49.
3. Ralph Ellison, *Invisible Man* (New York: Vintage Books, 1972), 13–14. Hereafter, this work is cited parenthetically in the text as *IM*.

**Figure 1.** Armstrong, mugging during a TV performance of Hoagy Carmichael's "Rockin' Chair." These two close friends, Armstrong and trombonist/blues singer Jack Teagarten, draw comedy from Carmichael's mock-sentimental lyrics and then add their own sexual and racial gags that are all part of the fun. (*Timex All-Star Jazz Show #1*, NBC, 1957)

his sound), but who, by night, was practicing both the phrasing and timbre of such blues singers as Ida Cox and, most emphatically, of the singing and trumpet playing of Louis Armstrong and his imitators. "Let that boy blow," Ellison recalls a neighbor saying of his fledgling efforts on horn. "He's got to talk baby talk on that thing before he can preach on it. . . . Now, try and make it sound like ole Ms. Ida Cox sings it."[4]

Ellison's main ambition while in college was to master European classical music sufficiently to write symphonies with an African American accent, sounding the depths of the spirituals and the blues. And it is interesting to consider that he held on to that ambition, only transferring the mode of expression to writing fiction thick with black talk and song: the trumpet player as novelist, his novel as Black New World Symphony.

4. Ralph Ellison, "Living with Music," in *Living with Music*, ed. Robert G. O'Meally (New York: Modern Library, 2001), 9.

**Figure 2.** Even in the presence of the fantastically beautiful Billie Holiday—at the top of her powers as a singer in 1947—it is Armstrong who steals the show. (*New Orleans*, Majestic Productions, Inc., 1947)

Through most of his childhood, Ellison (b. 1914) lived on or near Oklahoma City's Second Street, nicknamed Deep Second or Deep Deuce, which was a smaller version of Kansas City's famous Twelfth and Vine, that city's buckle of the black belt. Like Kansas City, Ellison's hometown specialized in hard-dancing big band blues alive with what Ellison always termed a *frontier* aspect, a lighter, more hopeful ring not as characteristic of, say, Muddy Waters or other blues artists of the Deep South. He grew up knowing the singer Jimmy Rushing and the guitarist Charlie Christian (with whom he had gone to school), and particularly favored the Armstrongian trumpeter/singer Hot Lips Page, that famously inventive, full-throated shouter of the blues. In his essays, Ellison remembers vividly the day in 1929 when Lester Young appeared in the local shoe-shine parlor, waiting in one of those elevated chairs to have his shoes done, wearing a heavy white sweater and a blue stocking cap, holding his "up-and-outthrust silver saxophone," and playing his magically fluid lyrical lines[5]—clearly inspired by fellow–New Orleanian

5. Ellison writes of Lester Young in "The Charlie Christian Story" and in "The Golden Age, Time Past," in *Living with Music*, 38, 60.

Armstrong—upsetting the town. Elsewhere, Ellison remembers first seeing Armstrong, also in 1929, as he performed in a black dance hall in Oklahoma City. The scene produced a memorable lesson in what Ellison has termed American "segregated democracy."[6] "Suddenly the place was filled with white women," he recalls. "Nothing like that had ever happened in our town before. His music was our music but they saw it as theirs too, and were willing to break the law to get to it. So you could see that Armstrong's music was affecting [the broad community's] attitudes and values"[7]—perhaps giving a hint of Armstrong the Civil Rights activist-to-be.

Beginning in the late 1940s, when it already had become commonplace to criticize Armstrong's public persona as pandering to whites, or Uncle Tomming, Ellison steadily and staunchly defended him. Indeed, Armstrong may be called the hero of Ellison's 1964 book of essays (the book that novelist Paule Marshall has brilliantly termed Ellison's true second novel), *Shadow and Act*. Armstrong also opens and closes *Invisible Man*; in its prologue, he appears as that novel's most complexly evocative artist-as-direction-giver: the one inside whose art the most discerning reader may hear a highly charged history of black Americans. From the vantage point of decades later, it is interesting to consider these sell-out charges against Armstrong and to watch Ellison's defenses of him in light of the sudden onslaught of anti-Ellison criticism from black students and artists of the 1960s and 1970s, for whom, like Armstrong, Ellison began to look suspiciously detached, elitist, and Uncle Tommish.[8] (Doubtless one reason for Ellison's failure to complete his ultimately unfinished novel was the shock of finding himself classified by his friends' college-age children and their classmates as some sort of racial opportunist.)

Among some of Ellison's defenses of Armstrong's comic smile was his observation that it was the entertainer's style to wear a smile on stage, simple as that. Armstrong's was a generation, before Charlie Parker's, that was less abashed about the entertainer's role as joy-bringer, good-time roller. "By rejecting Armstrong they thought to rid themselves of the entertainer's role. And by way of getting rid of the role, they demanded, in the

6. This phrase is used in Ellison's personal essay called "On Being the Target of Discrimination," in *The Collected Essays of Ralph Ellison* (New York: Modern Library), 821.
7. Ralph Ellison, "Ralph Ellison's Territorial Vantage," interview by Ron Welburn, in *Living with Music*, 28–29.
8. See James McPherson, "Indivisible Man," in *Conversations with Ralph Ellison*, ed. Maryemma Graham and Amritjit Singh (Jackson: University Press of Mississippi, 1995), 173–91.

name of their racial identity, a purity of status which by definition is impossible for the performing artist."[9] In the end, as Dizzy Gillespie's extroverted performance style clearly indicated, the beboppers were entertainers, too—even when, as eventually in Miles Davis's case, audiences came to see him turn his back on them as if in disdain.

But entertainment with a smile has a distinctive social value, says Ellison. Especially in times of national stress, we depend on the good work of such musical joy-bringers. During the Great Depression, for instance, jazz served the general welfare by helping to lift the spirits; and through the twentieth century, Ellison adds, black American art often gave the whole nation a lift.[10] Further, in an interview of 1976, the writer proclaims "Ellison's Law": If blacks could laugh (even if only laughing to keep from crying), who could dare to frown?[11] (A sobering corollary, he goes on to say, is that "whatever happens to blacks will accrue eventually, one way or another, to the nation as a whole. This is their dark-visioned version of the broader 'American Joke.'")[12]

Indeed, Ellison's take on Armstrong's deeply humorous art does recall Henry James's assessment of the American joke as a secret definitive national gift, "that American humor of which of late years we have heard so much."[13] We live, Ellison writes, in the "United States of Jokeocracy," "a land of masking jokers."[14] What could be more definitively American than Louis Armstrong, smiling? If it is a national gift, this humor, perhaps it is in line with Kenneth Burke's idea of the comic frame of reference in art as the window on the world through which one could see the most: comedy as the clearest view of salvation. "Comedy," writes Burke, "should enable us to be *observers of ourselves while acting*. Its ultimate end would not be *passiveness* but *maximum consciousness*. [It should allow] one to 'transcend' himself by noting his own foibles . . . [and should] provide a rationale for locating the irrational and the non-rational."[15] The Armstrongian smile as an American icon of optimism, an emblem of good cheer (Figure 3).

9. Ralph Ellison, "On Bird, Bird-Watching, and Jazz," in *Living with Music*, 69.
10. Ellison discusses this in "Homage to Duke Ellington," in *Living with Music*, 77–86.
11. Ellison said this in conversation with the author in May 1976.
12. Ralph Ellison, "An Extravagance of Laughter," in *Collected Essays*, 185–86.
13. Henry James, "Nathaniel Hawthorne," in *Henry James: Literary Criticism, Essays on Literature, American Writers, English Writers* (New York: Library of America, 1984), 352.
14. Ralph Ellison, "It Always Breaks Out," *Partisan Review* (spring 1963): 16; "Change the Joke and Slip the Yoke," in *Collected Essays*, 109.
15. These lines from Burke's *Attitudes toward History* (1937) are quoted in "An Extrava-

**Figure 3.** In *Rhapsody in Black and Blue* (1932), Armstrong plays a dream-figure dressed in a leopard skin and performs "Shine" as well as "(I'll Be Glad When You're Dead) You Rascal, You." Krin Gabbard has argued that Armstrong's mighty physique and musical artistry upstage the film's primitivist fantasies. (*Rhapsody in Black and Blue*, Paramount Pictures, 1932)

Nor, in this view, is such American humor necessarily a shield of deflection or avoidance. Writing about the Americanness of Duke Ellington's slyly humorous habits of spoken and musical expression in a way that brings Armstrong to mind, Ellison gives insight into the humor in jazz, and perhaps into defining a process that helps power the creation of much U.S. art as an indigenous art form. Ellington's sense of humor, Ellison says, is as full of mockery

> as the dancing of those slaves who, looking through the windows of a plantation manor house from the yard, imitated the steps so gravely performed by the masters within and then added to them their own special flair, burlesquing the white folks and then going on to force the

---

gance of Laughter," in *Collected Essays*, 185. The italics are Burke's; the brackets and ellipses, Ellison's.

steps into a choreography uniquely their own. The whites, looking out at the activity in the yard, thought they were being flattered by imitation, and were amused by the incongruity of tattered blacks dancing courtly steps, while missing completely the fact that before their eyes a European cultural form was becoming Americanized, undergoing a metamorphosis through the mocking activity of a people partially sprung from Africa. So, blissfully unaware, the whites laughed while the blacks danced out their mocking reply.[16]

This is an American process of creating art through a dynamic system of exchanges—including what Henry Louis Gates terms "signifyin(g)" and what Robert Farris Thompson terms "dances of derision"—that often come with a coolly calculated smile. Armstrong's smile, then, as a complex piece of signifying, in the African American way.

In a masterful essay called "An Extravagance of Laughter," Ellison studies "the blackness of Negro laughter" as he riffs hilariously on the twice-told tales of the colored citizen's "laughing barrel." According to many a tale, laughing barrels were strategically placed in the walkways of Southern towns so that if a Negro felt too turbulent a gale of laughter coming on, he or she could howl down into one of these laughing barrels and thus preserve the public calm and civic peace.

> The barrels were by no means an elegant solution of what whites regarded as a most grievous and inelegant problem. After all, having to observe the posture of a Negro stuck halfway into a laughing barrel . . . rising and falling . . . was far from an aesthetic experience. Nor was that all, for often when seen laughing with their heads stuck in a barrel and standing, as it were, upside down upon the turbulent air, Negroes appeared to be taken over by a form of schizophrenia which left them even more psychically frazzled than whites regarded them as being by nature. . . . It appeared that in addition to reacting to whatever ignorant, harebrained notion had set him off in the first place, the Negro was apt to double up with a second gale of laughter, triggered, apparently, by his own mental image of himself laughing at himself laughing upside down. It was, all whites agreed, another of the many Negro mysteries with which it was their lot to contend, but whatever its true cause, it was most disturbing to a white observer.[17]

16. Ellison, "Homage to Duke Ellington on His Birthday," in *Living with Music*, 84.
17. Ellison, "An Extravagance of Laughter," in *Collected Essays*, 651–52.

Here, then, is jazz as a rippling, subversive comic art, deflating self and others in a cakewalking communal celebration and bash.[18] Riffing, too, in "Extravagance," on Du Bois's thesis of doubleness and clairvoyance, Ellison also notes in this essay that the view from inside the laughing barrel was ironically such that "when a Negro had his head thrust into a laughing-barrel he became endowed with a strange form of extrasensory perspective—or second sight."[19]

These passages about Ellington (and, it seems to me, also about Armstrong) and about laughing barrels suggest that American-style comedy offers modes of self-reflection, ways of seeing ourselves and others without taking ourselves too seriously. And it is one of the mightiest engines of unself-conscious American art, art that is most characteristically American: Armstrong, looking at the lead sheet of a song such as "Shine," or "Ochie Chornie," laughing at what's expected of him, seeming to comply, then mocking the expectation and the falsely accommodating self, winking at his audience, laughing as he helps create a new form of American expression and art. Here is Armstrong employing a rich comedy indeed: comedy as our national artistic strategy and, in James's term, truly our national "gift."[20]

18. With all this going on in this music, small wonder Plato had his doubts about the place of *musika* in his republic: Pouring so directly into the soul, how easily music could lead the unsuspecting student astray. See *The Republic*.

19. Ellison, "An Extravagance of Laughter," in *Collected Essays*, 191.

20. See Ellison, "Going to the Territory" (1980), in *Collected Essays*: "Verbal comedy was a way of confronting social ambiguity. Being familiar with racial violence—we were living in the aftermath of the race riots that followed World War I, remember—we learned quite early that laughter made the difficulties of our condition a bit more bearable. We hadn't read Henry James at that time, but we realized nevertheless that American society contained a built-in joke, and we were aware, even if James wasn't (or did not choose to admit), that this joke was in many ways centered in our condition. So we welcomed any play on words or nuance of gesture which gave expression to our secret sense of the way things really were. Usually this took the comic mode, and it is quite possible that one reason the popular arts take on an added dimension in our democracy lies in an unspoken, though no less binding, agreement that popular culture is not to be taken seriously. Thus the popular arts have become an agency through which Americans can contemplate those aspects of our experience that are deemed unspeakable.

"Perhaps this is what was left to such comedians as Redd Foxx to notify us of, that since the 1950s a major change has occurred in our attitudes toward racial minorities. Thus when he, a black comedian, makes remarks about ugly white women which once were reserved only for black women, he allows us to bring attitudes and emotions that were once tabooed into the realm of the rational, where, protected by the comic mode, we may confront our guilt and prejudices and perhaps resolve them" (607–8).

Harder to embrace is Ellison's contention that we Americans need this highly charged comic process *sometimes even when it means putting up with offensive racial stereotypes.* Throughout American history, Ellison says, "the northerner found the southerner strange. The southerner found the northerner despicable. The blacks found the whites peculiar. The whites found the blacks ridiculous. Some agency had to be adopted which would allow us to live with one another without destroying one another, and the agency was laughter, was humor. If you can laugh at me, you don't have to kill me. If I can laugh at you, I don't have to kill you."[21] And in the process of laughing at the comic dupe, a human identification is made—something perhaps more important, he says, than eliminating the offending comic image or its perpetrator. Recall Invisible Man's comically thwarted effort to discard the metal bank in the stereotypical shape of a grotesquely smiling Negro head;[22] even in shards, the heavy item can't be thrown away by the young black man because, offensive as it is, it is nonetheless part of his American cultural luggage. Wanted or not, it is one of his densely significant *gifts.* What the young man learns is that if he can anticipate the uses by his enemies of such racist images as this one, maybe he can deploy them for his own strategic purposes—to "overcome 'em with yeses, undermine 'em with grins, agree 'em to death and destruction," as his grandfather advised (*IM,* 16).

Ellison implies that Louis's laughter might be taken as part of a strategy to create a freer space in which to make art: a way to "make poetry out of being invisible," as Invisible Man puts it, extolling Armstrong's art. Taken as a clown or fool, Armstrong is invisible and thus ironically freer to experiment with his art, without the pressures that typically go with the official recognition of "high art." Furthermore, deriving from African, European, and Native American people, with their many traditions of mask wearing, and specifically from multinational New Orleans, where masquerade is intrinsic to carnival (and where, in 1949, Armstrong came home to the Crescent City as the painted and highly decorated King of the Zulus, the Afro-Indian monarch of mockery), no wonder Armstrong the performer was a masked man. As such, he operated in the American/African American traditions of wearing one face and concealing another: of Benjamin Franklin

21. Ralph Ellison, "American Humor," a transcribed speech of 11 April 1970, quoted in Elwyn E. Breaux, "Comic Elements in Selected Prose Works by James Baldwin, Ralph Ellison, and Langston Hughes" (Ph.D. diss., Fisk University, 1971), 148.
22. One source of the image of the undiscardable item may have been "Abu Kasem's Slippers," in Joseph Campbell, *The King and the Corpse: Tales of the Soul's Conquest of Evil* (Princeton, N.J.: Princeton University Press, 1971), 9–25.

playing Europe as a primitive, Ellen Craft made up to look like her slave husband's white master, Richard Wright pretending, at a whites-only library, to be a white man's errand boy and hangdog black dunce. Like Rinehart's hat in *Invisible Man*, Louis's face, which looked like a stereotyped happy darky's grin, permitted him to express his own complex sense of life through his music without ruffling the feathers of those who preferred to think him less than he was.

It is very important that Ellison calls Armstrong not just a masked man but a *trickster*. With his "sweat, spittle and facial contortions," writes Ellison, Armstrong was "the trickster" who "emphasizes the physicality of his music as he performs the magical feat of making romantic melody issue from a throat of gravel; and [who] some few years ago was recommending to all and sundry his personal [medicine] 'Pluto Water,' as a purging way to health, happiness and international peace."[23] All in good fun, as through the trickster's mask he projected "romantic melody" and sublime elegance. "Elegance turns up in every aspect of Afro-American culture," says Ellison, "from sermons to struts, pimp-walks and dance steps. . . . And if Louis Armstrong's meditations on the 'Potato Head Blues' aren't marked by elegance, then the term is too inelegant to name the fastidious refinement, the mastery of nuance, the tasteful domination of melody, rhythm, sounding brass and tinkling cymbal which marked his style."[24]

"*We wear the mask*," Ellison writes, "*for purposes of aggression as well as for defense*."[25] Does this mean that there is a more aggressive side to Armstrong's trickster-play? Recall Ellison's short story "Scalped Indians," where the jazz music in the distance is heard as the music of coping with chaos in the form of white antagonists: The trumpet is a soldier, Buster says, "'cause he's slipping 'em in the twelves and choosing 'em, all at the same time. Talking 'bout they mamas and offering to fight 'em. Now he ain't like that ole clarinet; clarinet so sweet-talking he just eases you in the dozens." Buster tells his friend that he will emulate the instruments' ways of dealing with enemies with the subtlety of the signifying dozens ("the twelves"): "You have to outtalk 'em, outrun 'em, or outfight 'em and I don't aim to be running and fighting all the time."[26] But one way or the other, "our life is a war," as Invisible Man's grandfather said before he died (*IM*, 16), and the music a call

23. Ellison, *Collected Essays*, 106–7.
24. "Study and Experience: An Interview with Ralph Ellison," *Massachusetts Review* (1977), reprinted in *Conversations*, 329.
25. Ellison, "Change the Joke and Slip the Yoke," in *Collected Essays*, 109; my emphasis.
26. Ralph Ellison, "A Coupla Scalped Indians," in *Living with Music*, 186–87.

to arms, a set of suggestions for approaches to battle. "This familiar music had demanded action," says Invisible Man, listening to Armstrong's "Black and Blue" (*IM*, 12).

This idea of Armstrong's more aggressive subversions is hinted at in a 1957 letter Ellison writes from Rome to his friend Albert Murray:

> Here, way late, I've discovered Louis singing Mack the Knife. Shake-speare invented Caliban, or changed himself into him—Who the hell dreamed up Louie? Some of the bop boys consider him Caliban but if he is he's a mask for a lyric poet who is much greater than most now writing. That's a mask for [the critic] to study, me too. . . . Hare and bear [are] the ticket; man and mask, sophistication and taste hiding behind clowning and crude manners—the American joke, man. . . . The only time he ever comes out from behind that mask is when he's cornered—that's when you have to watch him. Unless, of course, he's Mose, who has learned to deal with a hell of a lot more pressure.[27]

Louis as Brer Hare and Brer Bear (trickster and strong man), clowning while, behind the mask, he continued to assert "sophistication and taste." But also, very tellingly: Armstrong as Caliban, the New World slave learning Old Master's language well enough to curse him with it, while he laughs.

As a consummate player and singer of the blues, Armstrong was involved, day in and day out, with the comedy at the edge of tragedy that defines the fundamental blues mode—wherein typically the performer counts the teeming troubles of the world and then laughs at them, the tragic facts trumped by an ironically comic punch line. As a form, the blues are characterized by "unobtrusive irony" and a staunch refusal to be sentimental or mawkish, however lovelorn the themes. The "great human joke" in the blues, writes Ellison in 1954, is that "though we be dismembered daily we shall always rise up."[28] For Ellison, at its best, this joke's dark blue laughter offers not just release but perspective by incongruity[29] and even revelation, which helps explain the strangely violent outbursts of cathartic laughter in

27. Ralph Ellison, letter to Albert Murray, Rome, 2 June 1957, in *Trading Twelves: The Selected Letters of Ralph Ellison and Albert Murray*, ed. Albert Murray and John F. Calla-han (New York: Modern Library, 2000), 166. "Mose" is Ellison's slang term for the generic African American.
28. Ralph Ellison, "Introduction to Flamenco," in *Living with Music*, 100.
29. This phrase is Kenneth Burke's, from "Attitudes toward History" (1937), reprinted in *Perspectives by Incongruity*, ed. Stanley Edgar Hyman (Bloomington: Indiana University Press, 1964), 94–99.

"Flying Home," "On Being a Target of Racism," and "An Extravagance of Laughter."[30]

In 1966, Ellison tells a group at Langston University what he means by the blues as a tragicomic frame of mind: "I refer not simply to the song form, but to a basic and complex attitude toward experience. It is an attitude toward life which looks pretty coldly and realistically at the human predicament, and which expresses the individual's insistence upon enduring in the face of his limitations, and which is in itself a kind of triumph over self and circumstance. . . . I can only say that there is a part of my temperament which finds its expression in this crazy mixture of modes."[31] This Ellisonian perspective on the blues as funny and sad but still triumphal is congruent with his friend Murray's sense of the Saturday Night Function as a function indeed wherein one confronted the tragic facts of life at the same time that one sought to drive the blues-troubles away with hard partying to blues music, the blues being an intrinsic part of a rite of purification and of courtship and fertility—a comic victory of spring over winter, a bluesy laugh and shout as we rise again.[32] Listen to Armstrong sing the "St. James Infirmary Blues"[33]—as much a chilling meditation on the death of a young lover stretched out on a cold white table as it is a reflection on the singer's own death. Twice in the midst of one performance recorded in 1959, Louis cracks up laughing, as if the blues can squeeze humor out of (and thus help us cope with) even the most devastating losses, not excluding death itself.

• • • •

With these various ideas about Armstrong's art in mind—and in particular its comic arc—let us consider the prologue to *Invisible Man*, where the protagonist, hiding in his underground basement, says he owns one record player but plans to get five of them, all broadcasting Armstrong's "Black and Blue" at the same time. Ellison uses that song as his character's Proustian madeleine or *lieu de memoire*: sweet site of memory and spur to cultural excavation and consciousness. Beneath the surfaces of that song, he hears a wide variety of sounds, recalling Ellison's statements about the

---

30. Note also the explosion of laughter in chapter 10 of *Invisible Man*, where the protagonist is asked to sing a Negro spiritual at a party of political activists.

31. Ralph Ellison, unpublished transcription of a talk at Langston University, 1966, 5.

32. See Albert Murray, *Stomping the Blues* (New York: McGraw-Hill, 1976).

33. The version of "St. James Infirmary" I refer to appears on a CD entitled *Doctor Jazz, Louis "Satchmo" and His All Stars*, Blue Moon 3067, recorded 1959.

play of references that Ellison admired both in Armstrong and T.S. Eliot. In both cases, the impulse to quote "grows out of a similar and quite American approach to the classics, just as Armstrong and any other jazz musician of that period would take a theme and start improvising. Then he would pay his respects to *Aida*, to any number of operas, to light opera, or to religious music. All this . . . in the course of the improvisation."[34] Invisible Man hears a whole symphony of songs and stories—including the sounds of an old ex-slave woman, whose sons laugh eerily because their white father, whom she loved and hated, is dead, and who, for her own part, explains, "*I laughs too, but I moans too*" (*IM*, 10)—folded inside that tragic and (though we usually forget this part) uncannily *comical* song, "(What Did I Do to Be So) Black and Blue."

Standing, for a moment more, outside the novel, what on earth are we to make of "Black and Blue" itself, this strange dirge of 1929, often called the first racial protest song in the United States? "Black and Blue" was written by the black songwriting team of Andy Razaf and Thomas "Fats" Waller in response to a specific order by the gangster Arthur Flegenheimer (a.k.a. Dutch Schultz) that the new, all-black show he was bankrolling have "something with a little colored girl singing how tough it is being colored."[35] In its original setting for that show, *Hot Chocolates*, "Black and Blue" offered what appeared at first blush to be just what Dutch had in mind—a conventional piece of staged racial pathos: "Even a mouse, ran from my house," go the lyrics. "Feel like old Ned, wish I was dead."

But there is an uninvited twist of black laughter here. Instead of jerking tears from whites about "how tough it is to be colored," Razaf wrote "Black and Blue" as a mock-pathetic joke by a dark-skinned woman who reclines on a fluffy white bed shining with white satin sheets in a room flooded with white lights, and who sings about how Negro men preferred light-skinned women: Edith Wilson's line "browns and yellers *all have fellers*" got the show's biggest laugh. And while the line "I'm white inside, but that don't help my case" offends our ears in 2003, in 1929 these words stopped the laughter for a moment; they were so bold a subversion of what white U.S. audiences generally expected of a "colored" show tune (pathos, humor, sex), that Razaf later said that at the show's opening, only the (white) audience's tumultuous extravagance of laughter—and then its spirited standing ovation—kept Schultz from shooting him on the spot! One rule in this world,

34. Richard Kostelanetz, "An Interview with Ralph Ellison," in *Conversations*, 90.
35. Barry Singer, *Black and Blue: The Life and Lyrics of Andy Razaf* (New York: Schirmer Books, 1992), 216–20.

Razaf later said, seemed to be that you just didn't kill a man who'd written you a hit song.[36]

With Razaf's own agenda of subtle but highly significant subversion in mind, it is easy to wonder if "Black and Blue" may have been conceived for Louis Armstrong, who did appear in the show and evidently was present while the song was being created. Armstrong recorded "Black and Blue" that same year, 1929, editing it to erase the intraracial pathos and boomeranging stage comedy as he turned it into his own tragedy-haunted meditation on white racism and—beyond the issue of race in the United States—a philosophical reflection on the meaning of inevitable human suffering: What did any of us do to be so bruised by life, so beaten *black and blue*?

Listening to Armstrong's "Black and Blue" (and smoking a reefer) and wishing he had five record players to hear it properly, Invisible Man is struck by Armstrong's way of singing with and against the music's expected steady cadences—his way of swinging the song. You felt you were "never quite on the beat," Ellison's character says. "Sometimes you're ahead and sometimes behind. Instead of the swift and imperceptible flowing of time, you are aware of its nodes, those points where time stands still or from which it leaps ahead. And you slip into the breaks and look around. That's what you hear vaguely in Louis' music" (*IM*, 8).

Swinging (one thinks of Malcolm X's "we need to stop singing and start swinging") can have its aggressive as well as its pleasingly musical side. To make this point, Ellison has Invisible Man listen to "Black and Blue" at the same time that he recalls seeing a prizefighter boxing a yokel, landing a hundred scientifically timed blows while the yokel can only recoil in stunned helplessness. "But suddenly the yokel, rolling about in the gale of boxing gloves, struck one blow and knocked science, speed and footwork as cold as a well-digger's posterior," writes Ellison. "The yokel had simply stepped inside his opponent's sense of time." Between the breaks in this intense but nonetheless swinging performance of "Black and Blue," Invisible Man hears the instruments as characters in a story: "The unheard sounds came through," he says, "and each melodic line existed of itself, stood out clearly from all the rest, said its piece, and waited patiently for the other voices to speak. That night I found myself hearing not only in time but in space as well. I not only entered the music but descended, like Dante, in its depths" (*IM*, 7–9).

In a novel often criticized for being masculinist, Invisible Man hears

36. Singer, *Black and Blue*, 219.

a song first staged as a woman's song inside which he also hears an old woman who sings a spiritual "*as full of Weltschmertz as flamenco, and beneath that lay a still lower level on which I saw a beautiful girl the color of ivory pleading in a voice like my mother's as she stood before a group of slaveowners who bid for her naked body*." While the old singer of spirituals tells her story and moans[37] of love and hate for the white man she has killed to gain her freedom, her sons upstairs howl an uncanny laughter. Typical Ellison, and true to "Black and Blue," the scene is mixed with tragedy and comedy. "*I laughs too*," the woman says, "*but I moans too. He promised to set us free but he never could bring hisself to do it. Still I loved him . . .*" (*IM*, 10–11).

In short, even before Ellison began to work his magic on "Black and Blue," the song was a site of contestation over the meaning of black expression and history. Schultz called for minstrel-show style Negro pathos and received, from Razaf, a protest song gently ribboned in humor; Armstrong edited out the humor to intensify the protest song's racial edge and tragic thrust; and Ellison edited it still further, eliminating the song's dated language about "house" and "mouse," and "I'm white, inside"—compressing it to the bare, bluesy ten words of the song's title, "What did I do / to be so black and blue?" But what fascinates me most here is that Ellison's character's reflections on the song return to the idea of the song as a woman's plaint and moan, mixed with strange, ambiguous laughter and a boxer(-artist?)'s knockout blow. That Armstrong is made to deliver the lines only adds more punch to the meaning: It is a trickster's song, deep and wide with meaning and moaning, but not without the edged anger—the blackness of Negro laughter.

An Ellisonian perspective on Armstrong's humor can also help us confront the strange cartoon of 1932 in which, three years after his recording of "Black and Blue," Armstrong makes brief but captivating appearances. Before turning to this cartoon, called "(I'll Be Glad When You're Dead) You Rascal, You," we should pause to note that Ellison sometimes referred to comics (he wrote about comic books, but I believe his analyses could also apply to cartoons) as revealing much about the violence and mythology in American life. In *Invisible Man*, as the hero begins to sense the significance

---

37. As we consider the woman's laughter, let us not forget her moans: A "moan," according to the *OED*, is a sympathetic lamentation, an expression beyond words, associated with "to have in mind, to mean." It is the sound of what Nathaniel Mackey has termed "telling inarticulacy," an expression which, for all its difficulty to interpret, has its own truth-value and precision.

of black leadership from the periphery, he sees three quiet black boys on a subway platform who are studying comic books "in complete absorption." "Who knew," says Invisible Man, "they might be the saviors, the true leaders, the bearers of something precious. . . . What if history was not a reasonable citizen, but a madman full of paranoid guile and these boys his agents, his big surprise! His own revenge? For they were outside, in the dark with Sambo, the dancing paper doll; taking on the lambo . . . running and dodging the forces of history instead of making a dominating stand" (*IM*, 431).

In the cartoon called "(I'll Be Glad When You're Dead) You Rascal, You," we first see Armstrong and his band in a film clip without animation.[38] The ten-piece band plays the quick, jaunty lines of "High Society," with Armstrong, the elegantly dressed leader, playing lead trumpet and mock-conducting the others with cool, nonchalant flexing of his arms and upper body. After an animated clip introduces Betty Boop, the cartoon's star, again with Armstrong's "High Society" as sound track, the story line begins with Betty, noticeably darker in complexion now than in the introductory trailer, on safari in "the jungle" with her friends Bimbo the Dog and Koko the Clown, her "white hunters," who carry her on a kind of stretcher that floats and bumps her along in an erotic dance that keeps dog, clown, and even the stretcher itself smiling. Eventually, the strangely androgynous "natives," stalking the intruders at every step, snatch Betty from her protectors and take her prisoner. What ensues is a fantastic chase, with Bimbo and Koko strut-dancing at top speed into the darkening night, pursued by a lone "savage," who moves to the music of "(I'll Be Glad When You're Dead) You Rascal, You."[39] Soon, the dark chaser metamorphoses into an animated head—an immense and menacing stereotyped black primitive, though bodiless—which chases Bimbo and Koko while singing the lyrics of the song in Armstrong's voice! As if that were not enough, the disembodied "savage" head then metamorphoses into film footage of Armstrong's own head, singing the lyrics with more of a laugh than a real threat as in hot pursuit it flies, disembodied, through the air (Figure 4).

38. Several other Betty Boop cartoons feature film footage of musicians; for example, Cab Calloway, Don Redman, and Ethel Merman all make appearances as themselves, performing.

39. This song, by the black songwriter Sam Theard (or was it Charles "Cow Cow" Davenport, to whom it has sometimes been attributed?), was obviously an Armstrong favorite. He recorded it in 1931 for Okeh and then again as a single for Decca, and, yet again, as a duet with Louis Jordan, who had also recorded "Let the Good Times Roll" and "You Can't Get That No More," both by Sam Theard.

**Figure 4.** In the Betty Boop cartoon "(I'll Be Glad When You're Dead) You Rascal, You," Koko and Bimbo run from the singing head of a stereotyped black "savage," which metamorphoses into Armstrong's own singing, floating head. (Paramount Pictures, 1932)

Then, as if what we were watching were a variety show, the animated cartoon unfurls like a curtain to reveal more film footage of the Armstrong band, this time playing "Chinatown, My Chinatown," the leader now directing his men by flapping his arms, still some sort of (temporarily grounded) creature of the sky. "Looks like these cats're trying to cut me here sure 'nough," says Armstrong as a stage aside—suggesting that the band's music, too, is about a chase or competition—"Oh, but I'm ready," he says, "*I'm ready*!" To top things off, before Betty is rescued and the savages blown up by a volcano, Armstrong's drummer, Alfred "Tubby" Hall, has a cameo appearance, and he, too, changes from being a drummer into a jolly savage stirring the pot in which the "natives" plan that Betty will be stewed. As film image, Armstrong has the last word, delivered in front of his band with a kind of roar in the middle of the statement and with an explosive grunt at the end: "I'll be glad when you're dead, *Oooooh*, I'll be glad when you're dead, you rascal you. . . . *NNyuhnn*!!"

There is much to consider here: the subversive song itself, perhaps related in spirit to the ironic slave secular "Massa's in the Cold, Cold

**Figure 5.** In the cartoon "(I'll Be Glad When You're Dead) You Rascal, You," Koko the Clown runs so fast that his black suit is left behind, to reveal that he really is "white." He is running from Louis Armstrong's voice and floating head. (Paramount Pictures, 1932)

Ground"; the Fleischers' brilliant uses of jazz in other cartoons, particularly in those with Cab Calloway and their use of jazz, here and elsewhere, not so much as sound track but as starting point from which the action is derived— consider the cartoon's action as narrativizing Armstrong's music; the background of vaudeville and minstrelsy suggested by the cadences of the comedy and especially by Koko the Clown, who runs out of his black clown suit to reveal that he is "white" underneath (Figure 5); the marking then of Koko as Jewish, as while he runs he hits speeds recorded first in miles per hour and then by a phrase in Hebrew letters; "white" (though elsewhere sometimes also Jewish) Betty's coloring, which gets darker the deeper she runs into the "jungle"; Betty's wink, as if she and we the audience understand all this complex business as part of a joke we share in secret together.[40] And then there is the fascinating problem of Betty herself, whose Boop-Boop-a-Doop act was copied by the cartoons' producers, the Fleischer Brothers,

40. See Leslie Cabarga, *The Fleischer Story* (New York: Dacapo, 1976); and Charles Solomon, *The History of Animation: Enchanted Drawings* (New York: Knopf, 1989).

from the performance stylings of the popular white singer Helen Kane, who took the Fleischers to court, charging them with stealing her show. In a dramatic (Ellisonian) turn of events, the Fleischers defended themselves by appearing in court with a black singer known as Baby Esther, who gave evidence that *her* Boop-Boop-a-Doop singing bit preceded that of Helen Kane's.[41] In other words, Boop herself had, as it were, a black grandmother in her background. What's most enthralling, in the context of this essay, is the role played by Armstrong. Cast as a stereotyped primitive, he is also the highly polished leader of a band for which he is the conductor, singer, and principal soloist. And his song, despite its "fried chicken" lyrics and foolishness, is unmistakable in its aggressive declarations that its singer will be glad when "you"—the "whites" in the cartoon? Betty? the producers? the audience?—are all dead.

Armstrong's spirit pervades the whole cartoon: He is the Ellisonian masked man, the trickster who bursts through the scene to sing a song of anger and revenge. Of course, he agreed to make the cartoon as a promotional short subject, to advertise his traveling band and its recordings. But he also advertised a point of view that might be termed Ellisonian: that through all the comedy that can seem so simplistically stereotyped, the trickster with his trumpet projects his complicated cultural message. As with "Black and Blue" in Ellison's novel, through this cartoon and this song—including Armstrong's smiling disembodied head—a whole cultural history may be detected.

In the novel *Juneteenth*, Ellison's main character is Rev. A. Z. Hickman, a trombone-playing bluesman who has converted and been called to preach. His adopted son, Rev. Bliss, is an unreliable narrator, but he does get it right when he implies that what we need as a nation are the values of jazz, not finished stasis but a will to improvise. Here's Bliss:

> We seek not perfection, but coordination. Not sterile stability but creative momentum. Ours is a youthful nation; the perfection we seek is futuristic and to be made manifest in creative action. . . . Born in diversity and fired by determination, our society was endowed with a flexibility designed to contain the most fractious contentions of an ambitious, individualistic and adventurous breed. . . . Yes, and as we check our checks and balance our balances, let us in all good

41. See Klaus Stratemann, *Louis Armstrong on the Screen* (Copenhagen: JazzMedia, 1996), 17–26.

humor balance our checks and check our balances, keeping each in proper order, issuing credit to the creditable, minus to plus, and plus to minus.[42]

What Bliss and Invisible Man, who calls himself a "bungling bugler of words," and Armstrong, the trumpeter known for what Ellison terms his "rowdy poetic flight," recommend to all of us are the qualities of resiliency and spiritual equipoise that define the blues along with the music's awareness that the real secret of life is to make life swing. And swinging, as we have seen, is an extremely complex business: With its aggressive and defensive aspects, swinging is a fiercely comic mode; it is an act of checks and balances, defenses and aggressions.

• • • •

As a coda, let us look for a moment at Ellison looking at Armstrong and—as if to confirm the difficulty of getting a fix on the great musician's public image—misinterpreting the situation. In a letter to Murray, Ellison reports on his impression, from newspaper accounts, of the 1957 Newport Jazz Festival, where Armstrong's band appeared briefly. After a few songs, Armstrong played "The Star-Spangled Banner" as a farewell song and then led his band offstage, not to reappear. Loud talk backstage was heard by reporters. "Louis was wearing his ass instead of his genius," writes Ellison to Murray.[43] What Ellison did not know is that on that day, George Wein, the director of the Newport Jazz Festival, had arranged with Armstrong's manager, Joe Glazer, that Armstrong's fifty-seventh birthday, the day of the concert, would feature guests associated with Louis's career, including Ella Fitzgerald, who would replace Louis's regular singer, Velma Middleton, for the evening. No one told (or asked) Louis about these surprise plans, however. And his long-standing agreement with his manager was that he—Armstrong—alone would make all such artistic decisions while leaving bookings and payments to Glazer. What Ellison read were newspaper speculations about what had made Louis walk off in a huff. No one seemed to get the story straight. Instead of "showing his ass"—embarrassing himself by acting unprofessionally, for no good reason—Louis had been standing up for his own artistic program and colleague, even if doing so meant a showdown with powerful white men with whom he had long done business. Behind the

42. Ralph Ellison, *Juneteenth* (New York: Random House, 1999), 20–21.
43. Ellison, letter to Albert Murray, Rome, 17 August 1957, in *Trading Twelves*, 175.

stage smile on that day was a world of trouble, misread by those who were there and even by his best defender, Ralph Ellison.[44]

Louis's smiling face is the slipperiest of cultural masks to interpret. What lies behind it? Sometimes political anger; sometimes another, more genuine smile; sometimes a story of artistic integrity defended. Sometimes it is a wink or groan that shatters a maudlin tale to fragments. Sometimes it seems to say that not only is the real secret of life to make life swing but to make life swing hard, and with a smile. But watch out, for what Ellison said of himself evidently was just as true of Mr. Armstrong, too: When he was laughing the hardest, *he was usually preparing a punch for somebody*!

44. This version of what happened on that night at Newport comes from an August 2000 conversation with George Wein, whose information came firsthand, and from Armstrong himself.

# "Fingering the Jagged Grain": Ellison's Wright and the Southern Blues Violences

*Adam Gussow*

## "Brutal Experience" and Lyric Flight

If we are still capable of valuing our writers by the extent to which they embody the creed put forward by Pope in "An Essay on Criticism"—which is to say, by their ability to express "what oft' was thought" in words that henceforward become an indispensable touchstone—then Ralph Ellison's summary description of the blues in a 1945 review essay entitled "Richard Wright's Blues" is arguably the most important two sentences he ever wrote. Ellison's elders, including Sterling Brown and Langston Hughes, had previously struggled, with mixed success, to articulate what might be called the blues' animating paradox, their curious compressed yoking of tragedy and comedy. "Crudities, incongruities, of course, there are in abundance," observes Brown in his 1930 essay, "The Blues as Folk Poetry," "—annoying changes of mood from tragedy to cheap farce."[1] "[S]ad as Blues may be," responds Hughes somewhat more sympathetically in 1941, "there's almost

---

1. Sterling Brown, "The Blues as Folk Poetry," in Robert G. O'Meally, ed., *The Jazz Cadence of American Culture* (New York: Columbia University Press, 1998), 551.

*boundary 2* 30:2, 2003. Copyright © 2003 by Duke University Press.

always something humorous about them—even if it's the kind of humor that laughs to keep from crying."[2] Four years later, in his review of Wright's *Black Boy*, Ellison theorizes blues expressiveness with eloquent and indelible concision. "The blues," he proposes, "is an impulse to keep the painful details and episodes of a brutal experience alive in one's aching consciousness, to finger its jagged grain, and to transcend it, not by the consolation of philosophy but by squeezing from it a near-tragic, near-comic lyricism. As a form, the blues is an autobiographical chronicle of personal catastrophe expressed lyrically."[3] Ellison's formulation was enlarged almost immediately into a literary trend by Earl Conrad, a writer for the *Chicago Defender*. "I have been looking into 'The Blues School of literature,'" Conrad tells his audience in an article published in December of 1945, speaking of Wright, Ellison, and Chester Himes. He goes on to say:

> Each of these writers is individually highly sensitized, nervous, jittery, ultra-critical, cynical. They have produced what I call "The Blues School of Literature." I take the term "blues" from an essay written recently by Ralph Ellison, called "Richard Wright's Blues." Ellison too thinks and works in this vein, and Himes in his first novel, *If He Hollers Let Him Go*, also portrays one of those frustrated characters, Robert Jones, a man who has been hard hit and is pretty devoid of hope.[4]

I cite Conrad's remarks not because I think his grouping of Ellison with Wright and Himes is particularly astute—Ellison's sensibility is surely more skewed toward the comic side of the blues dialectic—but because Conrad is the first of many to embrace Ellison's definition of blues expressiveness and apply it to specific literary texts. Who among us, in introducing our students to the troubled joys that animate blues-based African American literary works, has not at some point invoked Ellison's "near-tragic, near-comic lyricism"? What better way of glossing the pleasure/pain dialectic that motivates Janie Crawford's quest for a true marriage in *Their Eyes Were Watching God*, or the violent laughter that psychologically liberates Ellison's Invisible Man more than once during his odyssey? If we deepen our analysis and trace the source of tragicomic lyricism in *Their Eyes* to specific blues songs, such as Memphis Minnie's "Bumble Bee Blues" and Bessie Smith's "Empty Bed Blues," we are merely ratifying the wisdom of Ellison's own foun-

2. Langston Hughes, "Songs Called the Blues," *Phylon* 2, no. 2 (1941): 145.
3. Ralph Ellison, "Richard Wright's Blues," in *Shadow and Act* (1964; reprint, New York: New American Library, 1966), 90. Hereafter, this work is cited parenthetically as RWB.
4. Earl Conrad, "Blues School of Literature," *Chicago Defender*, 22 December 1945, 11.

dational gesture, the amalgamating of blues orature and blues literature into an expressive continuum.[5] "[L]ike a blues sung by such an artist as Bessie Smith," Ellison writes of *Black Boy* in 1945, "its lyrical prose evokes the paradoxical, almost surreal image of a black boy singing lustily as he probes his own grievous wound. . . . *Black Boy* represent[s] the flowering—cross-fertilized by pollen blown by the winds of strange cultures—of the humble blues lyric" (RWB, 91).

More than fifty-six years later, we are still struggling to articulate a unified field theory of blues expressiveness, one centered in the manifold, generative, and profound interconnections that obtain between the "humble blues lyric" invoked by Ellison and African American literature as a whole. A number of critics, including Stephen Henderson, Sherley Anne Williams, Albert Murray, Gayl Jones, Elizabeth Schultz, Paul Garon, Stephen Soitos, Ann duCille, and Houston A. Baker Jr., have theorized various aspects of blues expressiveness, but most have restricted themselves to one or at most two genres—poetry, fiction, autobiography, blues lyrics themselves—and none has successfully articulated a comprehensive theory grounded in the particulars of both post-Reconstruction history and an emerging culture of blues performance.[6] A fresh start is needed, and a fresh reading of Ellison's foundational definition can help us make it.

5. The best available survey of Hurston's use of blues themes is Maria V. Johnson, "'The World in a Jug and the Stopper in [Her] Hand': *Their Eyes* as Blues Performance," *African American Review* 32, no. 3 (fall 1998): 401–14. See also my study, *Seems Like Murder Here: Southern Violence and the Blues Tradition* (Chicago: University of Chicago Press, 2002), for a reading of *Their Eyes Were Watching God* that invokes both "Bumble Bee Blues" and "Empty Bed Blues."
6. See Stephen E. Henderson, "The Blues as Black Poetry," *Callaloo* 16, no. 3 (October 1982): 22–30; Sherley Anne Williams, "The Blues Roots of Contemporary Afro-American Poetry," in *Chant of Saints: A Gathering of Afro-American Literature, Art, and Scholarship*, ed. Michael Harper and Robert B. Stepto (Urbana: University of Illinois Press, 1979), 123–35; Albert Murray, *The Blue Devils of Nada: A Contemporary American Approach to Aesthetic Statement* (New York: Pantheon, 1996), esp. 143–83; Gayl Jones, *Liberating Voices: Oral Tradition in African American Literature* (Cambridge: Harvard University Press, 1991), 195–96; Elizabeth Schultz, "To Be Black and Blue: The Blues Genre in Black American Autobiography," *Kansas Quarterly* 7, no. 4 (summer 1975): 81–96; Paul Garon, *Blues and the Poetic Spirit*, rev. ed. (San Francisco: City Lights, 1996); Stephen Soitos, *The Blues Detective: A Study of African American Detective Fiction* (Amherst: University of Massachusetts Press, 1996); Ann duCille, "Blues Notes on Black Sexuality: Sex and Texts of the Twenties and Thirties," in *The Coupling Convention: Sex, Text, and Tradition in Black Women's Fiction* (New York: Oxford University Press, 1993); Houston A. Baker Jr., *Blues, Ideology, and Afro-American Literature: A Vernacular Theory* (Chicago: University of Chicago Press, 1984).

One of the first questions any such theoretical investigation might address is whether *Black Boy* deserves, in fact, to be called a work of blues literature, since it neglects—indeed, refuses—to represent the blues culture that was thriving in the Mississippi and Arkansas of Wright's youth, and contains nary a trace of the "humble blues lyric[s]" Ellison invokes. Just where *is* Wright's presumed blues expressiveness sourced, since it apparently doesn't result from contact with the blues musicians, including Charley Patton, Big Joe Williams, and Bessie Smith herself, who were ceaselessly traversing his native landscape? In the summer of 1921, when Wright was fourteen and living in Jackson, he made a brief and disillusioning tour of the Mississippi Delta as a "secretary-accountant" to W. Mance, an illiterate black insurance agent. "I saw a bare, bleak pool of black life and I hated it," he writes in *Black Boy*. "[T]he people were alike, their homes were alike, and their farms were alike."[7] Where young Wright saw a bleak pool of undifferentiated black life, devoid of the individuating and cathartic expressiveness enabled by blues culture, bluesman David "Honeyboy" Edwards (b. 1915) speaks in his autobiography of a Delta childhood animated and enriched by the blues—but also marked by the violence that was a key component of blues sociality:

> Mama . . . could play guitar and harp. She'd put a guitar across her lap with a pocket knife and play "Par-a-lee" on it. We was all kind of musical people. Didn't none of her family but her play music, but on my father's side was musicians. He played violin and guitar but he got rid of them after I got up to be a little size; he quit playing.
>
> Papa used to hold country dances on a Saturday night, sell whiskey and play guitar at the house. Sometimes he'd go off to play at jukes. He got in a fight one time at one of them Saturday night dances. My daddy got to fighting and hollering with a guy and they run out of the dance and into the field. My daddy had a plaid shirt on and this guy Jack shot at him with a Winchester rifle. The bullet just missed Papa, but it shot a hole through his shirt! Then he quit playing.[8]

Although Wright was not, according to biographer Hazel Rowley, "tempted by saloons, shooting craps, or houses of ill repute" after moving to Memphis with his mother in 1925, he did occasionally visit the Palace The-

7. Richard Wright, *Black Boy (American Hunger)* (1945; reprint, New York: HarperPerennial, 1993), 161. Hereafter, this work is cited parenthetically as *BB*.
8. David "Honeyboy" Edwards, *The World Don't Owe Me Nothing: The Life and Times of Delta Bluesman Honeyboy Edwards* (Chicago: Chicago Review Press, 1997), 4–5.

atre on Beale Street during his two-and-a-half-year residence and listen to the "dynamic" (if hardly legendary) Gertrude Saunders sing the blues.[9] Such meager experience marks Wright as a relative naïf on the matter of blues culture, at least when compared with blues-based writers such as Langston Hughes (who joyously immersed himself in the Harlem cabarets and Washington D.C.'s blues-rich Seventh Street neighborhood) and Zora Neale Hurston (a participant/observer who spent several months in the Polk County, Florida, jooks). As it happens, Ellison later backpedals on his early claims about Wright's literary bluesiness. "[F]or all of his having come from Mississippi," Ellison tells interviewer Robert O'Meally in 1976, "he didn't know a lot of the folklore. And although he tried to write a blues, he knew nothing about that or jazz."[10]

The "written" blues Ellison disparages here is almost surely not *Black Boy* but rather a blues song entitled "King Joe": thirteen stanzas Wright composed in 1941 at the suggestion of producer John Hammond in honor of boxer Joe Louis's recent triumphs. "King Joe," which was set to music by Count Basie and performed with something other than vernacular felicity by blues novice Paul Robeson ("[T]he man certainly can't sing the blues," Basie later mused), strained blues diction and prosody in a way that anticipates, unexpectedly, the syllabic propulsiveness of Jamaican dance hall–inflected rap: "Wonder what Joe Louis thinks when he's fighting a white man / Bet he thinks what I'm thinking, cause he wears a deadpan."[11] Although Wright would, in later years, return to the blues as a subject of occasional literary inspiration and reflection—in poems such as "Blue Snow Blues" and "The FB Eye Blues," liner notes for albums by Josh White and Big Bill Broonzy, a foreward to Paul Oliver's *Blues Fell This Morning: The Meaning of the Blues* (1960)—his aesthetic commitment to blues vernacular culture pales beside that of Hughes, Hurston, Sherley Anne Williams, August Wilson, Albert Murray, and Ellison himself.[12] Yet a crucial distinction needs to be

9. Hazel Rowley, *Richard Wright: The Life and Times* (New York: Henry Holt and Company, 2001), 43.

10. Ralph Ellison, "'My Strength Comes from Louis Armstrong': Interview with Robert G. O'Meally, 1976," in *Living with Music: Ralph Ellison's Jazz Writings*, ed. Robert G. O'Meally (New York: Modern Library, 2001), 283.

11. See Michel Fabre, *The Unfinished Quest of Richard Wright*, trans. Isabel Barzun, 2d ed. (Urbana and Chicago: University of Illinois Press, 1993), 237; and Rowley, *Richard Wright: The Life and Times*, 256–57.

12. For brief mentions of Wright's blues poetry and liner notes, see Fabre, *The Unfinished Quest of Richard Wright*, 516; Rowley, *Richard Wright: The Life and Times*, 227; and Craig Werner, "Bigger's Blues: *Native Son* and the Articulation of Afro-American Modernism,"

made here between blues *expression*—both lyric and literary—and blues *feeling*. Wright may not, as Ellison claimed, have known how to "write a blues" with anything like down-home veracity, and there is no record of him actually singing a blues, but it might certainly be argued that he *had* the blues as a Mississippi black boy, lived a life structured by blues feelings that he shared with his peers and elders—including the blues performers whom he chose later, as a writer, not to represent. The source of these blues feelings, as Ellison suggests, is a "brutal experience" composed of "painful details and episodes" that the blues subject, a subject engendered by this experience, chooses to keep "alive in [his or her] aching consciousness." What I want to do in the pages that follow is update and expand Ellison's theory of blues expressiveness, aligning Wright's "brutal experience" with the blues lyric and literary tradition in a way that begins to account, among other things, for the iconic, tropic power of guns, knives, and other blues weapons within that tradition. I use my articulations of Ellison's theory, in turn, as a way of glossing Ellison's master blues text, *Invisible Man*. Throughout this endeavor, I take as my cue Ellison's memorably concrete image: The blues, he claims, are an impulse not merely to dwell on one's brutal experience but to "finger its jagged grain"—as though brutal experience of the blues-producing variety had lodged within it a rough-hewn blade, or a shard of splintered bone.

My central, and Ellisonian, claim: Blues expressiveness is grounded in, and significantly shaped by, the encounter of working-class black folk with violence in the Jim Crow South, and with versions of that violence later encountered by, and propagated by, black folk who migrated north. There is more to the matter than this, of course: Blues expressiveness is also surely grounded in the spatial mobility made possible by an emergent post-Reconstruction southern railway system and in the sonic textures engendered by that system's horizon-bound trains (Houston Baker, Albert Murray); in the consolidation of a mass blues audience, with the emergence of a race records market and its attendant technologies of reproduction (Jeff Todd Titon, Daphne Duval Harrison); in the domain of the sexual, through which post-Emancipation freedom was explored by black male and female blues producers and consumers alike (Angela Davis).[13] Yet the southern vio-

---

in *New Essays on Native Son*, ed. Kenneth Kinnamon (New York: Cambridge University Press), 143.

13. See Baker, *Blues, Ideology, and Afro-American Literature*; Albert Murray, *Train Whistle Guitar* (1974; reprint, Boston: Northeastern University Press, 1988); Jeff Todd Titon, *Early Downhome Blues: A Musical and Cultural Analysis*, 2d ed. (Chapel Hill: University of North

lence of which I speak is, I would argue, a more comprehensive influence on black blues lives, blues feelings, and blues song than these other three domains, and in fact subtends all three. This violence consists of three distinct but interlocking violences, which might be termed *disciplinary* violence, *retributive* violence, and *intimate* violence.

Disciplinary violence is white-on-black violence that aims, in white southern parlance, to keep "the Negro in his place"; it consists primarily of lynching, police brutality, and related forms of white vigilantism. When Ellison speaks in "Richard Wright's Blues" about "an elaborate scheme of taboos supported by a ruthless physical violence" (RWB, 95), he is offering a succinct definition of disciplinary violence as it functioned in Mississippi between 1890 and 1965. Little Brother Montgomery's 1936 recording, "The First Time I Met You," exemplifies the blues response to disciplinary violence, with the singer's cry, "Now my blues got at me, lord, and run me from tree to tree / You should have heard me begging, Mr. Blues, don't murder me."[14] Robert Johnson's preternaturally restless "Hellhound on My Trail" ("I got to keep movin' / I've got to keep movin' / blues fallin' down like hail") is similarly haunted by the presence of white violence in the landscape it evokes, in the mobility it both enacts and laments.

Retributive violence, somewhat rarer in both southern history and blues song, is black-on-white violence that strikes back at disciplinary violence and other forms of racist oppression, often with a kind of "badman" swagger. "Stackolee," which features a sheriff who is leery of confronting that "bad son-of-a-gun they call Stackolee," is an example of a badman blues ballad that flirts with retributive violence.[15] Luzanna Cholly, the nattily attired bluesman in Albert Murray's *Train Whistle Guitar*, is an example of threatened retributive violence as an existential stance. "[T]he idea of going to jail didn't scare him at all," Murray tells us,

> and the idea of getting lynch-mobbed didn't faze him either. All I can
> remember him ever saying about that was: If they shoot at me they

---

Carolina Press, 1994); Daphne Duvall Harrison, *Black Pearls: Blues Queens of the 1920s* (New Brunswick, N.J.: Rutgers University Press, 1990); Angela Davis, *Blues Legacies and Black Feminism: Gertrude "Ma" Rainey, Bessie Smith, and Billie Holiday* (New York: Pantheon Books, 1998).

14. Little Brother Montgomery, "The First Time I Met You" (1936), in *The Blues Line: A Collection of Blues Lyrics from Leadbelly to Muddy Waters,* comp. Eric Sackheim (1969; reprint, Hopewell, N.J.: Ecco Press, 1993), 391.

15. "Stackolee," in Henry Louis Gates Jr. and Nellie Y. McKay, eds., *The Norton Anthology of African American Literature* (New York: W. W. Norton and Co., 1997), 50.

sure better not miss me they sure better get me that first time. White-
folks used to say he was a crazy nigger, but what they really meant or
should have meant was that he was confusing to them. . . .They certainly respected the fact that he wasn't going to take any foolishness
off of them.[16]

Mamie Smith's 1920 recording, "Crazy Blues," represents retributive violence as badwoman swagger in a concluding couplet that goes, "I'm gonna
do like a Chinaman, go and get some hop / Get myself a gun, and shoot
myself a cop."[17]

Intimate violence, the third kind of blues violence, is black-on-black
violence driven by jealousy, hatred, and other strong passions, particularly
the so-called cutting and shooting (often in juke-joint settings) that cut a
remarkably wide swath through blues song and blues literature. Ma Rainey's
"See See Rider," which reaches its climax with a verse in which the singer
swears she's going to kill her abandoning lover with "a pistol just as long
as I am tall," exemplifies this sort of intraracial vengeance. Intimate violence is a particularly useful thematic and tropic axis around which to align
blues orature and blues literature; what might be called the "blues knife," for
example, surfaces not just in blues songs such as "Got Cut All to Pieces,"
"Good Chib Blues," and "Two-by-Four Blues," but also in blues novels such
as Walter Mosley's RL's Dream, Murray's Train Whistle Guitar, Gayl Jones's
Eva's Man, and Toni Morrison's Jazz; in blues poems such as Hughes's "In
a Troubled Key" and "Suicide"; in blues plays such as August Wilson's Ma
Rainey's Black Bottom and Seven Guitars; and in blues autobiographies by
"Honeyboy" Edwards, Henry Townsend, and others.

Wright may not have known how to "write a blues," as Ellison later
insists, but he did know how to evoke these three Jim Crow violences, disciplinary, retributive, and intimate, which together constitute much of the
"brutal experience" he suffered and survived, and which likewise reveal his
underlying affinity with the blues textual tradition I've just sketched out. In
this respect, Ellison's original characterization of Black Boy as a kind of literary "flowering . . . of the humble blues lyric" is apt. Not only were Wright (b.
1908) and Little Brother Montgomery (b. 1910) contemporaries who came of
age in the Delta, for example, but Montgomery's signifying protest against
lynching in "The First Time I Met You"—including the line "Mr. Blues, don't

16. Murray, Train Whistle Guitar, 13.
17. For an extended discussion, see Adam Gussow, "'Shoot Myself a Cop': Mamie Smith's
'Crazy Blues' as Social Text," Callaloo 25, no. 1 (winter 2002): 8–44.

murder me"—is uncannily echoed in *Black Boy*'s evocation of the terror produced by the phantasmic lynch mob. "I had already grown to feel that there existed men against whom I was powerless," Wright insists of his Deep South boyhood, "men who could violate my life at will. . . . I had already become as conditioned to their existence as though I had been the victim of a thousand lynchings" (*BB*, 87). Here is one audible blues note in Wright, a note born out of the black southern subject's confrontation with ineludable disciplinary violence. Another blues note can be heard when Wright reports a story he's been told about one woman's retributive response to such violence, a response that parallels Mamie Smith's fantasy of copicide. "One evening," Wright tells us,

> I heard a tale that rendered me sleepless for nights. It was of a Negro woman whose husband had been seized and killed by a mob. It was claimed that the woman vowed she would avenge her husband's death and she took a shotgun, wrapped it in a sheet, and went humbly to the whites, pleading that she be allowed to take her husband's body for burial. It seemed that she was granted permission to come to the side of her dead husband while the whites, silent and armed, looked on. The woman, so went the story, knelt and prayed, then proceeded to unwrap the sheet; and, before the white men realized what was happening, she had taken the gun from the sheet and had slain four of them, shooting at them from her knees. (*BB*, 86)

The tale of black retributive violence Wright relates here resonates strongly not just with "Crazy Blues" but with blues singer Josie Miles's 1924 recording, "Mad Mama's Blues," which threatens shotgun-wreaked vengeance against a blues-inducing world:

> Wanna set the world on fire, that is my one mad desire
> I'm a devil in disguise, got murder in my eyes
>
> Now I could see blood runnin' through the streets
> Now I could see blood runnin' through the streets
> Could be everybody layin' dead right at my feet
>
> . . . . . . . . . . . . . . . . . . . .
>
> I took my big Winchester, down off the shelf
> I took my big Winchester, down off the shelf
> When I get through shootin', there won't be nobody left.[18]

18. Josie Miles, "Mad Mama's Blues" (1924), Document Records CD DOCD5467.

In his review of *Black Boy*, Ellison evokes this sort of blues-toned retributive violence when he speaks of the "three general ways" in which black folk
confronted their destiny "in the South of Wright's childhood," the third way
being to "adopt a criminal attitude, and carry on an unceasing psychological
scrimmage with the whites, which often flared forth into physical violence"
(RWB, 94).

What interests Ellison far more than black "badman" (or badwoman)
vengeance against whites, however, is the linkage he glimpses in Wright's
Mississippi boyhood between white disciplinary violence (in particular,
lynching) and black intimate violence, an intimate violence that took the form
not of cutting and shooting but of beatings Wright suffered at the hands of
his mother and grandmother. "Wright saw his destiny," Ellison writes, ". . . in
terms of a quick and casual violence inflicted upon him by both family and
community" (RWB, 94). This family violence, the violence of black southern parents against their children, is viewed by Ellison as a problematic but
understandable attempt to suppress a rebellious individuality that, were it
expressed by these children, would be met with white reprisal against the
entire black community. Later, he elaborates: "One of the Southern Negro
family's methods of protecting the child is the severe beating—a homeo-
pathic dose of the violence generated by black and white relationships. . . .
Even parental love is given a qualitative balance akin to 'sadism'" (RWB,
101). We may certainly dispute Ellison's bleak, totalizing reading of black
family life under Jim Crow and Wright's similarly bleak vision; what cannot
be disputed is the degree to which Wright's vision of intimate violence as
the inflicting of passion-driven beatings on the people one is close to is a
*blues* vision, one that links him with both blues song and the blues literary
tradition.

In blues song, this sort of intimate violence issues more frequently
against a lover than a child—as when Robert Johnson, in "Me and the Devil
Blues," sings, "I'm goin' to beat my woman / until I get satisfied," or when
Muddy Waters, in "Oh Yeah," cries, "Oh yeaaah, someday I'm goin' to catch
you soon / cut you in the morning, whup you in the afternoon." The beatings that slowly infect the relationship between Janie and her third husband,
Tea Cake, in *Their Eyes Were Watching God*, are a literary rendering of
such intimate blues violence. Some might claim that what I am calling "intimate violence" in Wright's case—black southern elders whipping a child to
keep him in line—is actually a kind of second-order disciplinary violence,
the black internalization and reinscription of a white disciplinary violence

that those elders hope prophylactically to ward off. In *Black Boy*, however, boundaries between the two sorts of violences, disciplinary and intimate, begin to break down; the black disciplining gesture is resisted and thereby forced into the open, revealed to be no more than a form of passion-driven aggression essentially equivalent to a knife slashing. The starkest example of this is the moment where young Richard watches his Uncle Tom tear "a long, young, green switch from the elm tree" (*BB*, 186) and determines not to be beaten by the older man. Richard goes to his dresser drawer, gets out a pack of razor blades, and arms himself with "a thin blade of blue steel in each hand" (*BB*, 186–87). This gesture aligns him with the blues tradition of passion-driven, blade-borne intimate violence—with Bessie Tucker's "Got Cut All to Pieces" and Bea Ella Thornhill's disembowelment of Beau Beau Weaver in *Train Whistle Guitar*. "I've got a razor in each hand!" young Richard warns his uncle in "a low, charged voice." "If you touch me, I'll cut you! Maybe I'll get cut too, but I'll cut you, so help me God!" (*BB*, 187). If intimate violence is the mode through which southern blues people express their fiercest blues feelings, then young Richard's gesture of revolt transforms the scene of incipient parent-child discipline into a kind of incipient juke-joint brawl—albeit a brawl bereft of both the blues music and blues sociality that give intimate violence its cultural heft.

This lack is significant. Fully articulate blues violence is part of an expressive continuum that includes both the lyric transformations of that violence into blues song and the cathartic release occasioned by the collective urgings of the juke-joint ritual. We might contrast young Wright's rebellion against Uncle Tom with a similar rebellion described by St. Louis bluesman Henry Townsend in his recently published autobiography, *A Blues Life*. Townsend, who was born in Shelby, Mississippi, in 1909, the year after Wright was born in Natchez, is reborn as a rambling bluesman the day he learns, as a nine year old, that his father is going to beat him for blowing snuff in his cousin's eyes. "[M]y daddy was gonna get me for that," he claims,

> and that's when I first left home. You don't know how bad it hurts my feelings for me to think that somebody is gonna physically interfere with me, like hitting on me. You don't know how bad it hurts me. My heart jumps and tears in two like busting a string. I can't stand that. I don't dish it out and I can't stand it. I've been whipped but it wasn't a pleasant thing for the man that whipped me—or me—I'll tell you that.
> . . . I didn't give [my daddy] no chance [to whip me]. I caught the

train. I didn't know where I was going—I didn't care. I knew I wasn't gonna stay there and get a whooping.[19]

Wright is the Mississippi black boy who silently suffers the blues of disciplinary and intimate violence, finally rebelling when pressed to the breaking point but escaping only later to exorcise his blues as a literary autobiographical chronicle up north. He has, in Trudier Harris's memorable phrase, "no outlet for the blues," or at least no musical outlet for them.[20] Townsend, by contrast, is the Mississippi black boy who refuses to stay put and allow those particular blues to be inflicted on him; his boyhood escape to East St. Louis is a creative liberation, the first step into an eventual self-ownership defined by a mastery of blues song's expressive vocabulary. Townsend, significantly, is a blues lyricist as well as performer; when I visited with him backstage at B. B. King's Blues Club in New York in the summer of 2001, he mentioned pridefully that he was the composer of the blues standard "Every Day I Have the Blues." It's tempting to imagine the future author of lines such as "Nobody loves me, nobody seems to care / Worries and troubles, you know I've had my share" as a bitterly rebellious but also euphoric nine-year-old runaway riding the rails north, away from his father's blows. It's also tempting to see these lines as the crystallization of young Richard Wright's plight: "Every Day I Have the Blues" is the "humble blues lyric" from which *Black Boy* seems to have sprung, even if Wright himself was incapable of singing that song in so many words.

If one fingers the "jagged grain" of blues expressiveness by paying attention to the way in which a linked set of southern-born violences circulates within blues orature and literature and unites them as an expressive field, it becomes clear that *Black Boy* stands both at the margins of the blues textual tradition and at the very center. The fact that it scrupulously erases all traces of a thriving Mississippi blues culture from the landscape it describes, with the ideological intent of depicting the unrelieved bleakness of black southern life, makes it marginal. Where, amid such desolation, are the belted-out blues songs described by James Cone as "an expression of fortitude in the face of a broken existence"?[21] Where is the tempo-

19. Henry Townsend, as told to Bill Greensmith, *A Blues Life* (Urbana and Chicago: University of Illinois Press, 1999), 6–7.
20. See Trudier Harris, "No Outlet for the Blues: Silla Boyce's Plight in *Brown Girl, Brownstones*," *Callaloo* 18, no. 2 (spring–summer 1983): 58.
21. James H. Cone, "The Blues: A Secular Spiritual," in *Write Me a Few of Your Lines: A Blues Reader*, ed. Steven C. Tracy (Amherst: University of Massachusetts Press, 1999), 236.

rary but vital liberation claimed by black Mississippians—including "Honey-boy" Edwards's father—every Saturday night in the jooks? Yet to the extent that Wright's own *life* is an expression of fortitude in the face of a broken existence defined in large measure by its subjection to and participation in disciplinary, retributive, and intimate violence, including young Richard's desperate, razor-waving rebellion against the beating threatened by Uncle Tom, *Black Boy* is an exemplary blues text, one animated by the deepest and most representative of southern blues feelings. That it can plausibly be claimed to be both marginal and exemplary helps explain Ellison's second thoughts about Wright's status as a blues writer and our own uncertainties about how to categorize his ambivalent attitude toward African American vernacular music.[22]

### Ellison's Violent Blues Humors

The wounded black bodies produced by disciplinary violence mani-fest at several points in *Black Boy*—most notably, the bodies of Uncle Hoskins and an acquaintance of Wright's named Bob, both of whose lynchings-by-shooting are related to Wright by others—but these bodies are represented in a sketchy, fleeting way. The traumatic effect they have on young Wright, as markers of malefic white power, is out of proportion with the distinctly unspectacular representations themselves. At one of the few moments in *Black Boy* where retributive violence is imaged—the story about the black woman who wraps a shotgun in a sheet to avenge the death of her mob-murdered husband—Wright is similarly circumspect; this story com-pels his attention by the sheer fact of the woman's audacity rather than the morbid details of the revenge-murders she commits. (Bigger Thomas's mur-der and dismembering of Mary Dalton in *Native Son*, with its splattering of blood and crunching of bone, comes, by contrast, to seem like compensa-tory exaggeration, a providing of the gruesome details that the "whispered tales" of Wright's youth forced young black men to imagine rather than wit-ness.) The most graphic spectacle of abjection imaged by Wright in *Black Boy*, in fact, are the beatings he suffers at the hands of his family, exemplary instances of intimate violence:

> "You almost scared us to death," my mother muttered as she stripped the leaves from a tree limb to prepare it for my back.
>
> I was lashed so hard and long that I lost consciousness. I was

22. See Werner, "Bigger's Blues," 146.

> beaten out of my senses and later found myself in bed, screaming,
> determined to run away, tussling with my mother and father who were
> trying to keep me still. I was lost in a fog of fear. A doctor was called—
> I was afterwards told—and he ordered that I be kept abed, that I be
> kept quiet, that my very life depended on it. My body seemed on fire
> and I could not sleep. Packs of ice were put on my forehead to keep
> down the fever. (*BB*, 7)

If intimate violence produces graphic images of a wounded blues body in *Black Boy*, where disciplinary and retributive violence only sketchily represent the body's violation, then all three violences conspire, in Wright's imagination, to evoke a portrait of southern black blues life as a desperate and humorless struggle against an abjection that registers on young Richard's flesh as a series of traumatic shocks.

   Ellison's representations of the blues-engendering and blues-expressing violences and the wounded black bodies they produce function somewhat differently in this regard—a result, in large measure, of his insistence on redeeming desperation with humor rather than seconding it with condemnation. He steers clear of the deepest blues engendered by white-on-black violence, refusing to hold those experiences quite so mercilessly in "aching consciousness" as Wright holds them. This divergence arises, it might be argued, from the fact that social relations between blacks and whites were considerably more benign in Oklahoma during Ellison's boyhood than they were in Mississippi during Wright's, granting Ellison a more detached perspective on the Deep South's egregious folkways.[23] Ellison knows, for example, that lynching is a source of agony for black folk, as his short story "A Party Down at the Square" amply evidences; but his decision to make the narrator of that story a white boy who admires the lynchers, rather than a black witness who shudders at them, reveals an inclination—perhaps more instinctive than conscious at that early moment in his career—to evade helpless abjection in favor of very dark satire.[24] The same satirical impulse is at work in *Invisible Man*, where Ellison places in the mouth of Dr. Bledsoe, the Booker T. Washington stand-in, a statement of infernal purpose that echoes a pronouncement made by white Mississippi demagogue James Vardaman. "I'll have every Negro in the country hanging on tree limbs by morning," thunders Bledsoe, "if it means staying where

23. Ralph Ellison, "Remembering Richard Wright," in *Going to the Territory* (1986; reprint, New York: Vintage Books, 1987), 198–99.
24. Ralph Ellison, "A Party Down at the Square," in *Flying Home and Other Stories* (New York: Vintage Books, 1996), 3–11.

I am."[25] One can hardly imagine Wright changing the joke and slipping the yoke in this manner. In an essay entitled "An Extravagance of Laughter," Ellison evokes a related form of disciplinary violence, southern policing, in a way that rejects Wright's bitter pronouncements about "days lived under the threat of violence" for a considerably more benign stoicism. "I gave Jeeter Lester types a wide berth," Ellison acknowledges of his college days in Alabama, "but found it impossible to avoid them entirely—because many were law-enforcement officers who served on the highway patrols with a violent zeal like that which Negro slave narratives ascribed to the 'paterollers' who had guarded the roads during slavery. . . . (Southern buses were haunted, and so, in a sense, were Southern roads and highways). . . . [E]ven the roads that led *away* from the South were also haunted; a circumstance which I should have learned, but did not, from numerous lyrics that were sung to the blues."[26]

Ellison knows that the "white death" invoked by Wright haunts the southern roads traveled by black folk, a haunting hinted by bluesmen such as Robert Johnson in "Hellhound on My Trail" and "Crossroads Blues," but he isn't rendered psychologically brittle by this violence. The spectacle of abjection represented by the lynched black body doesn't function in Ellison's imagination as a destabilizing phantasm, the way it does in Wright's "Big Boy Leaves Home" and his extraordinary lynching poem "Between the World and Me." Yet it certainly functions for Ellison as literary capital, as an existential challenge to be given aesthetic form and ethical weight. The tropes of spectacle lynching, for example, surface in the celebrated battle royal scene of *Invisible Man*, where the narrator is kicked by Mr. Colcord onto the electrified carpet. "It was," he tells us, "as though I had rolled through a bed of hot coals. It seemed a whole century would pass before I would roll free, a century in which I was seared through the deepest levels of my body to the fearful breath within me and the breath seared and heated to the point of explosion" (*IM*, 28). When lynching victims were burned—as the black victim in "A Party Down at the Square" is burned—the ritual was often referred to by whites as a "Negro barbecue." Ellison is drawing on that ritual here— not, as Wright does, to image black abjection as a form of protest but instead to dramatize the capacity of the wily black blues subject to *resist* tragedy with the help of improvisational dexterity and a salvific sense of absurdity. What Ellison's Invisible Man is always seeking, often without knowing it, is

25. Ralph Ellison, *Invisible Man* (1952; reprint, New York: Vintage Books, 1972), 141. Hereafter, this work is cited parenthetically as *IM*.
26. Ralph Ellison, "An Extravagance of Laughter," in *Going to the Territory*, 167, 180.

the half-comic insight that wrings blues transcendence out of misery and frustration.

Retributive violence, black-on-white violence with political rather than criminal intent, rears its head on the second page of *Invisible Man*, and the instrument of retribution is an exemplary blues knife, a knife deployed against oppressive whiteness with gutbucket panache and a raging sense of grievance. "Oh yes, I kicked him!" exclaims the narrator, speaking of a "tall blond man" who has called him "an insulting name" and repeatedly cursed him after the two men have accidentally bumped into each other one night on the street and begun to struggle:

> And in my outrage I got out my knife and prepared to slit his throat, right there beneath the lamplight in the deserted street, holding him in the collar with one hand, and opening the knife with my teeth— when it occurred to me that the man had not *seen* me, actually; that he, as far as he knew, was in the midst of a walking nightmare! And I stopped the blade, slicing the air as I pushed him away, letting him fall back to the street. I stared at him hard as the lights of a car stabbed through the darkness. He lay there, moaning on the asphalt; a man almost killed by a phantom. It unnerved me. I was both disgusted and ashamed. I was like a drunken man myself, wavering about on weak-ened legs. Then I was amused: Something in this man's thick head had sprung out and beaten him within an inch of his life. I began to laugh at this crazy discovery. Would he have awakened at the point of death? Would Death himself have freed him for wakeful living? But I didn't linger. I ran away into the dark, laughing so hard I feared I might rupture myself. (*IM*, 4–5)

Knives that show up in blues literary texts almost always do damage, from the razor with which "the little woman" in a Mississippi juke-joint slits her abusive husband's throat in "Honeyboy" Edwards's autobiography, to the knife that Levee plunges into Toledo's back at the end of *Ma Rainey's Black Bottom*, to the knife that leads Bea Ella Thornhill to get rechristened "Red Ella" after she eviscerates Beau Beau Weaver in *Train Whistle Guitar*. These blues blades are instruments of a raging passion that rarely subsides with-out bloodshed. The Invisible Man's knife is an exception. The hysterical laughter that wells up in him at the absurdity of his situation and causes him to run away without using his knife—a violence-defusing laughter—is, in fact, deliberate surrealism, a calculated divergence from the harsh truth of blues culture. Ellison has taken what might be called the "hardening" laughter that colors blues lyricism and deployed it with a pacifist, or at least meliorist, intent. The correct application of laughter to blues passions, he seems to say, can defuse those passions, dissipate—as explosive hilarity—the violence with which they demand to be expressed. This is a creative and extremely fertile misreading of the tragicomic moment within blues lyricism.

Blues people may have told violent stories and sung violent songs that were annealed with humor, but that humor was in large measure a way of dealing with the fact that blues culture was—or could be—a fearsomely violent thing, rippling with passions and grievances that mere laughter could *not* defuse. "They tell me she shot one old man's arms off, down in Mississippi," bluesman Johnny Shines recalls of blues singer Memphis Minnie, chuckling at the memory. "Shot his arm off, or cut it off with a hatchet, something. Some say shot, some say cut. Minnie was a hell-raiser, I know that!"[27] This sort of blues laughter was a way of maintaining psychological equilibrium in the face of a Jim Crowed social environment rendered deadly by the double-barreled threat of white disciplinary violence and black intimate violence. Ellison transforms this blues laughter, in his book's opening scene, into something different: a psychological tool for defusing one's *own* violence. There is little evidence to suggest that this is the way in which blues people in the Deep South actually dealt with the rage, terror, and sadness that white disciplinary violence engendered in them. They may have sometimes grinned in the white man's face, as Levee's father grins in the face of the white men who have raped his wife, but these grins dissolved neither their aggrieved blues feelings nor their fantasies of violent retribution. There is a great deal of evidence to suggest, in fact, that blues people expressed their blues feelings either by murdering the white men who had wronged them, as Levee's father does, or, far more likely, by redirecting those feelings at an acceptable target—which is to say, by using guns and knives against each other on juke-joint Saturday nights or in Chicago recording studios.

I have taken pains to stress Ellison's creative divergence from the harsh realities of blues violence in this opening scene of *Invisible Man* as a way of clarifying what he tries to do in his novel's justly celebrated blues performance, the so-called Trueblood episode. What intrigues me is what Ellison chooses to elide from Jim Trueblood's world: both the disciplinary violence that Ellison himself acknowledges was something that "haunted" the South in the form of "Jeeter Lester types," and the feelings of bitterness

27. Paul and Beth Garon, *Woman with Guitar: Memphis Minnie's Blues* (New York: Da Capo Books, 1992), 69–70.

that Trueblood might be expected to harbor, bluesman that he is, after his wife Kate has furiously attacked and grievously wounded him. My first claim about disciplinary violence isn't entirely true; in fact, white violence rears its head once, at the very beginning of Trueblood's tale, when the share-cropper tells the narrator and Mr. Norton how the "biggity school folks up on the hill," which is to say higher-class black folk, have tried to shut him up. "[T]hey sent a fellow out here, a big fellow too, and he said if I didn't leave they was going to turn the white folks loose on me. It made me mad and it made me scared" (*IM*, 52). But Trueblood's fear of white reprisal rapidly evaporates in the face of region-wide and financially remunerative white fas-cination with his tale of dream-provoked incest. The rest of Trueblood's nar-ration has been scrubbed clean of the sort of "haunting" redneck threat that Ellison images in both "A Party Down at the Square" and "Flying Home." Ellison's satiric purpose—the revenge of the earthy black-blues Id on the uplift-oriented black middle-class Superego—leads him to shade the truth here. He makes the white folks Trueblood's "friends" and the "biggity" black school folks Trueblood's ineffectual antagonists.

The same charge of creative divergence from harsh blues truth may be leveled at Ellison's depiction of Trueblood as a passive sufferer of his wife's aggrieved barrage of household items. Bluesmen do not generally let blows directed at their persons go unanswered. The life stories of bluesmen such as Skip James, Henry Townsend, and Leadbelly offer a great many vengeful—or simply vigorous—reprisals against violent male and female intimates, but few examples of blows withheld in the face of violent provoca-tions. The closest real-life parallel to Trueblood's willful passivity is offered by "Honeyboy" Edwards, in the form of a confession about his wife, Bessie. In his autobiography, he admits,

> Most of the time when we did fight, I would be the cause of it. Because I would come in drunk, jump on her sometimes. Which I had no busi-ness doing.
>
> She'd cut on me! I'd be wanting to fight and she'd cut me up! She'd be right on me with that pocketknife. I got cuts all over me. Bessie was tough; she was bad with a razor blade.[28]

Ellison gets the bluesman's wife exactly right, in other words: Kate's will-ingness to use anything and everything as a rage-communicating weapon against her no-good husband—including, in turn "[l]ittle things and big

28. Edwards, *The World Don't Owe Me Nothing*, 199.

things," "[s]omethin' cold and strong-stinkin'," something that sounds "like a cannonball," a double-barrel shotgun, some unnamed thing that digs into Trueblood's side "like a sharp spade," an iron, and finally an ax—places her squarely in the blues tradition of intimate violence as *expressive* violence (*IM*, 61–63). Surely this is the most remarkable inventory of improvised blues weapons the blues tradition has to offer! Too, Ellison quite properly fore-grounds the wounded blues body—Trueblood's body, in this case: the "scar on his right cheek" (*IM*, 50), the "wound" around which "flies and fine white gnats" (*IM*, 53) swarm—in a way that connects him with blues subjects as various as August Wilson's Levee, Henry Townsend, and the unnamed nar-rator of Wanda Coleman's "Identifying Marks," a poem about the scars that failed romance and domestic violence leave on a black woman's body and soul. Ellison's portrait of Trueblood also offers an accurate representation of the bluesman's ethos exemplified here by Edwards's surprisingly candid self-judgment: the continuing struggle to "do right" even when one finds one-self doing wrong.

What Ellison's blues portrait finesses, however, is precisely the blues-man's own violent tendencies. Not all bluesmen are as willing to cut and be cut as "Honeyboy"; B. B. King's whole career is built on his explicit public renunciation of violence, symbolized by his frequent and loving references to his female-gendered guitar, Lucille. But there is little precedent in either blues song or blues literature for Trueblood's astonishing willingness to be crucified by his wife.

Or is there a precedent? One is reminded, boomerang-like, of the impossibility of making any firm pronouncement about so dialectical an art as blues song. Surely Trueblood's willingness to suffer his enraged wife's blows is anticipated by the humble blues lyric that goes, "It's my own fault baby / treat me the way you wanna do."

The problem with making clear and comprehensive pronouncements about blues, as Ellison knew, is that blues are grounded in paradox—above all, the paradox that was African American life under Jim Crow. How can one be both free and encircled? That was the situation of southern blues people: free in name, significantly freer than one had been as a slave, but also thoroughly hemmed in by white disciplinary violence, part of the "bru-tal experience" Ellison invokes in his celebrated definition. How can music possibly do justice to this paradox? It can chronicle personal catastrophe, squeeze from that chronicle a near-tragic, near-comic lyricism, and hope for the best. That particular definition of the blues is Ellison's; it remains indel-ible, and provocative, after all these years.

# Ralph Ellison and the Problem of Cultural Authority

*Kenneth W. Warren*

In her controversial essay "Reflections on Little Rock," originally written for *Commentary* magazine but published in the 1959 volume of *Dissent*, Hannah Arendt questioned the wisdom of the NAACP for placing children on the front lines during the 1957 school integration crisis in Little Rock, Arkansas. Insisting on her *"sympathy for the cause of the Negroes as for all oppressed or under-privileged peoples,"* Arendt nonetheless faulted the desegregation effort for having contributed to recent social trends "abolishing the authority of adults." Civil rights leaders were denying both "their responsibility for the world into which they have borne their children" and their "duty of guiding them into it."[1] Arendt's critique of the NAACP's tactics and strategy derived from her general fear, reiterated throughout her writings during the 1950s, that a failure to distinguish properly between the political and social realms of human behavior gravely threatened political freedom.[2] The chief error of what she termed "forced integration" was that

1. Hannah Arendt, "Reflections on Little Rock," *Dissent* 6, no. 1 (winter 1959): 46.
2. Elisabeth Young-Bruehl's *Hannah Arendt: For Love of the World* (New Haven, Conn.: Yale University Press, 1982), 318–22, is especially good in tying Arendt's interventions into

*boundary 2* 30:2, 2003. Copyright © 2003 by Duke University Press.

it confused the political realm with the social realm and thus failed to recognize that what "equality is to the body politic—its innermost principle—discrimination is to society" (*FLW*, 51). The point she drew in her reflections was that forcing "parents to send their children to an integrated school against their will means to deprive them of the rights which clearly belong to them in all free societies—the private right over their children and the social right to free association" (*FLW*, 55).

Predictably, Arendt's comments did not strike a positive note among liberal readers. Not only had *Commentary* found the article problematic when Arendt originally submitted it (and consequently attached conditions for publication that led Arendt to withdraw it [*FLW*, 313–15]), but *Dissent*, in agreeing to publish it, had insisted on preceding "Reflections" with a disclaimer ("We publish it not because we agree with it—quite the contrary!") and on following it with two essays, by David Spitz and Melvin Tumin, respectively, attacking Arendt's arguments.[3] In deference to Arendt, *Dissent* also agreed to give her space in a subsequent issue to reply to her critics, and in her response, Arendt elaborated her argument in the following way:

> The point of departure of my reflections was a picture in the newspapers, showing a Negro girl on her way home from a newly integrated school; she was persecuted by a mob of white children, protected by a white friend of her father, and her face bore eloquent witness to the obvious fact that she was not precisely happy. The picture showed the situation in a nutshell because those who appeared in it were directly affected by the Federal Court order, the children themselves. My first question was: what would I do if I were a Negro mother? The answer: under no circumstances would I expose my child to conditions which made it appear as though it wanted to push its way into a group where it was not wanted.[4]

Arendt focused on the news photograph of a young black girl being taunted by white teenagers and adults in an attempt to make vivid the charge she had leveled in her original essay: The desegregation crisis in Little Rock represented the triumph of mob rule—the "sorry fact" that "the town's law-abiding citizens left the streets to the mob, that neither white nor black

---

social crises of the 1950s to Arendt's *The Human Condition*, published in 1957. Hereafter, *For Love of the World* is cited parenthetically as *FLW*.

3. Editors, Untitled Note, *Dissent* 6, no. 1 (winter 1959): 45.

4. Hannah Arendt, "A Reply to Critics," *Dissent* 6, no. 2 (spring 1959): 179.

citizens felt it their duty to see the Negro children safely to school."[5] Her elaboration amounted to a reiteration of her main charge that school desegregation, as pursued in Little Rock, had devolved into the evacuation of all legitimate authority, particularly parental authority, from the scene of the crisis.

Arendt's critics were not confined to the pages of *Dissent*, and of these critics perhaps the most significant was Ralph Ellison, who took advantage of several occasions to mention what he felt was Arendt's severe misreading of the Little Rock events. In "The World and the Jug," Ellison—no doubt relishing the irony of his gambit—disparaged Irving Howe's "Black Boys and Native Sons" by observing that Howe, who, as editor of *Dissent*, had distanced himself from Arendt's position on Little Rock, had now "written with something of the Olympian authority that characterized Hannah Arendt's 'Reflections on Little Rock.'"[6] This Olympian distance, which derived from Arendt's (and Howe's) lack of cultural knowledge of the Negro's situation in the South, had been fatal to the accuracy of their analyses. Both writers, Ellison contended, had missed the full human dimension of the situations they were observing.

Ellison subsequently built his case against Arendt in Robert Penn Warren's *Who Speaks for the Negro* when he remarked that Arendt's criticisms of black mothers had overlooked the way in which the black parents in Little Rock were instilling in their children an "ideal of sacrifice" necessary to move the nation forward on its quest for true democracy. In alleging that Negro parents were "exploiting their children during the struggle to integrate the school," Arendt had demonstrated her "failure to grasp the importance of this ideal among Southern Negroes caus[ing] her to fly way off into left field." Arendt clearly had "absolutely no conception of what goes on in the minds of Negro parents when they send their kids through those lines of hostile people." What she had missed was that the parents had placed their children in harm's way at Central High because they were "aware of the overtones of a rite of initiation which such events actually constitute for the child, a confrontation of the terrors of social life with all the mysteries stripped away. And in the outlook of many of these parents (who wish that the problem didn't exist), the child is expected to face the terror and contain his fear and anger precisely because he is a Negro American."[7] Reiterating

5. Arendt, "Reflections," 49.
6. Ralph Ellison, "The World and the Jug," in *The Collected Essays of Ralph Ellison*, ed. John F. Callahan (New York: Modern Library, 1995), 156.
7. Interview with Ralph Ellison, in Robert Penn Warren, *Who Speaks for the Negro?* (New York: Random House, 1965), 343–44.

a favorite theme that being a Negro in America required a stern discipline, Ellison found in Little Rock further evidence of the Negro's capacity to forge and express a sense of humanity not circumscribed by the narrow limits of the Jim Crow South. His point was not lost on Arendt, who, shortly after *Who Speaks for the Negro* was published, wrote to Ellison, saying, "It is precisely this ideal of sacrifice which I didn't understand."[8]

Arendt's concession, however, was only partial. As Elisabeth Young-Bruehl points out, although Ellison was the only one of her critics to whom Arendt "gave ground," she "remained convinced that education should not be the sole or even the most important source of social or political change" (*FLW*, 317). By contrast, Ellison was more the social interventionist in matters of education, arguing that among the failures of American education was that "many American children have not been trained to reject enough of the negative values which our society presses upon then."[9] Nonetheless, Arendt and Ellison were in accord on some crucial points in their readings of the Little Rock crisis and in their thoughts on society in general. In regard to the former, both presumed that the only legitimate agency to be reckoned with on the scene at Central High School was parental agency. Reading the children's unhappiness through their facial expressions, Arendt believed that the Little Rock Nine were on the frontlines solely at the behest of, or through abdication of, the authority of their parents. Arendt's reading took for granted that parents had the final say in determining whether or not their children participated in the battle to integrate the nation's schools. Likewise, Ellison's rebuttal of Arendt's "Reflections" focused on "the minds of Negro parents." Thus, although they drew diametrically opposed conclusions as to whether or not it had been exercised, both agreed that parental authority was the focal point of the event.

Yet the children who participated in Civil Rights struggles in Little Rock and elsewhere often did so either without the approval of, or over the objection of, their parents. For example, the 1951 student strike at Moton High School in Farmville, Virginia, was spearheaded by sixteen-year-old Barbara Johns, niece of Vernon Johns, who preceded Martin Luther King Jr. as pastor of the Dexter Avenue Baptist Church in Montgomery, Alabama. Barbara Johns had become outraged by the failure of local authorities to "fulfill commitments to improve the conditions of the high school set aside for black students," where students were forced "to sit in the shacks with coats

8. Arendt to Ralph Ellison, 29 July 1965, Library of Congress, cited in *FLW*, 316.
9. Ralph Ellison, "What These Children Are Like," in *Collected Essays*, 549.

on through the winter."[10] Fed up with the situation and acting without the approval of her parents, Johns organized a student strike and, in conjunction with other students, "sent out appeals to NAACP lawyers, who, completely misreading the source of the initiative, agreed to come to Farmville for a meeting, provided it was not with 'the children.'" Although the resulting suit was one of those that contributed to the NAACP's attack on school desegregation in the 1954 *Brown v. Board of Education of Topeka* case, the organization's tactics were clearly not centered on making heroes and martyrs of children, who had thrust themselves into the middle of a social and political movement.[11]

More directly related to the Little Rock crisis are the reminiscences of Melba Patillo Beals, one of the Little Rock Nine. In recounting how she came to be one of the students who defied segregation, Beals recalled somewhat painfully having made the decision on her own. She was among those who raised her hand "[w]hen my teacher asked if anyone who lived within the Central High School District wanted to attend school with white people." And having raised her hand in response to the teacher's question, Beals had set in motion a process in which her parents were placed in the position of reacting to, rather than directing, their daughter's actions. To be sure, Beals did not always feel comfortable having made such a momentous decision without consulting her parents. In the long period before divulging her decision to them she recalled agonizing, "When had I planned on telling them? Why did I sign my name to the paper saying I lived near Central and wanted to go, without asking their permission?"[12] Yet, however keen Beals's discomfort, her hardships were willingly undertaken and not thrust upon her by her parents.

That these young women acted without (and in Johns's case, in defiance of) immediate parental authority does not mean that black adults played no role in shaping the scene that unfolded in Little Rock. The family histories of Beals and Johns testify that the home life of both girls was far from a political vacuum and that the girls' political sensibilities were partially shaped by the family circle. Yet these young women were also taking responsibility for shaping the world they were preparing to inherit. As important as black parents were, the stories of Johns and Beals also show that

10. Taylor Branch, *Parting the Waters: America in the King Years, 1954–63* (New York: Simon and Schuster, 1988), 22.
11. Branch, *Parting the Waters*, 20.
12. Melba Patillo Beals, *Warriors Don't Cry: A Searing Memoir of the Battle to Integrate Little Rock's Central High* (New York: Pocket Books, 1994), 32.

parents were far from being the only initiators of actions leading to school desegregation. Young people were themselves keeping abreast of national court rulings and faulting the behavior of local officials. It was in part their awareness of these larger events that prompted these students to go forward even when their parents and grandparents counseled caution. In fact, these young women were able to go forward because they were readers of the news in addition to being creatures of their culture.

Nonetheless, in interpreting the Little Rock event, Arendt and Ellison accorded student agency a minor or nonexistent role. Instead, they described the young people as, respectively, victims of misplaced adult activism or cultural apprentices being trained into the discipline of the Negro's life world. Ellison echoed his opinion about the Little Rock Nine in an interview with Richard Stern that appeared in print in *Shadow and Act* under the title "That Same Pain, That Same Pleasure." Here, Ellison asked, rhetorically, "How do you account for Little Rock and the sit-ins? How do you account for the strength of those kids?" By way of an answer, he pointed to their heritage as both Negroes and Americans. The "thin-legged little girls who faced the mob in Little Rock" were avatars of "those human qualities which the American Negro has developed despite, and in rejection of, the obstacles and meannesses imposed upon us." Even more so, "the spirit which directed their feet is the old universal urge toward freedom."[13] However powerful and compelling Ellison's sentiments may be, his interpretation, in effect, looks past the children as individuals compelled by their own motives in order to see them as the fulfillment of something ancient. Facing what may have been an unprecedented moment in American life, Ellison described it as something "old." The Little Rock Nine had not broken with the past—they embodied it.

This is not to say that Ellison always valued the past over the present. On the contrary, the Ellisonian project often called for criticizing tradition and convention. As much as he revered the past, he also believed "that to embrace uncritically values which are extended to us by others is to reject the validity, even the sacredness, of our own experience."[14] Respecting one's own experience often meant challenging the truths imposed by authority and questioning the values handed down from one generation to the next. The children in Little Rock might have been avatars of an "old universal urge," but they were also acting out of motivations deriving from having come of age in a world that was in many ways unlike that of their par-

13. Ralph Ellison, "That Same Pain, That Same Pleasure," in *Collected Essays*, 79, 80.
14. Ralph Ellison, "Hidden Name and Complex Fate," in *Collected Essays*, 208.

ents. The culture and traditions that authorized these youthful challenges to segregation were themselves part of the Jim Crow world that was under assault; consequently, "these children" could fulfill the dreams of the previous generation only by challenging that generation's authority and wisdom.

Ellison's remarks on the Little Rock crisis were not merely responses to the events of the late 1950s. They also reflected some of the concerns that had shaped the writing of *Invisible Man* (1952) and remained the focus of his essays and interviews in the years following the publication of his novel. In his writings, Ellison continuously probed the nature of American and Negro identities and their interrelation to one another, as well as the ways that both Negro culture and American democracy, though fashioned within the constraints of slavery and segregation, did not merely reflect those conditions but pointed toward their transcendence. The sometimes positive, sometimes negative effects of having lived as a Negro and as an American meant that the counsels of one's elders were often laced with ambiguities that could make them more of a burden than a comfort to the social initiate. And though the protagonist of *Invisible Man* represents a rather extreme case of a young person prematurely burdened with the responsibility of addressing the nation's social problems, his difficulties give us some insight into Ellison's understanding of what the children at Little Rock's Central High signified.

Obsessed with doing what he ought to do, the protagonist of *Invisible Man*, not surprisingly, is confounded at those moments when, as with his grandfather's deathbed instructions, his policy of following to the letter the commands of white authority—saying "yes" when *they* expect you to do so—is described as a means of corroding the very logic on which authority depends. Through the words the old man confides to his grandson ("overcome 'em with yeses" he tells the boy. "Undermine 'em with grins, agree 'em to death and destruction"), obedience becomes defiance. Adding to the young man's confusion is the fact that there is no obverse—defiance does not automatically translate into obedience. The protagonist does indeed speculate momentarily that if whites truly knew something about the mind of blacks in the South, they would "have desired me to act just the opposite, that I should have been sulky and mean" rather than cheerfully compliant. Yet he also declares that he was "afraid to act any other way because they [whites] didn't like that at all."[15] As far as Ellison's naïf can tell, black obedience is the only prescribed course for getting along in the segregationist

15. Ralph Ellison, *Invisible Man* (New York: Vintage Press, 1990), 17. Hereafter, this work is cited parenthetically as *IM*.

South, and yet, according to his grandfather, being black and obedient was also to undermine the very people whom one was attempting to appease.

The social order of Jim Crow America, which Ellison knew both inside and out, was one that asserted black/white racial difference as both the ground and the goal of social and political life. Racial difference had to be taken for granted as the natural order of things, and yet, somewhat contradictorily, this difference also had to be continually enforced as if it could exist only by fiat. It was this tension between the idea of race as something natural and the idea of race as something merely imposed that signaled an instability in the nation's racial order that Ellison's novel—through plot and metaphor—was only too eager to exploit. The impossibility of guaranteeing white purity (the spoiled white paint at the Liberty Paint factory is one of the novel's most obvious metaphors for this) opened up an avenue for social critique that Ellison was to take repeatedly in his writings over the course of his career. The nation's white supremacist regime could always be embarrassed by its own inability to cordon off whiteness from blackness and to segregate black from white throughout all of the many tiers of human experience. Thus, if authority in the South (and in the nation, for that matter) depended on being always able to distinguish black from white, authority would always find itself in crisis. To invoke another of *Invisible Man*'s organizing metaphors, authority could be maintained only through a willed blindness.

It was also true, however, that authority could not be challenged on the white side of the color line without facing the same threat on the black side. If the white college trustee, Mr. Norton, tumbles into psychosexual chaos as a result of the excessive willingness of a young black man, whom the trustee describes as "my fate" (*IM*, 42), to do his bidding, then so is the regime of the black college president, Mr. Bledsoe, rattled by the same will to obedience. With his power resting largely on his ability to stage-manage a presentation of black reality (in Bledsoe's words, "haven't we bowed and scraped and begged and lied enough decent homes and drives for you to show him?" [*IM*, 138]), Bledsoe's throne cannot avoid being shaken by the young man's alacrity to follow "the white line." White should not be black, but as the Invisible Man acts as chauffeur to the college trustee he admits, "I identified myself with the rich man reminiscing on the rear seat" (*IM*, 39).

To understand *Invisible Man*'s inveterate irreverence toward authority, black as well as white, one can and should start with what Ellison saw midcentury as the bankruptcy of black politics—what he called the "ambiguity of Negro leadership":

This was the late forties, and I kept trying to account for the fact that when the chips were down, Negro leaders did not represent the Negro community.

Beyond their own special interests they represented white philanthropy, white politicians, business interests, and so on. This was an unfair way of looking at it, perhaps, but there was something missing, something which is only now being corrected. It seemed to me that they acknowledged no final responsibility to the Negro community for their acts, and implicit in their roles were constant acts of betrayal.[16]

This is also to say that because Negro authority, on an everyday basis, demonstrated its illegitimacy, surrendering judgment to those in charge was either foolish or suicidal. Bledsoe, who tells the horrified narrator, "I've made my place . . . and I'll have every Negro in the country hanging on tree limbs by morning if it means staying where I am" (*IM*, 143), is a case in point: No crime is too heinous if its commission contributes to securing the position of black leadership, a term that turns out to be merely a different way of saying *tyranny*.

The corruption represented by Bledsoe is, of course, a matter of history. The reign of Jim Crow required whites to seek to undermine, suppress, or co-opt any political power they saw emerging among black Americans. It should go without saying that these efforts were not always, and could not have been, uniformly successful—force and fraud were often countered with resistance. Yet the extent to which the compromising of black political power had been successful became a leitmotiv in criticisms and representations of black political praxis. The lament of an Alabama minister of the black Methodist Episcopal Church writing to the *Chicago Defender* during the first great migration was far from unusual: "As leaders we are powerless for we dare not resent such or to show even the slightest disapproval."[17] During the decades between the Harlem Renaissance and the publication of *Invisible Man*, the ineffectualness, cowardice, and duplicity of black leadership was a common theme among African American authors, whether in Langston Hughes's poem "To Certain Negro Leaders," which sneered at those "Voices crying in the wilderness / At so much per word / From the white folks,"[18]

16. Ellison, "That Same Pain," 76–77.
17. Unsigned letter to the *Chicago Defender*, Newbern, Ala., 7 April 1917; "More Letters of Negro Migrants of 1916–1918," *Journal of Negro History* 4, no. 4 (October 1919): 420.
18. Langston Hughes, "To Certain Negro Leaders," in *The Collected Poems of Langston Hughes*, ed. Arnold Rampersad (New York: Vintage Books, 1994), 136.

or in Richard Wright's depiction of Reverend Taylor at the beginning of his short story "Fire and Cloud," which finds the black preacher bemoaning, in Depression-era America, "Here Ah is a man called by Gawd t preach n whut kin Ah do?"[19]

The peculiar features of the white-dominated regime of the South would have justified Ellison's treating the problem of black leadership as more of a practical than a philosophical or theoretical problem. The relative weakness and the constrained circumstances of blacks in positions of power during Jim Crow would seem to make their behaviors and habits a some-what sterile ground for exploring broader or more abstract questions about the nature of legitimate power and authority. A racially segregated America represented a simple abuse of power and the replacement of authority with tyranny. Yet from another angle these very same circumstances serve quite nicely to frame an inquiry into the idea of authority in the modern world as well as to highlight the way that Arendt and Ellison functioned as interlocu-tors. In her discussion of the nature of authority Arendt observed that the "most conspicuous characteristic of those in authority is that they do not have power."[20] Given that authority is often taken to be synonymous with power, Arendt's remark, on its face, may seem counterintuitive (the reason-ing behind Arendt's claim will be addressed in greater detail below), but her words open up the possibility that the relative powerlessness of black Ameri-cans during Jim Crow could prove to be less an obstacle than an aid to an investigation of the notion of authority. To be clear on this point, Arendt was not partial to the idea that victims of oppression enjoyed any clarity of insight regarding the nature of political freedom. Quite the contrary: In her prefatory remarks to "Reflections," she wrote, "*Oppressed minorities were never the best judges on the order of priorities in such matters and there are many instances when they preferred to fight for social opportunity rather than for basic human or political rights.*"[21] And several years later, in a letter to Mary McCarthy in which she comments vituperatively on recent trends in the Civil Rights movement, Arendt reiterated her rather dim view of the capacity of the oppressed to set proper political and intellectual priori-ties. In words that would more than pass muster in contemporary far-right political circles, Arendt complained, "Negroes demand their own curriculum

19. Richard Wright, "Fire and Cloud," in "Uncle Tom's Children," in *Richard Wright, The Early Works* (New York: Library of America, 1991), 356.
20. Hannah Arendt, "What Is Authority," in *Between Past and Future: Eight Exercises in Political Thought* (1961; reprint, New York: Penguin, 1993), 122.
21. Arendt, "Reflections," 46.

without the exacting standards of white society and, at the same time, they demand admission in accordance to their percentage in the population at large, regardless of standards. In other words they actually want to take over and adjust standards to their own level. This is a much greater threat to our institutions of higher learning than the student riots."[22] Once again, the combination of obtuseness and insight by Arendt derived from her commitment to the importance of maintaining the integrity of the public, social, and private spheres. In her view, blacks, as they had done in the Little Rock crisis, were carrying the principle of equality necessary to the public realm into the social realm, the very existence of which depended on granting groups the right to make discriminations and enforce their own standards. Arendt's use of the term *white society* was, of course, more damaging to her argument than she realized in that it conceded the very argument that many black activists were making, namely, that the educational standards in institutions of higher learning, which should have been based on intellectual ability and achievement, had, throughout the nation's history, been determined by the goal of preserving white dominance.

What makes Arendt's ruminations on authority illuminating in a discussion of Ellison and *Invisible Man*, however, is not her clarity or lack thereof on the various political aims of black Americans. Rather, the distinction she drew between authority and power is suggestive in working through a problem that Ellison pursues relentlessly in his writings. The challenge embedded in Arendt's attempt to pin down the nature of authority is to find some account of authority's "binding force" that does not rely on coercion, on the one hand, or persuasion, on the other. Arendt maintained that authority must be "more than advice and less than a command, an advice which one may not safely ignore." Authority assumes that "the will and the actions of the people, like those of children, are exposed to error and mistakes and therefore need 'augmentation' and confirmation through the council of elders." The authoritative character of the "augmentation" of the elders lies in its being mere advice, needing neither the form of command nor external coercion to make itself heard. Operating in a manner akin to the way that "the binding force of the *auspices*" revealed "divine approval or disapproval of decisions made by men," authority as it had existed in previous civilizations had been "sanctified" by a tradition that "preserved the

---

22. Arendt, letter to Mary McCarthy, 21 December 1968, in *Between Friends: The Correspondence of Arendt and Mary McCarthy, 1949–1975*, ed. Carol Brightman (New York: Harcourt, Brace, and Co., 1995), 229–30.

past by handing down from one generation to the next the testimony of the ancestors."[23]

In *Invisible Man*, the figure of the grandfather, whose words of advice may not be safely ignored by the protagonist, reveals the curious nature of the "testimony of the ancestors" in Ellison's world. The old man's words are not underwritten by force or violence—his is a wisdom that began when "I gave up my gun back in the Reconstruction." Neither are they simply an indication of the way that the adult world imparts knowledge to children— the narrator's parents warn their son "emphatically to forget what he had said" (*IM*, 16). But forget he cannot, and the binding force of his grandfather's words is such that the narrator feels, "I was carrying out his advice in spite of myself" (*IM*, 16). He obeys even when he tries to do otherwise, and disobeys when he intends to comply. What *Invisible Man* urges us to contemplate is the idea that if the existence of proper authority implies obedience, there may be no legitimate authority if, at every turn, obedience results in subverting or misconstruing the very commands it intends to follow. This problem, which does emerge from the specific racial landscape of the South, nonetheless opens onto the larger problem of how in the modern era one can ground authority. In his notes on the protagonist of *Invisible Man*, Ellison writes, "The boy would appease the gods; it costs him much pain to discover that he can satisfy the gods only by rebelling against them."[24] And if that boy is also, as Ellison calls him, "the Negro individualist" whose god is himself, he must in turn embark on the seemingly impossible task of rebelling against his own rebellion. Thus, the gods must speak only to be defied, and the children must defy only to be rebuked.

*Invisible Man*'s narrator introduces himself to us by admitting, "All my life I had been looking for something, and everywhere I turned someone tried to tell me what it was. I accepted their answers too, though they were often in contradiction and even self-contradictory" (*IM*, 15). Because he seeks authority around every corner, one could say that the narrator simply makes the mistake of believing that anyone able to offer a response to the questions he asks counts as an authority. This is, of course, an egregious error (and, one might add, a stupid one: why should anybody want to believe everything he's told?). Yet, if Ellison's novel is interested in establishing the possibility for legitimate authority, then one might say that the Invisible Man's

23. Arendt, "What Is Authority?" 123–24. Arendt quotes from Mommsen's *Romische Geschichte*, 2d ed., vol. 1.
24. Ralph Ellison, "Working Notes for Invisible Man," in *Collected Essays*, 344.

stupidity turns out to be fortunate. Authority in the novel may not necessarily be in crisis. The problem may simply be that the narrator lacks the discernment to determine when a voice ought to count as an authority. For Ellison's naïf, the simple fact that someone is able to give a response to his questions is sufficient to compel his trust that the answers offered by his respondent are based on considered judgment. Proper authority, however, would be able to emerge only when the narrator reaches a place where he learns to judge, and because the novel is a bildungsroman, the entire engine of the narrative is chugging along to get the narrator to the place where he can learn to discern.

The questions for which the Invisible Man is seeking authoritative answers, however, are by no means small ones: Who am I? How should I, as a young black man, live? When should I submit? When should I defy? And given the dangers that come with living in Jim Crow America, his very survival would seem to depend on his answering at least these questions successfully. Complicating the narrator's plight is that the nature of these questions might also lead us to wonder who, aside from the young man himself, is in a position to answer them? Indeed, the narrator's tautological declaration "I am nobody but myself" — a certainty he claims as the hard-won discovery of his "painful boomeranging" — points toward an almost anarchistic answer to the problem of authority in which each individual acts as his own authority (*IM*, 15). Keeping one's own counsel opens up the possibility for self-authorization.

Ellison's story, however, gives us ample reason to doubt the efficacy of this solution. Late in the novel, when the protagonist seeks to avoid being physically attacked by the followers of Ras the Exhorter, he dons a disguise of a hat and dark glasses, precipitating a sequence in which he is repeatedly mistaken for Bliss Proteus Rinehart. Equally comfortable as a preacher, numbers runner, gambler, and ladies man, Rinehart represents a figure whose identity, ever shifting, cannot determine behavior from moment to moment. Described by Ellison as "the personification of chaos," Rinehart stands for "a country with no solid past or stable class lines; therefore he is able to move about easily from one to the other."[25] In such a country, the "natural" course of action would be to do as one likes, consulting no authority higher than one's whims or desires. However, as shown by the protagonist's near fatal experience while masquerading as Rinehart, *Invisible Man* is a novel that does not endorse surrendering to the chaos that would

25. Ralph Ellison, "The Art of Fiction: An Interview," in *Collected Essays*, 223.

result from unchecked self-authorization. Rather, Ellison's fiction strives to balance a necessary flouting of authority with a corresponding deference to some idea of order.

It is, of course, no news to readers of Ellison that order cannot be established in a once-and-for-all-time manner. Instead, the novel suggests that what order exists is best seen as an ongoing process that begins with the discovery that the patterns imposed on chaos are merely imposed and do not derive their authority from accurately representing things as they are. The reality of human existence as defined by Ellison is that we are surrounded by chaos, which means that all orderly and authoritative representations of reality are falsifications whose inadequacies will get exposed, given enough time. Positively speaking, this knowledge does arm the protagonist (and presumably the reader) with reasons for not acceding to the authority of Bledsoe, Jack, or Ras and their demands for complete submission. But as useful as this knowledge is in providing reasons not to conform to certain patterns, it offers no clear guidelines for selecting one pattern over another. When should one heed the counsel of authority? From the standpoint of representational adequacy, all coherent patterns fall short of the truth. As bad as, say, Brother Jack's vision might be, it is no blinder than any of the other visions the novel makes available.

There is one potential remedy that *Invisible Man* offers as the narrator winds his story toward its conclusion. He insists, "A plan of living must never lose sight of the chaos against which that pattern was conceived" (*IM*, 580). That is, patterns of conduct should always at some point call attention to the fact that they are fictive and not given. Presumably, this would prevent any individual from believing he or she has the right to impose a plan of living on someone else. This injunction is fair enough, and very much in accordance with liberal theories of individual restraint, in which one person's rights end at the point where the other fellow's nose begins. Ellison's narrator, however, extends the scope of this adage beyond the realm of individual conduct in asserting the importance of never "losing sight of the chaos" by saying that this truth "goes for societies as well as for individuals" (*IM*, 580). But extending this truth from individuals to societies is far from straightforward, because societies necessarily impose obligations on others. Societies always infringe on the individual's absolute freedom. How can an effort not to lose sight of chaos help create a plan to which the individual might willingly accede?

Here is where the novel's advocacy of a pattern of order that anticipates, makes room for, or otherwise acknowledges chaos seeks to find its authorization not in logical argument but rather in aesthetic practice. The Invisible Man begins his peroration by reciting a line—"Open the window and let the foul air out"—from a Louis Armstrong performance. The song in which the line appears is known as "I Thought I Heard Buddy Bolden Say," or "Funky Butt," the latter of which is also the name of the club where the young Louis Armstrong began his education in jazz improvisation. As Armstrong wrote in his autobiography, "At the corner of the street where I lived was the famous Funky Butt Hall, where I first heard Buddy Bolden play. He was blowing up a storm."[26] Ellison's metonymic allusion to one of the birthplaces of jazz almost obviates the need for the clarification of the lyric the narrator provides when he says, "Of course Louie was kidding, *he* wouldn't have thrown old Bad Air out, because it would have broken up the music and the dance, when it was the good music that came from the bell of old Bad Air's horn that counted." By this definition, jazz is a form made perfect by its imperfection—a vision of the plan made complete by virtue of its composer having left a hole for the intrusion of disorder. There is, then, no need to banish or exile the bad in order to have the good, a truth the narrator acknowledges when he remarks with great satisfaction that "Old Bad Air is still around with his music and his dancing and his diversity" (*IM* 581). In paralleling music, dancing, and diversity, the narrator suggests that the formula for making good art is the same as that for making a just society. "Diversity is the word. Let man keep his many parts and you'll have no tyrant states" (*IM*, 577). A good society would be like a good jazz song.

The protagonist puts this idea forward quite seriously, and the novel wants us to see this formulation as being the right one. The narrator's sentiments, after all, resemble those that Ellison expressed three years after the publication of *Invisible Man* in an essay titled "Living with Music," in which he declared, "The delicate balance struck between strong individual personality and the group during those early jam sessions was a marvel of social organization." Recounting his own youthful attempts to become a musician, Ellison insisted that he "had learned too that the end of all this discipline and technical mastery was the desire to express an affirmative way of life through its musical tradition, and that this tradition insisted that each artist achieve his creativity within its frame. He must learn the best of the past, and add to it his personal vision."[27] Learning to be a good artist appears to be a lot like learning how to live well and democratically. Yet, as much as

26. Louis Armstrong, *Satchmo: My Life in New Orleans* (London: Peter Davies, 1958), 25.
27. Ellison, "Living with Music," in *Collected Essays*, 229.

one might want to accede to Ellison's lesson, there are reasons to resist this conclusion. In touting Armstrong's singing, the narrator is not just arguing that keeping the bad air is ethically and politically sound. It is equally important that putting the two together *sounds* good. That is, the narrator accepts the bad air with the good because he likes the sound of the music he hears blaring from the horn of Bad Air. The narrator can get away with this justification because we all like (or he presumes that we should like) Armstrong. But it leaves one to wonder what would happen if we didn't? Given the diversity of human tastes, the linking of liking with authority would appear to raise almost as many problems as it solves. If there is no disputing tastes, there is no adjudicating of them either. An arbiter of taste could only be arbitrary.

If neither representational adequacy nor aesthetic compatibility determines whether or not we should respect a particular authority, then where are we to turn? Perhaps back to what Ellison called "the validity, even the sacredness, of our own experience." As a defense against the theories of those who claimed to know something about their lives, Negroes (as Ellison was to admonish Irving Howe in his "World and the Jug" essay) had to depend "upon the validity of their own experience for an accurate picture of the reality which they seek to change, and for a gauge of the values they would see made manifest."[28]

At first glance, this move seems to take us back to the idea of each individual navigating according to his or her own internal compass. In this case, however, the plural pronoun is hardly accidental. Ellison always sought to place individual experience within a larger group context, whether "Negro," "American," or some combination of the two. In fact, Ellison's larger point was that, had we the courage to admit it, the inescapable combination of the two was not only the truth of our individual experiences but also the inescapable implication of America's founding documents. It comes as no surprise to anyone familiar with Ellison's writings that the ideas expressed in the founding texts of the American republic underwrote the seriousness with which he approached the artistic enterprise. The title he gave to a 1967 lecture, "The Novel as a Function of American Democracy," exemplifies his many musings on the relationship between art and society. He "emphasize[d] that the American nation is based upon revolution, dedicated to change through basic concepts stated in the Bill of Rights and the Constitution. It is dedicated to an *open* society. . . . With such a society, it seems only natural that the novel existed to be exploited by certain personality

28. Ellison, "The World and the Jug," 161.

types who found their existence within the United States."[29] There was, then, a necessary correlation between America's founding documents, the art of the novel, the aesthetics of the jazz musician, and the actual experiences of Americans.

Acknowledging these truths meant acknowledging the Negro's humanity, a truth, Ellison felt, that white America was still unwilling to face but that Negro Americans, of necessity, had known all along. And knowing something about their own humanity—the Invisible Man's grandfather, for example, "never had any doubts about his"—placed black Americans somewhere ahead of whites in the struggle to make sense of the world. In his final effort to make sense of his grandfather's words, the Invisible Man speculates: "Was it that we of all, we, most of all, had to affirm the principle, the plan in whose name we had been brutalized and sacrificed—not because we would always be weak nor because we were afraid or opportunistic, *but because we were older than they, in the sense of what it took to live in the world with others?*" (*IM*, 574; my emphasis).

The Negro as Ellison knew him had never been young—naïve, perhaps, as is the hero of Ellison's only completed novel, but not someone who came into the world unknowing. That is, while there is much that Ellison's protagonist doesn't know, it is more so the case that he seems to have forgotten things rather than having not yet learned them—remembering himself is to remember his past. This position, which Ellison had reached even before the publication of *Invisible Man* in 1952, became doubly important in the early 1960s, when he found it necessary to counter Stanley Elkins's assertion, in his controversial study *Slavery*, that the Negro, as a result of the closed society of plantation slavery, had been a perpetual child.[30] Ellison's response before the fact was that the Negro could not have afforded himself such a luxury. Childhood had never been an option, as one could see in the courage of the children in Little Rock, who in some curious way were not really children. Ellison's conclusion was that were the Negro merely to accept his second-class status—had the children of Little Rock merely acceded to the desires of segregationists—the vision of American democracy would fail in its attempt to compel assent to its credos, and that equality, its innermost principle, would become a dead letter.

29. Ralph Ellison, "The Novel as a Function of American Democracy," in *Collected Essays*, 757. Perhaps not so coincidentally, Arendt's "What Is Authority" concludes by making recourse to the "act of foundation" (140–41).
30. Stanley M. Elkins, *Slavery: A Problem in American Institutional and Intellectual Life* (Chicago: University of Chicago Press, 1976), 130.

The problem, then, is not, as Houston Baker has recently charged, that *Invisible Man* lacks any trace of "the courage of nine black boys and girls braving white mobs to attend formerly segregated precincts of an Arkansas public school."[31] There is in the novel's relentless deconstruction of plans of order the very critical posture that helped sharpen the attack on Jim Crow. What Ellison was to wrestle with continually in his post–*Invisible Man* writings, however, was the awareness that the energies let loose by the Civil Rights Movement could not be expected to run smoothly in the cultural grooves laid down by the past. For no matter how much Ellison and his novel had contributed to the transformative energies that were on the scene in Little Rock, he, and his novel, too, could not escape becoming part of a past that would be questioned and perhaps repudiated by those newcomers (to use Arendt's word) who were more than willing to make the world their own.

31. Houston A. Baker Jr., *Critical Memory: Public Spheres, African American Writing, and Black Fathers and Sons in America* (Athens: University of Georgia Press, 2001), 34.

# "Jack-the-Bear" Dreaming: Ellison's Spiritual Technologies

*John S. Wright*

The year following the 1952 publication of *Invisible Man*, at the presentation ceremony for the National Book Award he had just won, Ralph Ellison told his audience that if he were asked in all seriousness what he considered to be the chief significance of *Invisible Man* as a fiction, he would reply, first, "its experimental attitude," and, second, "its attempt to return to the mood of personal moral responsibility for democracy which typified the best of our nineteenth century fiction."[1] That his first novel had won such an award he acknowledged as a clear sign of crisis in the American novel, a sense of crisis that he and the other "younger novelists" of the time shared.

On the aesthetic level, Ellison's experimental novel had developed out of his own reaction to a growing uncertainty about the formal possibilities of the novel—an uncertainty that led him to reject both the forms of the "tight, well-made Jamesian novel" and the "hard-boiled novel" of Hemingway, which had been a center of literary revolt among apprentice writers of the 1930s.[2] The narrative experiment that Ellison created to fill the void

1. Ralph Ellison, *Shadow and Act* (New York: Random House, 1964), 102.
2. Ellison, *Shadow and Act*, 178–79.

*boundary 2* 30:2, 2003. Copyright © 2003 by Duke University Press.

moved consciously from naturalism to expressionism to surrealism, from the world of "facts" to the world of dream and nightmare, from the determined to the disordered.

Over the past half century since its publication, successive generations of scholars engaged in interpreting *Invisible Man* have devoted no small measure of attention to the musical sources of the book's experimental attitude—to jazz and blues, in particular—in part because of the manifest autobiographical impress of musical experience on Ellison's sensibility. Those of us who have approached the novel in that vein have searched out, with great industry, the vernacular folk traditions and shape-shifting trickster archetypes that, along with jazz and blues players, seem to embody improvisational and experimental stances toward life and art. And we have betrayed no sign of shyness in excavating the eclectic mosaic of literary models and movements, "ancestors" and "relatives," that demonstrably helped expand Ellison's sense of aesthetic possibility.

In this context, however, Ellison's own frequent, almost incantatory allusions to the primacy of technique have perhaps helped reinforce narrowly aestheticist readings of the sources of his experimental attitude. For those of us who have cultivated with determined seriousness such readings of Ellison's technique, there may be a joke in this, precisely that kind of wry disjunction between illusion and reality that Ellison routinely turns to comic effect in his fiction and essays.

For if technique is, in Kenneth Burke's phrase, a kind of "God-term" in Ralph Ellison's critical vocabulary, this is not, I want to suggest, because of any implied superhuman powers in the how and the what of literary method, style, or manner. To rephrase one of the resonant scriptural texts of black sermonic traditions, it is not literary technique alone whose "ways are mysterious, their wonders to perform." Rather it may be because, in Ellison's use, the concept of technique routinely suggests both the literal, organizational, procedural part of executing a work of fiction *and* that much broader system of applied sciences and practical arts by which any society provides its members with those things needed or desired—technology, in other words. Over the course of his career—in critical essays and reviews, in short stories and interviews, in his novel and his novel-in-progress—Ellison used *technique* as a *synthesizing* term, referring to a way of making connections between the world of art and the world of our mechanized material civilization. He used it in *this* sense more insistently than as a reference to a set of operations peculiar to literary text making. In tracking Ellison's allegiances as an artist and a man, then, we should not be surprised to find his notions of technique having *less* to do with the sense of the term prevalent in the autotelic New Criticism promoted by John Crowe Ransom, Allen Tate, Robert Penn Warren, and company in the 1930s and 1940s, and *more* to do with the notions of technics and technology proffered by Lewis Mumford in those same decades in his wide-ranging, often highly speculative cultural criticism about science, utopia, architecture, religion, and "the myth of the machine." Mumford elaborated his sense of technique in a series of books that included *The Golden Day* (1924), *Technics and Civilization* (1934), and *Art and Technics* (1952).

*Invisible Criticism*, Alan Nadel's study of Ralph Ellison and the American canon, provides one of the rare explorations of Ellison's connection to Mumford's "neotechnic" terrain. In a pivotal chapter, Nadel first recounts Mumford's *Golden Day* as an archetypal drama of the prototypical American locked in losing combat with the ascendant machine age, then very deftly reads "Jack-the-Bear's" descent into dreamlike chaos at a Southern bordello—dubbed likewise "The Golden Day"—as a punning Ellisonian riff on Mumford's dismissive treatment of slavery and race as issues in the conflict that led to civil war.[3] Nadel accuses Mumford of writing fiction, not history, in his account of the antebellum culture of Emerson, Thoreau, Whitman, Hawthorne, and Melville as the "Golden Day" abruptly ended by the Civil War, only to be followed by the epoch of the Trust and the Machine. To buttress this reading of Mumford's book as "an ode to a period that never existed," Nadel quotes a personal letter he received from Ellison himself:

> It wasn't that I didn't admire Mumford. I have owned a copy of the sixth Liveright printing of THE GOLDEN DAY since 1937 and own, and have learned from, most of his books. I was simply upset by his implying that the war which freed my grandparents from slavery was of no real consequence to the broader issues of American society and its culture. What else, other than sheer demonic, masochistic hell-raising, was that bloody war all about if not slavery and the contentions which flowed there-from? As a self-instructed student I was quite willing for Mumford to play Aeschylus, Jeremiah, or even God, but not at the price of his converting the most tragic incident in American history into bombastic farce. For in doing so he denied my people the sacrificial role which they had played in the drama.[4]

3. Alan Nadel, "Invisible Man in the Golden Day," chap. 4 in *Invisible Criticism: Ralph Ellison and the American Canon* (Iowa City: University of Iowa Press, 1988), 85–103.
4. Ralph Ellison, quoted in Nadel, *Invisible Criticism*, 158.

This is classic Ellisonian infighting, and it leaves no doubt about the grounds of difference on which Ellison's send-up of Mumford's Golden Day proceeds. It does not, however, gainsay what Ellison *shares* with Mumford about interpreting the culture of the closing three antebellum decades— their absolute import in shaping American values and literature. Nor does it deny the extent to which Ellison shares Mumford's sense of the *omnipresence* of technology and the machine, and the artist's moral obligation to envision aesthetic possibilities for the machine that will not reinforce the fragmenting, life-denying, dehumanizing conditions created by capitalist technology.

Mumford's notion of the ideal relation between art and technics is in fact closely allied with that revealed in Ellison's work, and it is precisely in Ellison's conceptualization of the "experimental attitude" which culminated in *Invisible Man* that such a relation is most explicitly articulated. "What has been missing from so much experimental writing," he asserts in "Brave Words for a Startling Occasion," has been "the passionate will to dominate reality as well as the laws of art. This will is the true source of the experimental attitude."[5] The clues Ellison gives us about its development in his own life direct us first not to art but to technology—to the applied sciences, to the systems, mechanical and electrical, whereby our means of transportation and communication, the configuration of our landscape, our very sense of time and space and consciousness were being transformed during the decades of Ellison's boyhood and maturation as an artist.

The very first question of the very first interview framed in *Shadow and Act*, the 1961 exchange titled "That Same Pain, That Same Pleasure," called on Ellison to clarify "the way in which you as a Negro writer have vaulted the parochial limitations of most Negro fiction"—a question whose presumptions about "Negro fiction" I hope have withered over the past forty years. Answering that it was "a matter of attitude," and calmly contradicting any assumptions that his own life might resemble traditional "portraits of the artist," Ellison recalls,

> Like so many kids of the twenties, I played around with radio—building crystal sets and circuits consisting of a few tubes, which I found published in the radio magazines. At the time we were living in a white middle-class neighborhood, where my mother was custodian for some apartments, and it was while searching the trash for cylindrical ice-cream cartons which were used by amateurs for winding tun-

5. Ellison, *Shadow and Act*, 105.

ing coils that I met a white boy who was looking for the same thing. I gave him some of those I'd found and we became friends. . . . His nickname was Hoolie and for kids of eight or nine that was enough. Due to a rheumatic heart Hoolie was tutored at home and spent a great deal of time playing by himself and in taking his parents' elaborate radio apart and putting it back together again, and in building circuits of his own. . . . It didn't take much encouragement from his mother, who was glad to have someone around to keep him company, for me to spend much of my free time helping him with his experiments. By the time I left the community, he had become interested in shortwave communication and was applying for a ham license. I moved back into the Negro community and began to concentrate on music, and was never to see him again, but knowing this white boy was a very meaningful experience. It had little to do with the race question as such, but with our mutual loneliness (I had no other playmates in that community) and a great curiosity about the growing science of radio. It was important for me to know a boy who could approach the intricacies of electronics with such daring and whose mind was intellectually aggressive.[6]

That the impress of technology on consciousness and communion would remain a fixture of his life, and finally effect a fusion with the musical and the literary, Ellison had earlier acknowledged in a 1955 essay for *Hi Fidelity* magazine, titled "Living with Music." In the course of recalling the intimate battle history of his audio-system warfare with a musically committed but painfully untalented would-be classical singer in the apartment next door, Ellison also recounted his intense reengagement in the late forties with the electronics world that, after a great technological leap forward, suddenly interposed itself between his records, his typewriter, and his ears roughly midway in the course of his long labor with the experimental novel:

> I had started music early and lived with it daily, and when I broke I tried to break clean. Now in this magical moment all the old love, the old fascination with music superbly rendered, flooded back. . . . If I was to live and write in that apartment, it would be only through the grace of music. I had tuned in a [Kathleen] Ferrier recital, and when it ended I rushed out for several of her records, certain now that deliverance was mine.

6. Ellison, *Shadow and Act*, 23–24.

But not yet. Between the hi-fi record and the ear, I learned, there was a new electronic world. . . . It was 1949 and I rushed to the Audio Fair. . . . I had hardly entered the fair before I heard David Sarser's and Mel Sprinkle's Musician's Amplifier, took a look at its schematic and, recalling a boyhood acquaintance with such matters, decided that I could build one. I did, several times before it measured within specifications. And still our system was lacking. . . . I built a half a dozen or more preamplifiers and record compensators before finding a commercial one that satisfied my ear, and, finally, we acquired an arm, a magnetic cartridge and—glory of the house—a tape recorder. All this plunge into electronics, mind you, had as its simple end the enjoyment of recorded music as it was intended to be heard. I was obsessed with the idea of reproducing sound with such fidelity that even when using music as a defense behind which I could write, it would reach the unconscious levels of the mind with the least distortion.[7]

David Sarser and Mel Sprinkle and their "Musician's Amplifier" represented a new phase of audio science and technology in the modern world, which brought high-order musicianship directly into the design processes of laboratory audio engineering, and brought also into the public domain a new cult of audiophile high fidelity, which spread far beyond the radio magazines Ellison had absorbed in his youth and into the world of high-culture literacy embodied in magazines such as the venerable *Atlantic Monthly*. Sarser was a Juilliard-trained, Stradivarius-owning violinist who played in the NBC Symphony Orchestra under Maestro Arturo Toscanini. Sarser in fact became Toscanini's personal advisor on audio technology and recording, and he went on to become the musical director of NBC's Opera Hour, Hallmark's Hall of Fame, and to record Frank Sinatra, Bing Crosby, Perry Como, Dinah Washington, and Maurice Chevalier while inventing literally dozens of patented audio devices.[8]

The experimental musician's amplifier that Sarser and Sprinkle designed for sale in kit form in 1949, and that Ellison built and rebuilt while wrestling with his experimental novel, grew out of the obsession Sarser shared with Ellison to create a technology of sound reproduction—focused at that point on the development of "high efficiency vacuum tube triode

7. Ellison, *Shadow and Act*, 193–94.
8. John Conly, "They Shall Have Music," *Atlantic Monthly* 207, no. 2 (February 1961): 100–103.

amplifiers"—capable of producing a spectrum of frequencies beyond both the high and low ends of human audibility, but which at the same time would render its mechanical and electronic components "invisible" to the listening ear.[9] When asked if he considered himself an artist, a technician, or a musician, Sarser routinely responded, "I'm a musician. All my formal training has been in music. I've played in many different orchestras. And when war broke out it was my music that saved me. Everything I've done in my life has been because of my music. Everything else has been a hobby." In offering one key to his legendary success, he said, "I was never afraid of what I didn't know."[10]

As Ellison's commentary in "Living with Music" suggests, at the "level of technique" Sarser served as an adult analogue in Ellison's interwoven technologico-musical evolution to his boyhood crystal-set co-experimenter, Hoolie. Though now as a mature artist, Ellison understood, as he could *not* have as a boy, that the technical media through which we hear music (the physical systems and spaces) cannot be separated from our ability to experience the music itself. Because music's meaning is embodied in its physical quality, we cannot separate music's rhetoric—its "words"—from its physical reality, its "delivery."[11] The obsession that Sarser and Ellison both confessed became, in those early years of "high fidelity," itself the object of vernacular joking; audiophile insiders began quipping about a strange new distortion of sensibility and consciousness dubbed "audiophilia nervosa,"[12] manifest in all the peculiar social behaviors, violations of etiquette, and listening practices of the new cult's fervent devotees—devotees who numbered among their representations in fiction Ellison's reefer-smoking, audio-obsessed dedicated dreamer, "Jack-the-Bear."

Psychologically speaking, "the goals that lie at the end of a chain of condensers, resistors, and vacuum tubes"[13] were only partly aesthetic: Ellison financed the completion of *Invisible Man* in part by building systems for other audiophiles. Here, as part of a pattern we as readers have

9. Melvin Sprinkle, "A High Efficiency Triode Amplifier," *Radio and Television News*, May 1950, 55–57, 134–37.

10. Quoted in Gillian Newson, "David Sarser: A True Recording Idol," in *Who's Who in the Roxio Discussion List Community*, available at roxio.com, 26 Oct. 2001.

11. Keith Jarrett, foreword to Robert Harley, *The Complete Guide to High-End Audio*, 2d ed. (Albuquerque, N.M.: Acapella Publishing, 1998), xviii.

12. Julius Segal, "A Psychologist Views Audiophilia," *High Fidelity: The Magazine for Music Listeners*, September 1955, 50.

13. Segal, "A Psychologist Views Audiophilia," 50.

probably understated over the years, we can glimpse Ellison focused for a moment on the first and least acknowledged corner—revolutionary technological modernity—of what he often posited as the triangular design of African American identity, whose complementary corners are, second, the changing fate of being "American," as mysterious and uncertain as that may be, and, third, the "racial predicament," with its complex legacy of oppression, repression, and possibility.

In "Some Answers and Some Questions" posed for the magazine *Preuves* in 1958, Ellison addresses directly the problematic role of modern industrial evolution in the "spiritual crisis of the Negro people of our times" and its potential dangers for the future of a "genuine Negro culture." He sees that role to be as ambiguous in African American life as in the life of any modern people:

> It depends on how much human suffering must go into the achievement of industrialization, upon who operates the industries, upon how the products and profits are shared and upon the wisdom used in imposing technology, upon the institutions and traditions of each particular society. Ironically, black men with the status of slaves contributed much of the brute labor which helped the industrial revolution under way; in this process they were exploited, their natural resources were ravaged and their institutions and their cultures were devastated, and in most instances they were denied anything like participation in the European cultures which flowered as a result of the transformation of civilization under the growth of technology. But now it is precisely technology which promises them release from the brutalizing effects of over three hundred years of racism and European domination. Men cannot unmake history, thus it is not a question of reincarnating those cultural traditions which were destroyed, but a matter of using industrialization, modern medicine, modern science generally, to work in the interest of these peoples rather than against them. Nor is the disruption of continuity with the past necessarily a totally negative phenomenon; sometimes it makes possible a modulation of a people's way of life which allows for a more creative use of its energies. . . . One thing seems clear, certain possibilities of culture are achievable only through the presence of industrial techniques.
>
> It is not industrial progress per se which damages peoples or cultures; it is the exploitation of peoples in order to keep the machines

fed with raw materials. It seems to me that the whole world is moving toward some new cultural synthesis, and partially through the discipline imposed by technology.[14]

However our own experience of machine society may lead us now to evaluate this technological ethos Ellison embraced at midcentury, his own reflections then seem bound up with those of Mumford in the same kind of "antagonistic cooperation" that characterizes so many of Ellison's engagements with leading thinkers of the era.[15] Mumford's monumental studies of the development of technology and the history and culture of the city; his extra-academic generalist's readiness to trespass constantly across disciplinary boundaries in the effort to define "organic" connections between different realms of thought and experience; his troubled awareness of the historic abuse of technology and the apparent human inability to control the aggression and power lust that threaten ecological disaster and global conflagration; his utopian strain of belief in the redemptive possibilities of a humane technology mediated by a new "vitalistic," "gestaltic" perception of the "complicated interdependences" of all things—all these facets of Mumford's thought seem to resonate on the *cooperative* side of Ellison's intellectual confrontation with the author of *The Golden Day*.

But lest I overstress that convergence, I want to turn for a moment to the pivotal juncture where Ellison's technological ethos and Mumford's ultimately diverge. The impetus of Mumford's career carried him from an early focus as a critic primarily of American literature and the arts—with painting, architecture, and technology as simply *part* of the mix—to ever larger questions of human history and destiny *centered* increasingly on the origin, meaning, and potential of technology. The fate of urban culture, the possibility of constructing a global technological utopia that was *not* technocratic, the hopes and frustrations of large-scale urban planning—all impelled Mumford toward a collectivizing, macrocosmic vision that made the specific technology and symbolism of architecture his prime nexus for locating and evaluating the social meanings of the machine.[16]

The artisan, not the artist, became the locus of Mumford's utopian hopes for democracy; and he professed a profound ambivalence about the modern artistic imagination as a means of "human salvation" from the dep-

14. Ellison, *Shadow and Act*, 255–56.
15. Ellison, *Shadow and Act*, 143.
16. Robert Casillo, "Lewis Mumford," in *Dictionary of Literary Biography*, vol. 63 (Detroit: Gale Research Inc., 1988), 184–200.

redations of the machine and technologized science. "Though each new invention or discovery may respond to some general human need, or even awaken a fresh human potentiality," he writes in "Utopia, the City, and the Machine,"

> the only group that has understood those dehumanizing, totalitarian threats are the *avant-garde* artists, who have caricatured the system by going to the opposite extreme. Their calculated destructions and "happenings" symbolize total decontrol: the rejection of order, continuity, design, significance, and a total inversion of human values which turns criminals into saints and scrambled minds into sages. In such anti-art, the dissolution of our entire civilization into randomness and entropy is prophetically symbolized. In their humorless deaf-and-dumb language, the *avant-garde* artists reach the same goal as power-demented technicians, but by a different route—both seek or at least welcome the displacement and eventual elimination of man.[17]

For Ellison, if frequent forays into the world of cultural criticism inclined him at all toward Mumford's salvific grander "organicism," his vocation as a novelist drove him instead to seek the "universal" in the particular, the macrocosm in the microcosm, and less to dreams of artisanal utopia than to psychotherapeutic models of personal healing mediated by the artistic imagination. "More than any other literary form," he argues in 1957 in "Society, Morality, and the Novel," the novel "is obsessed with the impact of change upon *personality*. . . . Man knows that even in this day of marvelous technology and the tenuous subjugation of the atom, that nature can crush him, and that at the boundaries of human order the arts *and* the instruments of technology are hardly more than magic objects which serve to aid us in our ceaseless quest for certainty."[18] It is not, then, technology as a vast alienating system of machines moving through history with implacable force that preoccupied Ellison; it is technology as an extension of human lives, as something *someone* makes, *someone* owns, something *some* people oppose, most people *must* use, and *everyone* tries to make sense of. However dreamlike and surreal, the processes of living, through which technology acquires personal and social meaning, are what prevail in Ellison's

17. Lewis Mumford, "Utopia, the City, and the Machine," in *Interpretations and Forecasts, 1922–1972: Studies in Literature, Biography, Technics, and Contemporary Society* (New York: Harcourt Brace Jovanovich, 1975), 257.
18. Ralph Ellison, *Going to the Territory* (New York: Random House, 1986), 244–46.

"experimental attitude." And more than architecture, it is the impact on personality of the new technology of *electrification* and the machinery of the electric age that defines the crucial contexts of value in his novelistic experiment with the forms of fiction, consciousness, and democracy.

One of the things differentiating *Invisible Man* most dramatically from the other African American fictions of its time is this absorption with the immediate effects of the technological environment on the human imagination and spirit, and on the blurring line between reality and illusion, the natural and the artificial—as the "technoscape" replaces the landscape, and as the very nature of human perception is changed by the pervasive presence of the artificial. During the years of Ellison's literary novitiate, other black writers created fictions rooted in the ethos of blues and jazz—Langston Hughes, in *Not without Laughter*, for instance; other black writers fabricated characters immersed in the tales and trickster traditions of African American oral lore—perhaps none more extensively than Zora Neale Hurston; other black writers, such as Chester Himes, in *If He Hollers*, and Richard Wright, in *The Long Dream*, brought the world of dreams to center stage; and other writers—here William Attaway's *Blood on the Forge* served as Ellison's reference point—dramatized the epic migration from the feudal Southern landscape to the urban, industrial modern North. None, however, attuned these crucial facets of African American life as consciously as Ellison would to the new world of social and psychic meanings created by technological change, and none attempted to fuse them *all* into the odyssey of a single black personality whose distinctive consciousness is mediated pervasively by technology.

In *Invisible Man*, the conflicts between personal and public values, between psychic power and political power, between the ethic of material progress and the spiritual potential of the solitary soul, are dramatized through technological experience. From the punning structural and thematic frame appropriated from H. G. Wells's science fiction classic *The Invisible Man*, to the controlling optical metaphors and hyper-illuminated underground "sound stage" of Jack-the-Bear's monologue-in-flashback, technologically altered perceptions reverberate. The confrontations with such human antagonists as the Southern white bigwigs at the Battle Royal, A. Hebert Bledsoe, Mr. Norton, Lucius Brockaway, the Liberty Paints doctors, and the Brotherhood's Jack reflect the challenges to "natural," autonomous values and self-consciousness presented by the new "artificial" environment of machines and by what Mumford calls the "megamachines," the machinelike human organizations that convert the "raw material" of humanity into automatons, robots, and "zombies"—as the crazy vet at the novel's Golden Day calls Jack-the-Bear. The "characters" he becomes conscious of emerge from the dramatic series of agons with machines and technology, including the electrified rug, the electric gauge-laden paint boiler, and the electrifying hospital machine that gives him the equivalent of a prefrontal lobotomy. Transported from site to site in his new Northern home by electrified streetcars and subway trains, and driven finally underground by the boomerangs of fate, Jack-the-Bear ultimately grapples with the forms and formlessness of his life and identity in the artificial illumination made possible by electrification. Why electrification and electric machinery more than the other technologies of the time? Let me offer some suggestions, the first of which Ellison understood from deep personal experience.

The period from 1880 to 1940, as David Nye's history of that new technology details, was the period when, spurred by startling scientific inventions and an aggressive new social class of entrepreneurial engineers, we embarked on the mammoth technological process of "electrifying America."[19] Americans adopted electrical technologies across a vast spectrum of social, political, economic, and aesthetic contexts, reconfiguring the whole texture of national experience. Electricity changed the appearance and multiplied the meaning of the landscapes of ordinary life, its aboveground and underground transport systems. Electricity created new ties between city centers and separated outlying districts such as Harlem, created the huge network of electric cables and transformers that made possible assembly-line factories (such as Liberty Paints), electrified homes, and the new experience of night space that fascinated painters and photographers and spawned a new species of phantasmagoric public spectacles along the "Great White Way."[20] Electrification created the "mass media" as we know it—the radio, the phonograph, the telephone, the movies—along with a newly verbalized entertainment taste for onstage "live wires," "human dynamos," and "electrifying performances," the taste that Ellison, during his boyhood in a small town on the edge of the Oklahoma frontier, was attempting to gratify in the early 1920s by obsessively mastering the techniques and concepts of crystal-set circuitry, vacuum tubes, and winding coils.

The impact of electrification on Ellison's maturing literary imagination, though, had other sources, contemporary and historic. If during Elli-

---

19. David Nye, *Electrifying America: Social Meanings of New Technology* (Cambridge: MIT Press, 1990).
20. Nye, *Electrifying America*, 51.

son's coming of age electricity was, in the public mind, a sign of Thomas Edison's inventive genius and the hallmark of specifically *American* progress, it was also a "mysterious power Americans had long connected— as far back at least as Mumford's mid-nineteenth century Golden Day—to magnetism, the nervous system, heat, power, . . . , sex, health, and light."[21] In his own day, Mumford himself was not immune to the supernal allure of urban electrification, as he rhapsodizes autobiographically in his *Sketches from Life*: "I saw the skyscrapers in the deepening darkness become slowly honeycombed with lights until, before I reached the Manhattan end, these buildings piled up in a dazzling mass against the indigo sky. . . . Here was my city, immense, overpowering, flooded with energy and light. . . . The world at that moment opened before me, challenging me, beckoning me. . . . In that sudden revelation of power and beauty all the confusions of adolescence dropped from me, and I trod the narrow, resilient boards of the footway with a new confidence."[22]

Prospects for electrification notwithstanding, such confidence had been more elusive for the Civil War generation, and the Golden Day had been ended, Mumford writes, by a war "between two forms of servitude, the slave and the machine. . . . The machines won; and the war kept on. . . . The slave question disappeared but the 'Negro' question remained."[23] Mumford read the era's abolitionism as unenlightened moral righteousness "oblivious to the *new* varieties of slavery . . . practiced under industrialism."[24] But Ellison's own ancestral moorings in the Golden Day inverted Mumford's allegory of dark and light, blindness and sight. Instead, Ellison read the social crises of the Golden Day more in accord with the phalanx of transcendentalist millenarians, social reformers, spiritualists, and abolitionists who aligned themselves with Emerson's "Party of Hope" and who heeded Walt Whitman's call to "sing the body electric" as an anthem to the new democratic vistas in which electricity—"the demon, the angel, the mighty physical power, the all-pervading intelligence," one of Hawthorne's characters calls it[25]—would be bound up with the realm of human spirit more profoundly than the machine had ever been.

21. Nye, *Electrifying America*, 155–56.

22. Lewis Mumford, *Sketches from Life: The Autobiography of Lewis Mumford—The Early Years* (New York: Dial Press, 1982), 129–30.

23. Quoted in Nadel, *Invisible Criticism*, 88.

24. Nadel, *Invisible Criticism*, 90–94.

25. Clifford, in Nathaniel Hawthorne, "The Flight of the Owls," chap. 17 in *The House of the Seven Gables*, quoted in Nye, *Electrifying America*, 1.

At the same time that Ellison's moral allegiances to the literary lights of Mumford's Golden Day reinforced his own allegorical sensitivity to the tropes of electrification, his ties to the Jazz Age artists against whom his own literary experiment had to be defined—Hemingway and Fitzgerald, in particular—made the electrified technoscape an almost inevitable site of interpretive confrontation and revision. Ellison's critique of the writers of the twenties resounds throughout his critical essays, but perhaps nowhere more cogently than in the aforementioned "Society, Morality, and the Novel," where he contends that the "organic" moral-aesthetic struggle during the Golden Day against slavery both in *this* world and in the world of spiritual values had its trajectory broken by the failure of Reconstruction and the signalizing Hayes-Tilden Compromise of 1876. The consequent moral evasions and materialism of the Gilded Age, Ellison posits, "prepared for the mood of glamorized social irresponsibility voiced in the fiction of the twenties, and it created a special problem between the American novelist and his audience. . . . [The] novel, which in the hands of our greatest writers had been a superb moral instrument, became morally diffident and much of its energy was turned upon itself in the form of technical experimentation." In Hemingway's case, Ellison argues, "the personal despair which gave the technique its resonance became a means of helping other Americans to avoid those aspects of reality which they no longer had the will to face."[26] The unfaced and enduring problem of race, and its relationship to the health of democracy, loomed largest here in Ellison's mind, and despite that element of Hemingway's "technique" which recognizes that what is left out of a fiction is as important as what is present, the want of a *black* presence in Hemingway's pivotal images of America marks the moral evasion Ellison detected as real and aesthetically indefensible.

To see F. Scott Fitzgerald in Ellison's eyes requires a closer acquaintance with the "little man at Chehaw Station," the hypothetical crossbred connoisseur, critic, and trickster whom the Tuskeegee concert pianist Hazel Harrison foisted pedagogically on Ellison during his college student days as the ideal audience and goad for would-be American artists. Internalizing the little man as an alternate authorial persona, Ellison notes that in Fitzgerald's *The Great Gatsby*, the narrator, Nick Carraway, "tells us, by way of outlining his background's influence upon his moral judgments, that his family fortune was started by an Irish uncle who immigrated during the Civil War, paid a substitute to fight in his stead, and went on to become wealthy from war

26. Ellison, *Going to the Territory*, 252, 255.

profiteering." Quick to see the symbolic connections between this ances-tral moral legacy and Gatsby's illusory rise and fatal end, Ellison's little man represents a possible "saving grace" for both Fitzgerald and his doomed protagonist:

> The little man, by imposing collaboratively his own vision of America upon that of the author, would extend the novel's truth to levels below the threshold of that frustrating social mobility which forms the core of Gatsby's anguish. Responding out of a knowledge of the man-ner in which the mystique of wealth is intertwined with the American mysteries of class and color, he would aid the author in achieving the more complex vision of American experience that was implicit in his material. As a citizen, the little man endures with a certain grace the social restrictions that limit his own mobility; but *as a reader*, he demands that the relationship between his own condition and that of those more highly placed be recognized. He senses that the American experience is of a whole, and he wants the interconnection revealed.[27]

Fitzgerald's failure, however, to incorporate the little man's experi-ence into his own diminished his fiction for readers of the highest standard, Ellison counsels; and by the little man's corollary logic, Jay Gatsby, whose murder-by-mistake might have been averted—had the black man who wit-nessed the real driver of the death car *not* been left voiceless and discon-nected from the novel's action—pays with his life.

Now, in case it seems that I have strayed too far from Ellison's own electrified technoscape, let me try to make those connections clearer. For both Hemingway and Fitzgerald, as for many of their American peers, elec-trification helped chart, fictively, "the changes in values and self-perception that came with modernity."[28] But for them, as for writers such as Eugene O'Neill, the very real connections between the modern drama of electri-fied technological change and the modern drama of race went unperceived. O'Neill, who "electrified" his own early career with three "Negro plays"—*Emperor Jones*, *The Dreamy Kid*, and *All God's Chillun*—also produced a play called *Dynamo* in 1929, in which the stark contrasts between tradition and modernity, between the certainties of Protestant fundamentalism and the morally indeterminate universe of Darwin, Freud, and Einstein, are dra-

27. Ellison, *Going to the Territory*, 13–14.
28. Nye, *Electrifying America*, 284.

matized onstage in the opposing images of two family homes, one pious and *un*electrified, the other fully electrified and infused with the worship of electricity. The worlds of O'Neill's "Negro plays" and *Dynamo*, however, are kept mutually exclusive in his dramaturgical imagination: The characters of the Negro plays are confined to the expressionist jungle of Jungian primitivism, while the electrified world of *Dynamo* is kept imperturbably white.

In Hemingway's work also, electrification takes on broad spiritual and metaphysical import divorced from racial implication. One of the classic examples of Hemingway's style and technique especially pertinent to Ellison, the much anthologized 1933 story, "A Clean, Well-Lighted Place,"[29] deploys electric light not just as a pragmatic substitute for older forms of illumination but as a sign of the existential force that, in a modern world darkened by the loss of meaning, both holds back the void and, within the frame of enveloping spiritual darkness, solidifies and confirms the fragile reality of human existence. Two waiters sit in a Spanish café, one old, one young; one wise but wearied by the ways of the world, the younger one naïvely confident about his life and its prospects—"I have confidence. I am all confidence," he declares. The older waiter is no longer religious but still seeks human communion; the younger one is void of empathy and absorbed in personal pleasure. The two converse about a customer after he leaves, an old man who has recently attempted suicide, and whom the two waiters, at the insistence of the younger, have put out of the bright, cheery bodega so they can close for the night.

Arguing that they should have permitted the customer to stay and to share the café's lighted communion rather than send him home to drink alone, the older waiter acknowledges that he, too, is one of those "who like to stay late at the cafe . . . with all those who do not want to go to bed. With all those who need a light for the night." After the young waiter leaves, *he* stays on, reluctant to close, and, after asking himself *why* he needs a "clean, well-lighted place," realizes that it offers the aura of order in answer to "a nothing that he knew too well." On his own way home in the darkness, without the light, he holds back the void by reciting a parody of the Lord's Prayer—"Our nada who art in nada, nada be thy name thy kingdom nada thy will be nada in nada as it is in nada"—before retiring sleeplessly to await the light of day.

Like Hemingway and O'Neill, Fitzgerald recognized that the new technology of illumination "was far more than a utilitarian prop for home economics": Electricity confronted the modern world with new ways to express

29. Ernest Hemingway, "A Clean, Well-Lighted Place," in *The Fifth Column and the First Forty-Nine Stories* (New York: Scribner's Sons, 1939), 477–81.

and understand the self.[30] Nye points to *The Great Gatsby* as a modern fable in which electricity becomes, literally, a tool of self-creation. Nick Carraway's first images of Gatsby come from the extravagant lawn parties where caterers mount "enough colored lights to make a Christmas tree of Gatsby's enormous garden."[31] The lights conjure up the mood of grand spectacle for Gatsby's guests, who equate the parties with Coney Island amusement. His lights advertise Gatsby's success to the world, and making them more intensely visible makes that success *seem* more real—and more able to fascinate and draw Daisy to him from across the bay. They blaze brighter the closer he comes to regaining her, and brightest on the night a rendezvous is arranged. Gatsby's spectacular lighting asserts the self he has fabricated, multiplies his sense of worth, and answers Daisy's green light flashing at him across the bay. Gatsby *believed* in that green light, Nick Carraway concludes, "the orgiastic future that year by year recedes before us."[32]

From this juncture, the web of allusive connection to Ellison's worldview and fictional universe, if not absolutely straightforward, can be readily demonstrated, so some shorthand should serve to bring this excursion to a close. Ellison connected himself to Hemingway and Fitzgerald and their "lost generation" peers partly through a counterpointing sense of novelistic mission: "Ours is a task," he wrote, which, "whether recognized or not, was defined for us to a large extent by that which the novels of the twenties failed to confront, and implicit in their triumphs and follies were our complexity and our travail."[33] In *Invisible Man*, Ellison confronted the modernist tropes of electrification in Hemingway's "A Clean, Well-Lighted Place" and Fitzgerald's *The Great Gatsby* with revisionary narrative riffs bright with counterpointing implication, and anchored in the particular experience of technology and its social contexts that mark three centuries of African American life in the alloy bowels of the machine. Ellison reiterated through the years that this experience marked black men and women themselves as being hypermodern, self-fabricated creations, as far from the "primitives" of popular stereotype as Mumford's utopian "neotechnic" age is from Neolithic ooze. Alongside all the other things it would become, *Invisible Man* would also constitute a gloss on the techniques and technological consciousness of the American novel, from the Golden Day to the Jazz Age and beyond, and Ellison's fictive experiment in revolutionary technological

30. Nye, *Electrifying America*, 284.
31. F. Scott Fitzgerald, *The Great Gatsby* (New York: Scribner's, 1925), 39.
32. Fitzgerald, *The Great Gatsby*, 182.
33. Ellison, *Going to the Territory*, 257.

modernity would indeed carefully heed the little man at Chehaw Station's goad to incorporate the experience of multifarious "others" into its own and, with the combinatory energy of plural truths, to synthesize new thresholds of consciousness.

The famous framing prologue of Ellison's novel nigrifies, hyperbolizes, and renders comically surreal and ironic the controlling motifs of Hemingway's "clean, well-lighted place," something Robert O'Meally's work on the Hemingway-Ellison connection suggested some years ago.[34] That prologue created an entirely new kind of figure in American literature—a theory- and concept-toting, gadget-fabricating black "thinker-tinker,"[35] kin to Ford, Edison, and Franklin, and sufficiently deft with the techniques of electrification to shunt off enough purloined electricity from Monopolated Light & Power's local station to charge the 1,369 lightbulbs Jack-the-Bear has wired the ceiling of his underground retreat with to shed light on his invisibility. And with that creation Ellison rejected the social and spiritual assumptions on which the violence, social cynicism, and understatement in Hemingway's work were based—assumptions rendered questionable to Ellison by his place in the social order. "Light confirms my reality," Jack-the-Bear tells us, "gives birth to my form" (*IM*, 6). But the insight that has led him to this consciousness he has won from the master of formlessness, Bliss Proteus Rinehart, that "spiritual technologist" and man of multifarious parts who, with electrified guitar music and glowing neon signs—dark *green* neon signs—fishes Harlem street corners for "marks" ready to "Behold the Invisible" (*IM*, 495).

Rinehart orchestrates the Ellisonian riff on Gatsby's green light, with the scene of electric illusion transported from Gatsby's hyper-illuminated manicured lawns to Rinehart's Harlem storefront, "where a slender woman in a rusty black robe played passionate boogie-woogie on an upright piano along with a young man wearing a skull cap who struck righteous riffs from an electric guitar which was connected to an amplifier that hung from the ceiling above a gleaming white and gold pulpit. . . . The whole scene quivered vague and mysterious in the green light" (*IM*, 376). Both Jack-the-Bear's and Rinehart's "spiritual technologies" suggest one final facet of Ellison's fictive confrontation with the myth of the machine and the forms of the

---

34. See Robert O'Meally, "The Rules of Magic: Hemingway as Ellison's 'Ancestor,'" *Southern Review* 21 (1985): 751–69.
35. Ralph Ellison, *Invisible Man*, 2d international ed. (New York: Vintage, 1995), 7. Hereafter, quotations will be cited parenthetically as *IM*.

novel that we should bear in mind. That will to personal power and agency, which their shared facility with electrical power mirrors, manifests itself most directly in Jack's and Rinehart's *inventiveness*, their experimental *ingenuity*. "When you have lived invisible as long as I have, you develop a certain ingenuity. I'll solve the problem," Jack tells us (*IM*, 7). Unlike Rinehart, "that confidencing sonofabitch" whose own ingenuity knows no moral boundaries, Jack-the-Bear commits himself to community. And if in projecting himself as a "thinker-tinker" kin to Ford, Edison, and Franklin, we presume *that* community of the ingenious to be something alien to his own race, Ellison hints at one last underground illumination from his people's underground history. In the prologue, Jack-the-Bear makes a point of having wired his ceiling "not with fluorescent bulbs, but with the older, more-expensive-to-operate kind, the *filament* type. An art of sabotage, you know" (*IM*, 7).

Ellison *knew* from his early 1940s research and writing labors alongside Roi Ottley, Waring Cuney, Claude McKay, and company for the WPA manuscript project which culminated in the publication of *The Negro in New York* (1967) that, despite disclaimers to the contrary which rendered black technological innovators historically invisible,

> the bewildering array of technical inventions, which altered human life within a brief span, found Negroes in the vanguard. . . . But the machine age, which did so much to bring about divisions in the ranks of labor, put men out of work and caused protest from sections of the laboring population, [and] also brought whites new reasons to bolster their hatred of blacks. . . . When the "third rail" was invented [the electrified metal rail system which carries current to the motor of an electric railway or subway car] and electricity replaced steam on the elevated railways in this city, the white men, who lost their jobs as steam locomotive engineers because of the innovation, heaped all manner of abuse on the whole Negro race because its inventor was a Negro. After its installation, Negroes were not safe on the streets of New York. They were frequently attacked by persons aware only that a new-fangled electric device invented by some "damn nigger" had taken away their jobs. Violence subsided only when the company finally rehired the old engineers and taught them the new job of motormen. The inventor, Granville T. Woods, a native of Ohio, had arrived in New York in 1880 and soon after invented a system by which telegraphing was made possible between trains in motion, technically known as "induction telegraph." During the next thirty

years, until he died in New York City in 1910, he perfected twenty-five inventions, . . . was employed by Thomas Edison . . . and while working at his laboratory . . . the American Bell Telephone Company purchased his electric telephone transmitter.[36]

Moreover, one of Woods's black thinker-tinker peers, Louis Latimer, a draftsman who was the son of an escaped slave, not only made the drawings for the first Bell telephone from a design by Alexander Graham Bell but subsequently superintended the installation of the electric lighting systems of Philadelphia, of several Canadian cities, and of London, as well as of New York City itself—as *The Negro in New York* details. Though the "collective authorship" of this Harlem-based Federal Writers Project compendium effaces specific contributions by individual writers, the pertinent passage in *The Negro in New York*, with notably Ellisonian markers of diction, phrasing, and style, reveals that Latimer had patented his own pioneering electric lightbulb as early as 1881, that he became associated with Thomas Edison in 1896, and that, as a member of the "Edison Pioneers," it was he, the "Black Edison," who perfected the revolutionary carbon *filament*, which made the intense, smokeless, fireless, glowing orange "Edison light" throw off an illumination unlike anything seen before—and which fuels Jack-the-Bear's prologue epiphany.

The spiritual resolve and ingenuity of these invisible black theory and concept-toting technological innovators are what both Ellison and his nameless narrator have claimed in kinship; and the unrecompensed transgenerational spiritual costs of their world-altering electrodynamic "enlightenment" are what Jack-the-Bear's guerrilla war levies against Monopolated Light & Power. Ultimately for him, acts of sabotage and the writer's art of psychic illumination become inseparable facets of his own "spiritual technology"; and for us as readers, they become the underground laboratory site of one more "electrifying" Ellisonian joke—evidence that, waking or dreaming, in this thinker-tinker's theory and concept-toting world of high fidelity and calculated distortion, the ways of invisibility remain willfully and invariably mysterious, their wonders to perform.

36. Roi Ottley and William Weatherby, eds., *The Negro in New York: An Informal Social History, 1626–1940* (New York: Praeger Publishers, 1969), 140–43.

## Toward a Critical Genealogy of the U.S. Discourse of Identity: *Invisible Man* after Fifty Years

*Jonathan Arac*

### 1

I start with a key moment late in Ralph Ellison's *Invisible Man*, published in 1952. The moment comes near the end of the Harlem riot, a few pages before the protagonist falls underground, just before he transfixes with a spear the Afrocentric, Black nationalist agitator Ras, who is in turn hoping to hang our hero for allying himself to the white-directed Brotherhood. In a single sentence, the narrator sets himself against all the powers the book has conjured. These forces map as "un-American," subaltern-American, and hegemonic-American. They include Jack and the Brotherhood, which is a fictional group modeled on the Communist Party; they include Bledsoe, the president of the college for Negroes the narrator had been expelled from, modeled on Booker T. Washington's Tuskegee, which Ellison had attended; and they include the WASP establishment of Emerson and Norton. Here is the sentence:

My thanks to the many institutions that have sponsored, and the many colleagues who have discussed, earlier versions of this text given as talks, especially Herbert Grabes, who published some pages of this in the German publication *REAL* 17 (2001).

*boundary 2* 30:2, 2003. Copyright © 2003 by Duke University Press.

> I looked at Ras on his horse and at their handful of guns and rec-
> ognized the absurdity of the whole night and of the simple yet con-
> foundingly complex arrangement of hope and desire, fear and hate,
> that had brought me here still running, and knowing now who I was
> and where I was and knowing too that I had no longer to run for or
> from the Jacks and the Emersons and Bledsoes and Nortons, but
> only from their confusion, impatience, and refusal to recognize the
> beautiful absurdity of their American identity and mine.[1]

This passage signposts one beginning for a discursive cluster, involving
*identity*, that is still alive, and troubling, today.

My inquiry is still work in progress, the protraction of a beginning com-
menced long ago and extended through the publication of several books.
For my thoughts cast themselves again in the mode of critical genealogy:
I want to think about the 1950s—and, you will see, from there back to the
1930s—because I need this past in order to think about our time. This selective presentism tries to find somewhat obscure moments of the past that,
when brought to the present, both receive illumination and themselves cast
light.

My inquiry takes the form of critical genealogy, but also my topic
continues a problem I had defined in the last chapter of my book entitled
*Critical Genealogies*. I argued then, in 1987, that the impasses of American critical thinking would not be worked through until we had gotten ourselves straight with the thirties. I was thinking of the ways in which accu-
sations, from left and right alike, of communism and fellow traveling had
dug scars so deep that it seemed thought could not cross the barriers.
More broadly, the 1930s' political structure of Popular Front versus Fascism
seemed to prefigure the animosity in the 1980s between populist intellectual
ambitions of the Rainbow Coalition and the avant-garde tendencies associated with poststructuralism. In *Criticism and Social Change* (1983), Frank
Lentricchia tried to diminish the then powerful appeal of Paul de Man by
recovering the rhetorical criticism of Kenneth Burke, which was arguably
equally radical—in the sense of fundamentally challenging—but certainly
more left oriented. By 1987, some months after my *Critical Genealogies* had
appeared, the world learned that de Man had been closer to fascism than
any of us had known, or for the most part imagined, and in the nineties,
scholars went back to first editions to discover that Burke was closer to
communism than had been understood. Michael Denning, in his extraor-

1. Ralph Ellison, *Invisible Man* (1952; reprint, New York: Random House, 1992), 550.

dinary and controversial *The Cultural Front* (1996), developed the case for this more deeply left-affiliated Burke, whom Denning designated "a leading American Marxist of the 1930s" and "the major cultural theorist of the Cultural Front."[2]

Moreover, my *"Huckleberry Finn" as Idol and Target* (1997) itself is oriented around issues from the thirties in at least two crucial respects. First, I argue there that the hypercanonization of *Huckleberry Finn* in the 1940s was made possible by the downgrading of its rival, *Uncle Tom's Cabin*, and that this in turn was enabled via the critique of the genre of "protest novel," which had been developed by *Partisan Review* critics in the thirties as tools against two cultural forms sponsored by the Communist Party: proletarian fiction and popular front fiction. Lionel Trilling's put-down of John Steinbeck's "popular front" *Grapes of Wrath* (1939) and James Baldwin's of Richard Wright's "proletarian" *Native Son* (1940) illustrates this point. Second, the case for hypercanonization required an integral and basically positive relation between *Huckleberry Finn* and American culture. This relation was defined in the thirties by the right-affiliated critic Bernard DeVoto (Edmund Wilson's 1937 diptych, "American Criticism, Left and Right," counterposed DeVoto to Communist criticism).[3]

Let me contextualize DeVoto's impact. Mark Twain died in 1910, and in 1920, the new-model intellectual Van Wyck Brooks, a Harvard contemporary of T.S. Eliot's, authored a psychobiographical cultural critique, *The Ordeal of Mark Twain*, which suggested that Twain should be left behind as America grew up. Measured on the scale of great English and French writers—he names Jonathan Swift, Voltaire, and Charles Dickens—Brooks argued, Twain failed to achieve a major body of satiric art. In Brooks's analysis, Twain lost his outsider's radical perspective through his eagerness to be accepted by the dominant, genteel, corporate culture. For Brooks, because Twain was so widely read and loved, he provided an apt symptom for diagnosis of the national malady.

To answer Brooks involved a judgment of American culture as well as of Twain. DeVoto provided this in his 1932 *Mark Twain's America*, which concludes with an admonitory memento. As opposed to the optative mood motivating Brooks, whose America is still to be wished into being, DeVoto

2. Michael Denning, *The Cultural Front: The Laboring of American Culture in the Twentieth Century* (London: Verso, 1996), 444, 445.

3. Edmund Wilson, "American Criticism: Left and Right," originally in the *New Republic*, 1937, reprinted in his *The Shores of Light: A Literary Chronicle of the Twenties and Thirties* (New York: Farrar, Straus and Young, 1952), 640–61.

asserts a perfect indicative: "There is, remember, such an entity. It seems necessary to explain that America has existed, has had a past."[4] DeVoto was a figure in American letters and scholarship who is still not reckoned at his full consequence. He was the first real scholar of Twain; after *Mark Twain's America*, in 1942, he published an archivally based genetic study, *Mark Twain at Work*.[5] But there was much more: From 1935 until his death in 1955, DeVoto was the "Editor's Easy Chair" columnist for *Harper's*; before being denied tenure at Harvard, he had contributed to the founding of its doctoral program in American civilization, which occurred in 1937; and in the 1940s, he was a Pulitzer Prize–winning and best-selling historian of the American frontier. DeVoto, along with Constance Rourke's 1931 *American Humor: A Study of the National Character*, helped make available the meaning Ellison gave the term *American* in the passage I began from.[6]

Ellison now, nearly a decade after his death and almost ninety years after his birth, is a figure of compelling actuality in American culture. In the niche known as literary fiction, the major publishing event of 1999 was the appearance of Ellison's second novel, *Juneteenth*, which proved to raise controversy beyond the scope of this essay to address. My concern now is the public framing of its arrival. It was excerpted in the *New Yorker* and heralded in the *New Republic*, which devoted over twenty pages of multicolumn fine print to a review essay on Ellison's career by Shelby Steele and the first publication of materials from Ellison's collected correspondence, tantalizing bits from nearly sixty years of his adulthood. The nineties had already begun to seem the Ellison decade when in the wake of a *New Yorker* feature celebrating his eightieth birthday—by chance appearing just before his death—the Modern Library issued a volume of nearly nine hundred pages bringing together Ellison's *Collected Essays*. Is there another American critic so attractively and inexpensively compiled?

For the fortieth anniversary of *Invisible Man*, in 1992, the Modern

---

4. Bernard DeVoto, *Mark Twain's America* (Boston: Little, Brown, 1932), 321.

5. For more on DeVoto's crucial role in the study of Twain, see Jonathan Arac, "The Birth of Whose Nation? The Competing Claims of National and Ethnic Identity and the 'Banning' of *Huckleberry Finn*," in *Claiming the Stones/Naming the Bones: Cultural Property and the Negotiation of National and Ethnic Identity*, ed. Elazar Barkan and Ronald Bush (Los Angeles: Getty Research Institute, 2002), 306–9.

6. Ellison cites Rourke, for example, in "Society, Morality, and the Novel" (1957), "Change the Joke and Slip the Yoke" (1958), and his review essay on Leroi Jones's *Blues People* (1964). See *The Collected Essays of Ralph Ellison*, ed. John F. Callahan (New York: Random House, 1995), 103, 287, 703, 718.

Library had issued a handsome text of that novel and after Ellison's death commissioned a new foreword by novelist Charles Johnson, winner of the National Book Award and a MacArthur Fellowship. Johnson's essay sets the keynote for Steele's *New Republic* piece, but I'm sure that each is sincerely recounting true experience: They both emphasize that as young, culturally ambitious African Americans in the later 1960s, they were taught—largely by peer pressure—that Ellison offered nothing they should want, but each discovered, to the contrary, that Ellison was right on. Two themes emerge from these materials: the individual against the restrictions of groupthink, and Ellison's integrationist emphases against the separatist tendencies of Black Power and Black Arts. To rephrase these: the good of self-identity as a citizen, versus the bad of group identity as a minority. This impoverished choice between liberalism and identity politics is what today's most important thinking is trying to leave behind.

I can tell my own brief tale here, too. As a student in the era of the Vietnam War, I found Ellison's patriotic commitment to the idea of America more than I could abide. I had initially, around 1963, read *Invisible Man* with great excitement and admiration, but I turned away from it and him for decades, only returning to Ellison shortly before his death, when it became clear that he was a necessary part of my work on *Huckleberry Finn*. And yet these years of my distance from Ellison were also the years in which *Invisible Man* became the most canonical work of African American fiction. By 1975, for instance, it was taught at Princeton in a one-semester freshman general education course on American literature that made room for it by omitting *Moby-Dick*. Toni Morrison has certainly replaced Ellison as the most taught African American novelist, but I don't know that even *Beloved* has displaced *Invisible Man* as the most taught novel. It is striking that Steele's *New Republic* piece makes its case for Ellison via critique of *Beloved* as one more protest novel, repeating the gesture by which Baldwin had put down Wright fifty years earlier.

Let me offer two more brief registrations of Ellison's currency. The Pulitzer Prize–winning historian Leon F. Litwack recently published a massive study of black Southerners in the age of Jim Crow, that is, from 1890 to 1940. The book's first sentence reads, "Nowhere is the paradox of black life in the United States more graphically revealed than in Ralph Ellison's portrayal of the black odyssey in *Invisible Man*," and the first two and a half pages of the preface unroll from there in a discussion of the novel, awarding it the ultimate accolade, "No historian could have improved upon the scene."[7] The literary scholar Meili Steele published recently *Theorizing Textual Subjects: Agency and Oppression.* You can get a feel for the ambition and range of this fairly short but intensely serious book if I cite the titles of chapters three and four: "Language, Ethics, and Subjectivity in the Liberal/Communitarian Debate" and "Truth, Beauty, and Goodness in James's *The Ambassadors.*" The fifth chapter, which wraps up the argument and brings forward a solution, is "The Subject of Democracy in the Work of Ralph Ellison." It seems "we" now think Ellison can do everything for us: fictionalize, historicize, theorize.

In marking the extraordinary prestige that has accrued to the figure of Ellison as a subject for speculative discussion, I do not want to suggest that I find his work uninteresting or of poor quality, but there are important differences between what it means to read a text and what it means to stage a figure, and there may be more staging than reading going on.

Thinking about Ellison is part of figuring out how the thirties remain fruitful and nagging. *Invisible Man,* published in 1952 and presenting itself as of its moment, places the beginning of its action back some twenty years, and in the progress of the action there is nothing to indicate that the Second World War is ever reached. So it is set in the thirties, though it is part of its craft to make its temporal placement somewhat vague, even as much of its geography is very precise. And "the Brotherhood" in the novel, the theoretically directed, highly disciplined, left-wing agitation group to which the narrator belongs for nearly half the novel, offers an image of the Communist Party. To understand the novel, we must understand it as in large part an interpretation and representation of the thirties. It has been called an "'epoch-making'" novel in "the strict sense"; that is, "by its range of stories and corresponding attitudes," it "sums up an era."[8] Part of its richness for study now is that it condenses so much not only of the 1930s but also of the 1950s.

*Invisible Man* is also related to the thirties by its position in the world of literature. It is not a protest novel, though it has sometimes been read that way; as a negative bildungsroman that brings its protagonist close to politically explosive events without fully involving him in them, it is more like Flaubert's *Sentimental Education* than like the thirties' type. In its some-

7. Leon F. Litwack, *Trouble in Mind: Black Southerners in the Age of Jim Crow* (New York: Knopf, 1998), xi, xii.

8. Kenneth Burke, "Ralph Ellison's Trueblooded Bildungsroman," in *Speaking for You: The Vision of Ralph Ellison,* ed. Kimberly Benston (Washington, D.C.: Howard University Press, 1987), 350.

times weird and frequently dissociated first-person narration, *Invisible Man* is closer to the romantic genre that we can title from Gogol "The Diary of a Madman"—a thirties' exemplar of this would be Jean-Paul Sartre's *Nausea* (1938). Yet Denning argues persuasively that a fundamental gesture of thirties' left culture was to invite first-person narratives from a range of voices that would not have conventionally been thought worthy of authoring themselves. That is, he presents the thirties as the first wide-scale American multiculturalism. He redefines "proletarian literature" not as a genre but as what he calls, after Raymond Williams, a "literary formation."[9] From this point of view, Ellison's associations with *New Challenge*, *New Masses*, and the Federal Writers' Project place him squarely in the "cultural front."[10] And Ellison knew this. Once he became famous, he was in many essays and interviews equivocal about his relation to thirties' left culture, so further excavation and elucidation remain necessary, but the contours are clear.

Ellison is very clear about one debt he owes to the thirties, even though that clarity then requires further development. In his critical essays, one theorist is cited and alluded to more than any other: Kenneth Burke. This is not a secret. In Ellison's first collected volume of nonfictional writings, *Shadow and Act* (1964), the acknowledgments begin with his "special indebtedness to Stanley Edgar Hyman, with whom I've shared a community of ideas and critical standards for two decades, and to Kenneth Burke, the stimulating source of many of these."[11] So Ellison names himself and Hyman as sharing in ideas largely drawn from Burke, and, indeed, Hyman's 1948 book on what were then recent developments in literary and cultural criticism, *The Armed Vision*, devotes its culminating chapter to Burke as the figure who combines and shows how to carry forward the resources of this early, and perhaps now largely forgotten, phase of the theory movement. Ellison's chronology here takes himself and Hyman and Burke back into the 1940s, but in a 1977 interview, Ellison places his relation to Burke a good deal earlier and defines its importance very strikingly.

As he first came north to New York from Tuskegee in the summer of 1936, Ellison brought with him many things, but he encountered several specific areas of culture and politics that challenged him: "Marx and Freud were the dominant intellectual forces during that period, and I had become aware

9. Denning, *Cultural Front*, 201–3.
10. By far the fullest documentation and analysis of Ellison in this context appeared only after this essay was written. See the major new biography of Ellison's earlier life by Lawrence Jackson, *Ralph Ellison: The Emergence of Genius* (New York: Wiley, 2002).
11. Ellison, *Collected Essays*, 60.

of Freud even before finishing high school. Marx I encountered at Tuskegee—but how did you put the two together? I didn't know, so I read, I talked, I
asked questions and I listened. Such ideas concerned me as I turned from
music to literature."[12] Burke, in Ellison's account, made it possible to achieve
this connection. In the interview, he emphasizes that he learned from Burke
nothing about the craft of writing; it was a way of thinking that he learned, a
matter of what we now call *theory*: "What I learned from Burke was not so
much the technique of fiction but the nature of literature and the way ideas
and language operate in literary form." Here is Ellison's summary of the key
encounter:

> I first became interested in Burke after hearing him read his essay,
> "The Rhetoric of Hitler's Battle." It was a critique of *Mein Kampf*, and
> the time was 1937. I was absolutely delighted because in the essay,
> he made a meaningful fusion of Marx and Freud, and I had been
> asking myself how the insights of the two could be put together. . . .
> I began to grasp how language operates, both in literature and as
> an agency of oral communication. In college and on my own, I had
> studied a little psychology, a little sociology . . . but Burke provided a
> *Gestalt* through which I could apply intellectual insights back into my
> own materials and into my own life.[13]

Burke's essay on Hitler is an early instance of what we now call critical cultural studies, the close linguistic analysis of a mass-circulated contemporary
work in order to discern its (re)sources of power. The essay first appeared
in the *Southern Review*, edited from Louisiana State University by Cleanth
Brooks and Robert Penn Warren. Burke could please these Southern, conservative New Critics even while working with Marx and Freud—the interdisciplinary resources of theory that sixty years later are still the names of
our problems if not of our answers. Burke and Warren had become friends
in active intellectual exchange even earlier than Burke and Ellison, back in
the 1920s. So the authors of the two most important American midcentury
novels of political oratory, Warren's *All the King's Men* (1946) and *Invisible
Man*—both set in the thirties—were both in close dialogue with the most
notable left-wing critical analyst of Hitler's rhetoric.

I do not think it is widely registered in our contemporary critical aware-

12. *Conversations with Ralph Ellison*, ed. Maryemma Graham and Amritjit Singh (Jackson:
University Press of Mississippi, 1995), 346.
13. *Conversations with Ralph Ellison*, 363–64.

ness that Burke was, to the best of my knowledge, the first English-language critic to make extended, crucial use of the terms *identity* and *identification*.[14] He understood these terms as drawn from the repertory of psychoanalysis, and he used them both for matters of textual rhetorical analysis and for thinking larger social questions. The major point of reference is Freud's *Group Psychology and the Analysis of the Ego* (1921, translated 1922). If Constance Rourke and DeVoto helped establish the *American* for Ellison, Burke provided resources for a discourse of *identity*.

In Burke's 1937 *Attitudes toward History* (by *history* he means "primarily man's life in political communities"), he devotes ten pages in his "Dictionary of Pivotal Terms" to *Identity* and *Identification*.[15] The beginning of this discussion I find very strong:

> All the issues with which we have been concerned come to a head in the problem of identity. Bourgeois naturalism in its most naïve manifestation made a blunt distinction between "individual" and "environment," hence leading automatically to the notion that an individual's "identity" is something private, peculiar to himself. And when bourgeois psychologists began to discover the falsity of this notion, they still believed in it so thoroughly that they considered all collective aspects of identity under the head of pathology and illusion.[16]

Even though Burke had allied himself rhetorically with Marxism by his pejorative use of *bourgeois* to characterize the dominant strands of current thought, the Marxist journal *Science and Society* severely criticized *Attitudes toward History*, and Burke replied with "Twelve Propositions on the Relation between Economics and Psychology" (explaining that "economics and psychology" should be glossed as "'Marx and Freud'").[17] Here he explains directly the analytic function of his conception of identity: "The purely psychological concept for treating relations to symbols of authority, possession and dispossession, material and spiritual alienation, faith or loss

14. Burke's usages are earlier than any registered in the excellent "keywords"-like essay by Philip Gleason, "Identifying Identity: A Semantic History" (1983), reprinted in Werner Sollors, ed., *Theories of Ethnicity: A Classical Reader* (New York: New York University Press, 1996): 460–87.

15. Kenneth Burke, *Attitudes toward History*, rev. 2d ed. (Boston: Beacon Press, 1961), first page of unpaginated introduction.

16. Burke, *Attitudes toward History*, 263. The text is unchanged from the 1937 first edition.

17. Kenneth Burke, *The Philosophy of Literary Form: Studies in Symbolic Action* (1941), 3d ed. (Berkeley and Los Angeles: University of California Press, 1973), 305.

of faith in the 'reasonableness' of a given structure's methods and purposes and values, is that of 'identity.'"[18]

## 2

Insofar as Ellison's narrator, in the passage from which I began, names his identity as "American" and both "their[s] . . . and mine," he seems to agree with Burke that "identity is *not* individual."[19] Nonetheless, the reception of Ellison, and to a large degree Ellison himself, tends in a more individualistic direction. To help illuminate this issue in Ellison, to which I shall return in my final pages, I shift over to a second strand of identity discourse, also deriving from Freud, and perhaps also in dialogue with Burke, emerging from the thirties but reshaped by both World War and Cold War.

Before engaging with these further materials, it may be helpful to reflect on some of the fault lines in the meaning and usage of the term *identity*. In our current usage, the term seems wholly ambivalent along the axis of necessity and freedom: The term is used to name both what you can't help being and also what you choose to become. No doubt this saturation of the spectrum is one cause for the term's appeal. In its history as a term, *identity* has undergone transformation and reversal. Its fundamental sense is *sameness*, but it is nowadays understood within a discourse of difference. An OED citation from South Africa in the 1920s shows an understanding of "identity politics" absolutely opposite to what we would expect. The writer contrasts the "policy of subordination" and the "policy of identity." The policy of identity is faulted because it "refuses to acknowledge any real difference between Europeans and natives"—that is, it treats them as identical to each other.

A strange duplicity in the functioning of the term *identity* arises as we reflect on *Invisible Man*, and this complication needs untangling for Ellison to become most useful in our times. It could be said that *Invisible Man*, and Ellison's work as a whole, marks the cultural high point of the movement in U.S. life signified by the term *Integration* (a key Burke term). It was only in the 1890s, a full generation after the Civil War, that the Supreme Court authorized, in the case of *Plessy v. Ferguson*, the constitutionality of the "separate but equal" principle that undergirded American racial segregation. Elli-

18. Burke, *Philosophy of Literary Form*, 306; italics in original.
19. Burke, *Attitudes toward History*, 263.

son was born in the era understood to mark the nadir of relations between American whites and the no longer enslaved African Americans, a time, therefore, also when new commitments were being forged to equality. For instance, it was just a few years before his birth that the National Association for the Advancement of Colored People (NAACP) was founded. *Invisible Man* appeared just before the 1954 Supreme Court decision in *Brown v. Topeka Board of Education*, which declared the separate but equal principle no longer to hold. The period in which the canonical status of *Invisible Man* rapidly took hold was the decade of what we now call the Civil Rights Movement. But by the middle sixties, a challenge to liberal, integrationist goals and procedures had arisen among African Americans—what was sloganized as "Black Power." Ellison took a lot of heat for what became evident as his uncompromising resistance to the cultural and political program of racial separatism. So on behalf of an ideal of integration, Ellison resisted what we have come to call "identity politics."

But, we have seen, Ellison was profoundly committed to the idea of America. Like Martin Luther King Jr., he summoned the actually existing United States to transform itself in accord with its own stated principles of human equality, principles and statements that had themselves arisen out of revolutionary and civil warfare. His resistance to identity politics did not prevent him from affirming, and exploring, an American identity.

Burke, we have seen, took his starting premises on identity from Freud, yet the great terminological reference work for psychoanalysis by Jean Laplanche and J.-B. Pontalis has no entry for or discussion of identity. Its major entry is for *identification*. I quote the primary definition in full: "psychological process whereby the subject assimilates an aspect, property or attribute of the other and is transformed, wholly or partially, after the model the other provides. It is by means of a series of identifications that the personality is constituted and specified."[20] (It is sobering to find that the three key terms in this definition—*subject, other, personality*—have no entry; we must recognize that even the most characteristic notions within psychoanalysis, as is true for any discipline, are enmeshed in far larger philosophical and ideological networks.) Freudian *identification*, in this definition, is not a fixity but a "process"—transformative, disruptive, and productive. In conclusion, Laplanche and Pontalis emphasize that a "subject's

20. Jean Laplanche and J.-B. Pontalis, *The Language of Psychoanalysis* (1967), trans. Donald Nicholson-Smith (New York: Norton, 1973), 205.

identifications viewed as a whole are in no way a coherent relational system"—that is, the "whole" is that of an overdetermined, symptomatic structure, not an expressive totality.[21]

So where does the privilege of the term *identity* come from? I think from modern American social science, in a scholarly project across disciplines that flourished for several decades after World War II. I intend no nativist gesture like the current retrieval of pragmatist philosophy (which has also claimed Burke).[22] Rather, I aim to retrace a formation that rather suddenly lost its place, leaving a blank for the emergence of what we now know as Cultural Studies in the United States.[23] So I describe my undertaking as genealogical because it emphasizes discontinuity, the way a term changes meaning as it changes context, and because it points to sources that (I think) cause some discomfort to acknowledge.

What become the key texts and terms for the production of new knowledge have quite oblique relations to predecessors in a different discursive field, even when they echo each other. Many of the questions and hopes of current cultural studies repeat a major interdisciplinary project in the midcentury American social sciences. Already in the 1930s, the anthropological conception of culture began to achieve wide currency, marked by the great success of Ruth Benedict's *Patterns of Culture* (1934).[24] And after the war, to take one instance, at Harvard, Talcott Parsons from sociology, Clyde Kluckhohn from social anthropology, and Henry Murray from clinical psychology, with others, not only established major collaborative advanced research agendas but also inaugurated an undergraduate major

21. Laplanche and Pontalis, *Language*, 208.
22. For an example of such nativism, see the otherwise valuable essay by Timothy L. Parrish, "Ralph Ellison, Kenneth Burke, and the Form of Democracy," *Arizona Quarterly* 52, no. 3 (1995): 119. Parrish cites the relative neglect of Burke as proof that "American intellectuals prefer foreign accreditation to homegrown wisdom," and he plays down the extent to which Burke's value to Ellison came from his conjoining two European thinkers.
23. My sense of (inter-)disciplinary amnesia is strengthened by an important recent essay in intellectual history: David A. Hollinger, "The Disciplines and the Identity Debates, 1970–1995," in *American Academic Culture in Transformation*, ed. Thomas Bender and Carl E. Schorske (Princeton, N.J.: Princeton University Press, 1998), 353–71. Hollinger rightly emphasizes the emergence in the early seventies of a new discourse on identity that has been decisively important over the last several decades, but he gives no hint that this replaced a prior discourse hinged on the same key term.
24. On the "'discovery' of the concept of culture" in the 1930s, see Warren I. Susman, *Culture as History: The Transformation of American Society in the Twentieth Century* (New York: Pantheon, 1985), 153–58.

called "social relations" in the belief that a newly comprehensive, symboli-
cally mediated knowledge of human culture and society was possible.[25]

At Yale, the historian David Potter saw the challenge, and opportunity, for history in what he recognized as the emergence of "the term 'culture' in a new sense."[26] He saw the disciplines of psychology, sociology,
and anthropology as converging in this new sense of culture and as thereby
empowered to "displace history as the primary study of man" (xix). While the
behavioral sciences gained explanatory power through their emphasis on
"the nursery, the bathroom, and the bedroom" (65), historians were stuck.
The primacy of great-power politics had yielded to a democratic need to
include "the total experience of a people" (29), but the only familiar nonpoliti-
cal category for defining a people, that of race, had been wholly discredited
by Hitler, and yet the "compulsions of the medium" of narrative historiogra-
phy required a "unifying device" (30) by which historians could make their
subjects cohere. Potter concluded, "The concept of culture has given to the
study of society the same integrating effect which the Freudian concept of
the personality has given to the study of the individual" (35), and to rival
these, he proposed a conception of "national character."

Before leaving Potter, let me highlight the features in his discourse
that motivated my particular citations. I find it striking that this historian's historian, who won his reputation for political studies of the longer- and shorter-
term causes of the U.S. Civil War, had already by the early 1950s recognized
the crisis of narrative history, the need to construct conceptually a new subject of history if narrative were to be preserved, and the attractions of subject
areas drawn from intimate everyday life. His analysis was wholly prescient,
although his solution had little effect.

More broadly influential than Potter was Erik Erikson, who, in the
work that made his name, put the term "national characters" in scare quotes
and explained that he preferred "to call them . . . national identities."[27] This
was in 1950, shortly before Ellison's use of "American identity" in *Invisible*

25. Henry Murray importantly assisted the career of Erik Erikson in its early days, and
Parsons brought Burke to teach a graduate seminar in 1967, which I audited for several
meetings. On Murray and Erikson, see Robert Coles, *Erik H. Erikson: The Growth of His
Work* (Boston: Little, Brown, 1970), 33, 36.
26. David M. Potter, *People of Plenty: Economic Abundance and the American Character*
(Chicago: University of Chicago Press, 1954), 35. Subsequent quotations from this book
in this paragraph are cited parenthetically.
27. Erik H. Erikson, *Childhood and Society* (1950), 2d ed., rev. and enlarged (New York:
Norton, 1963), 285.

*Man.* Erikson—a failed artist and émigré lay psychoanalyst, trained by Anna Freud—mobilized the term *identity* to bring together culture and personality in his founding of the interdisciplinary zone known as psycho-history. I will refer here only to his first two books, *Childhood and Society* (1950) and *Young Man Luther* (1958), subtitled *A Study in Psychoanalysis and History*. Let me offer one telling example of the impact of Erikson's work. In Edward Said's first published piece on Palestinian politics and culture, dating back to the 1960s, he quotes almost a page from *Young Man Luther* on "identity crisis" to help characterize the then current moment in "Palestinian experience."[28]

Like Potter, Erikson mapped his place in relation to new developments in knowledge. Both Potter and Erikson posed the goal of a comprehensive integration that would advance knowledge by disciplinary transformation. Erikson placed his project in relation to three levels: the body, the self, and society, and therefore in relation to "three different scientific disciplines—biology, psychology, and the social sciences."[29] He regretted that "our thinking is dominated by this trichotomy," but he acknowledged that this limitation arises "because only through the inventive methodologies of these disciplines do we have knowledge at all." Nonetheless, any knowledge is "tied to the conditions under which it was secured," namely, in these cases: "the organism undergoing dissection or examination; the mind surrendered to experiment or interrogation; social aggregates spread out on statistical tables." At this point in his rhetoric, Erikson sounds surprisingly like Michel Foucault, but his direction is different. By conjoining disciplines, Erikson sought to restore the "total living situation." This holism joins Erikson's project closely to what has often been felt to be the distinctive value of literature.

Erikson's notion of identity was first formulated as what he called "ego-identity."[30] He is part of neo-Freudian ego-psychology, which puts him on the other side from Laplanche and Pontalis. For Erikson claimed that "psychosocial identity develops out of a gradual integration of all identifications. . . . [H]ere, if anywhere, the whole has a different character from the sum of its parts."[31] And for those parts, in a way wholly familiar in our dis-

---

28. Edward W. Said, *The Politics of Dispossession: The Struggle for Palestinian Self-Determination, 1969–94* (New York: Pantheon, 1994), 15. He dates the essay "1968–69."
29. All quotations in this paragraph are drawn from Erikson, *Childhood and Society*, 36–37.
30. Erikson, *Childhood and Society*, 42.
31. Erikson, *Childhood and Society*, 241.

course but, the OED suggests, quite new at the time, Erikson used all of the following adjectives to modify *identity*: cultural, ethnic, racial, religious, sexual, tribal—but also, emerging. And yet for all these differencings, the core meaning of identity for Erikson was "the ability to experience one's self as something that has continuity and sameness."[32]

Despite Erikson's brave stand against the University of California loyalty oath in 1950,[33] his project was enabled by the state's mobilization of intellectuals for national security. In developing his arguments for conceptualizing "group identities" analogously to individual identities, he drew on two major studies he had done. The first study was on Germany, "written for a U.S. government agency at the beginning of World War II, in preparation for the arrival of the . . . first Nazi prisoners."[34] This piece on "Hitler's Imagery and German Youth" appeared a few years after Burke's study of Hitler and is also an interpretive reading of *Mein Kampf*.[35] Erikson's second group study was on Russia, from work at Columbia's Research Project in Contemporary Cultures, "sponsored by the Office of Naval Research."[36] In evoking the loss of older, "primitive," "exclusive," "feudal," or "agrarian" identities in the face of "world-wide industrialization, emancipation, and wider communication,"[37] Erikson took his sense of history from modernization theory and from a sense of America's world-historical role: "We begin to conceptualize matters of identity at the very time in history when they become a problem. For we do so in a country that attempts to make a super-identity out of all the identities imported by its constituent immigrants; and we do so at a time when rapidly increasing mechanization threatens these essentially agrarian and patrician identities in their lands of origin as well."[38] In developing his

32. Erikson, *Childhood and Society*, 42.
33. See Coles, *Erik H. Erikson*, 155–58. In 1952, Burke's affiliations of the thirties made him too hot for the University of Washington. See the summary in Ellen W. Schrecker, *No Ivory Tower: McCarthyism and the Universities* (New York: Oxford University Press, 1986), 267, and for intriguing detail, *The Selected Correspondence of Kenneth Burke and Malcolm Cowley*, ed. Paul Jay (Berkeley and Los Angeles: University of California Press, 1990), esp. 306–13.
34. See Erik Homburger Erikson, "Hitler's Imagery and German Youth," *Psychiatry* 5 (1942): 475–93. Erikson here uses terms derived from the verb *to identify* but does not use *identity*. There is a useful discussion of this essay in Lawrence J. Friedman, *Identity's Architect: A Biography of Erik H. Erikson* (New York: Scribner, 1999), 166–72.
35. Erikson, *Childhood and Society*, 327.
36. Erikson, *Childhood and Society*, 359.
37. Erikson, *Childhood and Society*, 262, except for the term *exclusive*, which comes from 237.
38. Erikson, *Childhood and Society*, 282.

signature term *identity crisis*, Erikson boldly claimed his terrain: "The study of identity . . . becomes as strategic in our time as the study of sexuality was in Freud's."

These features of imperial totalization in Erikson's work explain why it has been, so far as I know, forgotten in the recent movement for cultural studies in the United States, and why, therefore, it may be repeated, perhaps in staging the figure of Ellison. As is also true of Ellison, there are features in Erikson's work that make it worth actively remembering. For example, when Erikson proposes the notion of the "psycho-historical," he avows the "risk [of] impurity . . . inherent in the hyphen" and thus ventures an identification without the security of identity. This new and impure undertaking is not harmonious and integrated; Erikson places himself amidst "the compost heap of today's interdisciplinary efforts."[39]

In explaining the genesis of his book on Luther, Erikson maps a complex temporality. In 1956, he was in Germany, at the invitation of Theodor W. Adorno, to commemorate Freud's centenary:

> When speaking about Freud to the students . . . , I remembered an event in my own early years, a memory which had been utterly covered by the rubble of the cities and by the bleached bones of men of my kind in Europe. In my youth, as a wandering artist, I stayed one night with a friend in a small village by the upper Rhine. His father was a Protestant pastor; and in the morning, as the family sat down to breakfast, the old man said the Lord's Prayer in Luther's German. Never having "knowingly" heard it, I had the experience, as seldom before or after, of a wholeness captured in a few simple words, of poetry fusing the esthetic and the moral: those who have suddenly "heard" the Gettysburg Address will know what I mean.[40]

Wrapped between Erikson's awareness of the "bleached bones" of German genocide and his evocation of Gettysburg and the slaughter of Americans, this anecdote of the man in his fifties recovers the joy of the man in his twenties in finding, as if for the first time, something forgotten from childhood. Between acknowledging his Jewish identity at the beginning of the anecdote and brandishing his American identity at the end, in the middle Erikson rediscovers a German identity. This uncanny repetition and multiplication of identities rejoins Burke's theory; one of his Twelve Propositions

---

39. Quotations in this paragraph come from Erik H. Erikson, *Young Man Luther: A Study in Psychoanalysis and History* (New York: Norton, 1958), 16.
40. Erikson, *Young Man Luther*, 10.

states that "the individual is composed of many 'corporate identities.'"[41] It rejoins, too, some of the actual practice of Ellison's novel, if not the rather balder position taking that makes the thirties of *Invisible Man* so much a product of the fifties.

## 3

I conclude by sketching a reading of *Invisible Man* that follows out the novel's argument on behalf of Cold War liberalism but that also finds in Ellison's text turbulences that open different possibilities. The figure framing my reading of Ellison is Walter Benjamin. In his "Theses on the Philosophy of History," composed after the Molotov-Ribbentrop Pact of 1939, Benjamin offered a horrified critique of the ideology of progress, which he grasped as undergirding the current sense of history from the bourgeoisie through the Social Democrats to the Communists. Ellison, too, writes into his novel a critique of progress, for the myth of progress belying the reality of catastrophe has long marked the history of African Americans in the United States.[42] *Invisible Man* discredits the terms *history* and *progress* and proposes in their stead the term *identity*. Perhaps, however, *identity* is just another modality of *progress*—replacing the myths of racial uplift and of communism with the myth of America. Yet Ellison's work also does something more than recuperate *progress*, and in this something more I find also a resonance with Benjamin, perhaps mediated through André Malraux, with whose work Ellison had become familiar by 1935 and whom he never failed to praise.

*Invisible Man* takes the form of a first-person account by its unnamed narrator, beginning with a prologue, set in the present time of 1952. The prologue establishes the trope of invisibility and begins to explore its ramifications, leading to an inquiry into how the character came to be as he is. The narrator goes back twenty years to follow his path from high school graduation in the Jim Crow South of the 1930s and his expulsion from a college modeled on the Tuskegee Institute, founded by Booker T. Washington, leading to his relocation to Harlem, where he becomes an agitational speaker on behalf of "the Brotherhood," a group modeled on the Communist Party. Having broken party discipline in response to the police murder

41. Burke, *Philosophy of Literary Form*, 307.
42. See Stephen Steinberg, "Up from Slavery: The Myth of Black Progress," *New Politics* n.s., 7, no. 1, whole no. 25 (summer 1998): 69–81; and for several specific examples close in time and milieu to Ellison, see Jonathan Arac, *"Huckleberry Finn" as Idol and Target* (Madison: University of Wisconsin Press, 1997), 12.

of Tod Clifton, an African American comrade, he is under party judgment as Harlem erupts into a riot, stirred by Ras the Exhorter, a West Indian Black Nationalist. In the course of the riot, fleeing for his life, the narrator falls into a coal cellar—which has been his base of operation ever since. After this account in twenty-five chapters and more than five hundred pages, the novel returns to the present with an epilogue.

In the prologue, the narrator strikes a keynote: "Beware of those who speak of the spiral of history; they are preparing a boomerang. Keep a steel helmet handy."[43] The spiral, a Hegelian figure of historical progress, adapted in many variants of Marxist discourse, and criticized by Benjamin in thesis XIII, gets reconfigured as a painful, even dangerous form of closure. The move from spiral to boomerang also enacts a discursive shift, from jargon to vernacular, in which the agency of retribution (the boomerang) comes from an incorporated, minoritized Other.[44] In the first chapter, the discourse of progress is specified in the context of "separate but equal" racism. On the narrator's high school graduation day, as valedictorian, he "delivered an oration in which I showed that humility was the secret, indeed, the very essence of progress" (17). And at college, the chapel oration concludes by invoking an "ever unfolding glory, the history of the race a saga of mounting triumphs" (131).[45] The ambiguities, even treacheries, within this discourse are figured in the meeting with the college president: "Suddenly he reached for something beneath a pile of papers, an old leg shackle from slavery which he proudly called 'a symbol of our progress.' 'You've got to be disciplined, boy,' he said" (138–39). The symbol of progress equally betokens oppression, and, as manipulated by the president, it seems to threaten the narrator with renewed subjection.

In his disillusionment after the murder of Tod, the narrator reflects, "My god, what possibilities existed! And that spiral business, that progress goo! . . . And that lie that success was a rising *upward*" (501–2). Here the figure of the Hegelian spiral and the language of progress are brought explicitly together and contrasted negatively to the world of "possibilities." The discourses of progressive history are thus represented as closing off

---

43. For a valuable essay that touches on some of the same topics as mine but to quite different overall purpose, see Robert G. O'Meally, "On Burke and the Vernacular: Ralph Ellison's Boomerang of History," in *History and Memory in African-American Culture*, ed. Geneviève Fabre and Robert O'Meally (New York: Oxford University Press, 1994), 244–60.
44. Ralph Ellison, *Invisible Man* (New York: Modern Library, 1992), 6. Subsequent references to this edition are cited parenthetically in the text.
45. Litwack, *Trouble in Mind*, offers many citations of, and some commentary on, such rhetoric. See the index under *uplift*; *progress* is not indexed.

possibility. This theme is resumed even more explicitly in the epilogue: "Like almost everyone else in our country, I started out with my share of optimism. I believed in hard work and progress. . . . But my world has become one of infinite possibilities" (566–67). Optimism is discarded but not replaced with pessimism; the text suggests that possibility, as freedom, is beyond any -*ism*: "Until some gang succeeds in putting the world in a strait jacket, its definition is possibility" (567).

The novel criticizes progressive history as exclusionary. In his very first conversation with Jack, his mentor in the Brotherhood, the narrator is told: "You mustn't waste your emotions on individuals, they don't count. . . . They're like dead limbs that must be pruned away so that the tree may bear young fruit, or the storm of history will blow them down anyway" (284–85). In the course of the riot, the narrator is impressed by a person named Dupre, who is leading a group in the looting of a building: "He was a type of man nothing in my life had taught me to see, to understand, or respect, a man outside the scheme until now. . . . The men worked in silence, now, like moles deep in the earth. Time seemed to hold" (538). Dupre was a lumpen to the Marxists, and a relic of shame to the Negro ideology of uplift, but at this crisis he is dynamic and effective. He and his men are described in language that resonates from Marx's revolutionary echo of Hamlet's "old mole," and this moment of profound category shifting, of schema breaking, stops time's designated trajectory, as is linguistically enacted in the tension between the past-tense narration and the reiterated "now." I think of Benjamin's contrast between the "homogeneous, empty time" of historicism and the explosive *Jetztzeit*.[46]

Thomas Pynchon's *Gravity's Rainbow*, motivated to large degree by reflection on Max Weber's "iron cage,"[47] adapted a rare term from Puritan theological discourse to name those who don't count, who are outside the scheme: the "preterite," those whom God had passed over. Ellison, like Pynchon, understands that historical preterition is an effect of power:

> History records the patterns of men's lives, they say. . . . All things, it is said, are duly recorded—all things of importance, that is. But not quite, for actually it is only those events that the recorder regards as

46. Walter Benjamin, "Theses on the Philosophy of History," in *Illuminations*, ed. Hannah Arendt, trans. Harry Zohn (New York: Schocken, 1969), 261.

47. Weber's great closing image in the *Protestant Ethic* is derived from the figure of "a man in an iron cage," in John Bunyan, *The Pilgrim's Progress*, part 1 (1678) (New York: New American Library, 1964), 38–39. Bunyan's footnote to his text explains, "despair is like an iron cage."

important that are put down, those lies his keepers keep their power
by. But the cop would be Clifton's historian, his judge, his witness,
and his executioner. . . .

I stood there with the trains plunging in and out, throwing blue
sparks. What did they ever think of us transitory ones? Ones such as
I had been before I found Brotherhood—birds of passage who were
too obscure for learned classification, too silent for the most sensitive
recorders of sound; and too distant from the centers of historical decision to sign or even to applaud the signers of historical documents.
We who write no novels, histories or other books. (432)

The narrator's, and Ellison's, act of writing intervenes to shift this structure.
More broadly, it is a recurrent claim of the novel as a form that it is the mode
by which subaltern history may be written more effectively than by those
means that power certifies as fact.

Ellison, again like Pynchon, stages scenes in which his narrator is
moved to reflect on alternative configurations of history. After the murder of
Tod, the narrator becomes aware of black street life in a way that neither
his education nor the Brotherhood had prepared him for, and he surmises a
role for the "boys" of the street: "What if Brother Jack were wrong? What if
history was a gambler, instead of a force in a laboratory experiment, and the
boys his ace in the hole? What if history was not a reasonable citizen, but a
madman full of paranoid guile and these boys his agents, his big surprise! . . .
For they were outside, in the dark . . . running and dodging the forces of history, instead of making a dominating stand" (434). In the spirit he invokes,
the narrator, in phrases I have withheld until now, breaks the decorum of his
own prose with punning, pathos, and echolalic play on the signifier: They
were "in the dark with Sambo, the dancing paper doll; taking it on the lambo
with my fallen brother, Tod Clifton (Tod, Tod)" (434). One hears now the German word for *death* in Tod's name. The epilogue affirms the importance of
all those "in the loud clamoring, semi-visible world, all that world seen only
as a fertile field for exploitation by Jack and his kind [that is, revolutionaries],
and with condescension by Norton and his [that is, the power elite], who
were tired of being mere pawns in the futile game of 'making history'" (565).
The narrator finally proclaims his own ignorance and indifference concerning the course of history. He does not know whether what he has learned
"has placed me in the rear or in the *avant-garde*." "*That*," he says, "is a lesson for history, and I'll leave such decisions to Jack and his ilk while I try
belatedly to study the lessons of my own life" (565).

This turn to the lessons of one's own life is sloganized in the book by the term *identity*, from which I began. In a proleptic experience early in his time in Harlem, the narrator encounters a street vendor of yams, and memories arise of the South he has left behind, culminating in a famous heteroglossic moment: "I yam what I am" (260), a tautology of identity that echoes the voice of God to Moses from the burning bush and also the words of the popular cartoon character Popeye the Sailor Man, while insisting as well on an African American inflection. We may now recall the climactic assertion of identity. In a single sentence, the narrator sets himself against all the powers the book has conjured, including Jack and the Brotherhood, Bledsoe the college president, and the WASP establishment of Emerson and Norton: "I looked at Ras on his horse and at their handful of guns and recognized the absurdity of the whole night and of the simple yet confoundingly complex arrangement of hope and desire, fear and hate, that had brought me here still running, and knowing now who I was and where I was and knowing too that I had no longer to run for or from the Jacks and the Emersons and Bledsoes and Nortons, but only from their confusion, impatience, and refusal to recognize the beautiful absurdity of their American identity and mine" (550). There is a bit more work to do, however schematically, before I conclude.

First, the discourse of identity and the discourse of history interact in the book's master trope of *invisibility*. Invisibility is the figure for the difference between identity as self-possession ("I am who I am") and as dispossession ("how they see me"), and in this text *dispossession* specifically means being (un)seen as preterite.

But in the language of seventeenth-century American Puritanism, there is another master trope that Ellison adapts: that of the jeremiad. The Americanist Sacvan Bercovitch has shown in the *American Jeremiad* (1978) that this form, originally a sermon of social lament, has a more powerful ideological force: It asserts the glorious model of "America" against the dreadful shortcomings of what I will call "actually existing Americanism."

Ellison employs this jeremiad strategy as the narrator, in the epilogue, thinks over the mystifying advice offered by his dying grandfather in the book's first pages: "He *must* have meant the principle, that we were to affirm the principle on which the country was built and not the men. . . . Did he mean say 'yes' because he knew that the principle was greater than the men, greater than the numbers and the vicious power and all the means used to corrupt its name?" (564). This is Ellison the patriot, who supported the Vietnam War.

Yet there remains an element that if not irrecuperable at least offers other possibilities. When Benjamin wrote that "the concept of progress has to be grounded in the idea of catastrophe,"[48] at least one reasonable gloss on "catastrophe" is "capitalism." And amidst all that Ellison shows of the misery produced by capitalism and the structures of racism by which it has flourished in the United States, he also recognizes in the new, commercial modes of popular entertainment made possible by new media forms a force that changes what history means and does. In the midst of street life after Tod's death, the narrator continues his reflections on the preterite who had escaped, he thought, even the most sensitive recorders of sound: "They'd been there all along, but somehow I'd missed them. . . . They were outside the groove of history, and it was my job to get them in, all of them. . . . I moved with the crowd, sweat pouring off me, listening to the grinding roar of traffic, the growing sound of a record shop loudspeaker blaring a languid blues. I stopped. Was this all that would be recorded? Was this the only true history of the times, a mood blared by trumpets, trombones, saxophones and drums, a song with turgid, inadequate words? My mind flowed" (436). Ellison supported himself while writing *Invisible Man* by freelancing as a hi-fi technician. The vinyl record gives a new meaning to the "groove" of history, as Ellison, the trumpet player and jazz critic, brushes against the Benjamin of the "reproducibility" essay.

48. Der Begriff des Fortschritts ist in der Idee der Kastastrophe zu fundieren. See Walter Benjamin, "Central Park," trans. Lloyd Spencer, *New German Critique*, no. 34 (1985): 50; and "N [Theoretics of Knowledge; Theory of Progress]," trans. Leigh Hafrey and Richard Sieburth, *Philosophical Forum* 15 (1985): 21.

# Books Received

Alexis, Jacques Stephen. *In the Flicker of an Eyelid*. Trans. Carrol F. Coates and Edwidge Danticat. Charlottesville: University of Virginia Press, 2002.

Anderson, William S., and Lorina N. Quartarone, eds. *Approaches to Teaching Vergil's Aeneid*. New York: Modern Language Association of America, 2002.

Barton, H. Arnold. *Sweden and Visions of Norway: Politics and Culture, 1814–1905*. Carbondale: Southern Illinois University Press, 2003.

Bean, Jennifer M., and Diane Negra, eds. *A Feminist Reader in Early Cinema*. Durham, N.C., and London: Duke University Press, 2002.

Beaulieu, Jill, and Mary Roberts, eds. *Orientalism's Interlocutors: Painting, Architecture, Photography*. Durham, N.C., and London: Duke University Press, 2003.

Berman, Sabina. *The Theater of Sabina Berman: The Agony of Ecstasy and Other Plays*. Trans. Adam Versényi. Carbondale: Southern Illinois University Press, 2003.

Bhagwati, Jagdish, ed. *Going Alone: The Case for Relaxed Reciprocity in Freeing Trade*. Cambridge: MIT Press, 2002.

Bloom, Clive. *Bestsellers: Popular Fiction since 1900*. New York: Palgrave, 2002.

Bloom, John, and Michael Nevin Willard, eds. *Sports Matters: Race, Recreation, and Culture*. New York: New York University Press, 2002.

Bloom, Marcus. *The Road of Excess: A History of Writers on Drugs*. Cambridge: Harvard University Press, 2002.

Brady, Mary Pat. *Extinct Lands, Temporal Geographies: Chicana Literature and the Urgency of Space*. Durham, N.C., and London: Duke University Press, 2002.

Brandom, Robert B. *Tales of the Mighty Dead: Historical Essays in the Metaphysics of Intentionality*. Cambridge: Harvard University Press, 2002.

Canagarajah, A. Suresh. *A Geopolitics of Academic Writing*. Pittsburgh, Penna.: University of Pittsburgh Press, 2002.

Carr, Robert. *Black Nationalism in the New World: Reading the African-American and West Indian Experience*. Durham, N.C., and London: Duke University Press, 2002.

Casteñeda, Claudia. *Figurations: Child, Bodies, World*. Durham, N.C., and London: Duke University Press, 2003.

Castleman, David. *Death Is My Shepherd*. White Bear Lake, Minn.: Artword, 2002.

Cazdyn, Eric. *The Flash of Capital: Film and Geopolitics in Japan*. Durham, N.C., and London: Duke University Press, 2002.

Craciun, Adriana. *Fatal Women of Romanticism*. New York: Cambridge University Press, 2003.

Dain, Bruce. *A Hideous Monster of the Mind: American Race Theory in the Early Republic*. Cambridge: Harvard University Press, 2002.

Doane, Mary Ann. *The Emergence of Cinematic Time: Modernity, Contingency, the Archive*. Cambridge: Harvard University Press, 2002.

Elliott, Michael A. *The Culture Concept: Writing and Difference in the Age of Realism*. Minneapolis: University of Minnesota Press, 2002.

Elliott, Michael A., and Claudia Stokes, eds. *American Literary Studies: A Methodological Reader*. New York: New York University Press, 2003.

Eng, David L., and David Kazanjian, eds. *Loss*. Berkeley: University of California Press, 2003.

Feldman, Jessica R. *Victorian Modernism: Pragmatism and the Varieties of Aesthetic Experience*. New York: Cambridge University Press, 2002.

Felman, Shoshana. *The Juridical Unconscious: Trials and Traumas in the Twentieth Century*. Cambridge: Harvard University Press, 2002.

Freedman, Carl. *The Incomplete Projects: Marxism, Modernity, and the Politics of Culture*. Middletown, Conn.: Wesleyan University Press, 2002.

Fubini, Riccardo. *Humanism and Secularization: From Petrarch to Valla*. Durham, N.C., and London: Duke University Press, 2003.

Greaney, Michael. *Conrad, Language, and Narrative*. New York: Cambridge University Press, 2002.

Hungerford, Amy. *The Holocaust of Texts: Genocide, Literature, and Personification*. Chicago: University of Chicago Press, 2003.

Iwabuchi, Koichi. *Recentering Globalization: Popular Culture and Japanese Transnationalism*. Durham, N.C., and London: Duke University Press, 2002.

Kellman, Tila L. *Figuring Redemption: Resighting Myself in the Art of Michael Snow*. Waterloo, Ontario: Wilfrid Laurier University Press, 2002.

Laughlin, Charles A. *Chinese Reportage: The Aesthetics of Historical Experience*. Durham, N.C., and London: Duke University Press, 2002.

Lavendar, Bill, ed. *Another South: Experimental Writing in the South*. Tuscaloosa: University of Alabama Press, 2003.

Lentricchia, Frank, and Andrew Dubois, eds. *Close Reading: The Reader*. Durham, N.C., and London: Duke University Press, 2003.

Miller, Nicholas Andrew. *Modernism, Ireland, and the Erotics of Memory*. New York: Cambridge University Press, 2002.

Naas, Michael. *Taking on the Tradition: Jacques Derrida and the Legacies of Deconstruction*. Palo Alto, Calif.: Stanford University Press, 2002.

Opdahl, Keith M. *Emotion as Meaning: The Literary Case for How We Imagine*. Lewisburg, Penna.: Bucknell University Press, 2002.

Pease, Donald E., and Robyn Wiegman, eds. *The Futures of American Studies*. Durham, N.C., and London: Duke University Press, 2002.

Polkinhorn, Harry, and Mark Weiss, eds. *Across the Line / Al Otro Lado: The Poetry of Baja California*. San Diego: Junction Press, 2002.

Punday, Daniel. *Narrative after Deconstruction*. Albany: State University of New York Press, 2002.

Rajan, Tilottama. *Deconstruction and the Remainders of Phenomenology: Sartre, Derrida, Foucault, Baudrillard*. Palo Alto, Calif.: Stanford University Press, 2002.

Roberson, Matthew. *1998.6*. Normal and Tallahassee, Fla.: FC2, 2002.

Sanders, Mark. *Complicities: The Intellectual and Apartheid*. Durham, N.C., and London: Duke University Press, 2002.

Sedgwick, Eve Kosofsky. *Touching Feeling: Affect, Pedagogy, Performativity*. Durham, N.C., and London: Duke University Press, 2003.

Shimakawa, Karen. *National Abjection: The Asian American Body Onstage*. Durham, N.C., and London: Duke University Press, 2003.

Stivale, Charles J. *Disenchanting Les Bon Temps: Identity and Authenticity in Cajun Music and Dance*. Durham, N.C., and London: Duke University Press, 2002.

Terán, Ana Enriqueta. *The Poetess Counts to 100 and Bows Out: Selected Poems*. Trans. Marcel Smith. Princeton, N.J.: Princeton University Press, 2003.

Valis, Noël. *The Culture of Cursilería: Bad Taste, Kitsch, and Class in Modern Spain*. Durham, N.C., and London: Duke University Press, 2002.

Weston, Kath. *Gender in Real Time: Power and Transience in a Visual Age*. New York: Routledge, 2002.

Wiegman, Robyn, ed. *Women's Studies on Its Own: A Next Wave Reader in Institutional Change*. Durham, N.C., and London: Duke University Press, 2002.

# Contributors

Jonathan Arac is Harriman Professor and chair of the Department of English and Comparative Literature at Columbia University and also a member of the *boundary 2* editorial collective. His publications include *Critical Genealogies: Historical Situations for Postmodern Literary Studies* (1987) and *"Huckleberry Finn" as Idol and Target: The Functions of Criticism in Our Time* (1997). His essay in this issue is the beginning of a larger inquiry into the emergence of identity as a major term in American intellectual discourse.

Kevin Bell is an assistant professor of English and comparative literary studies at Northwestern University. He works in philosophical aesthetics, British and American literary modernisms, and African American literature and film. He has just completed a book manuscript entitled *The Language of Wanting: Aesthetic Modernism and the Critique of Identitarian Violence*.

Adam Gussow is an assistant professor of English and southern studies at the University of Mississippi. For twelve years, he was the harmonica-playing half of Satan and Adam, a Harlem-based duo that toured internationally and recorded three albums on the Flying Fish label. Gussow's first book, *Mister Satan's Apprentice: A Blues Memoir* (1998), won the Keeping the Blues Alive Award in Literature from the Blues Foundation in Memphis. His second book, *Seems Like Murder Here: Southern Violence and the Blues Tradition*, was published last year.

Ronald A. T. Judy is professor of English at the University of Pittsburgh, where he teaches courses related to the fields of American literature and culture, African literature, Arab literature, contemporary Islamic thought, global English studies and literature, as well as literary theory, with a particular focus on modernism. He is a member of the editorial collective of *boundary 2*, and was the guest editor of a special issue of *boundary 2* on the philosophy of W. E. B. Du Bois, entitled *Sociology Hesitant: Thinking with W. E. B. Du Bois*, which was awarded second place in the category of Best Special Issue of 2001 by the Council of Editors of Learned Journals.

He is currently completing a book project tentatively called *The Last Negro or the Destruction of Categorical Thought: An Experiment in Hyperbolic Thinking.*

Robert G. O'Meally is Zora Neale Hurston Professor of Literature at Columbia University and has been the director of Columbia's Center for Jazz Studies since 1999. He is the author and editor of numerous books, including *The Craft of Ralph Ellison* (1980), *Living with Music: Ralph Ellison's Essays on Jazz*, and *The Jazz Cadence of American Culture* (1998), which was awarded the Deems Taylor Prize by the American Society of Composers, Authors and Publishers in 1999. O'Meally was nominated for a Grammy, for his work as coproducer of the five-CD box set called *The Jazz Singers* (1998). He lives in New York with his wife Jacqui Malone and their sons Douglass and Gabriel.

Donald E. Pease is the Avalon Foundation Chair of the Humanities at Dartmouth College. The author of *Visionary Compacts: American Renaissance Writing in Cultural Context* and the editor of eight volumes including *The American Renaissance Reconsidered, Cultures of United States Imperialism* (with Amy Kaplan), *Revisionary Interventions into the Americanist Canon, Postnational Narratives*, and, most recently, *The Futures of American Studies*, Pease is the general editor for the New Americanists book series at Duke University Press, the founding director of the Summer Institute for American Studies at Dartmouth, and the head of Dartmouth's Liberal Studies Program. In the Hilary term of 2001, Pease served as the Visiting Drue Heinz Professor of American Literature at Oxford.

Barry Shank teaches comparative ethnic and American studies in the Department of Comparative Studies at Ohio State University. His new book, *A Token of My Affection: A Cultural History of American Greeting Cards*, is forthcoming. He is beginning an investigation of the sonic strategies of abstraction and embodiment in the music of Yoko Ono.

Hortense Spillers is the Frederic J. Whiton Professor of English at Cornell University. During academic year 2002–2003, she was a guest professor in the Program in Literature at Duke University. A collection of her essays, *Black, White, and in Color: Essays on American Literature and Culture*, was published in April 2003. She is at work on a new project called "The Idea of Black Culture."

Kenneth Warren is the William J. Friedman and Alicia Townsend Friedman Professor in the Department of English at the University of Chicago. His second book, *So Black and Blue: Ralph Ellison and the Occasion of Criticism*, will be published in September 2003.

Alexander G. Weheliye is assistant professor of English and African American studies at Northwestern University, where he teaches African American and Afro-diasporic literature and culture, critical theory, and cultural studies. Currently, he is completing a book manuscript entitled *Phonographies: Grooves in Sonic Afro-Modernity*, which explores sound recording and reproduction and its impact on twentieth-century black culture, including literary, musical, and cinematic art. His work has been published in *Amerikastudien/American Studies*, *CR: The New Centennial Review*, and *Social Text*.

John S. Wright is the Morse-Amoco Distinguished Teaching Professor of African American & African Studies and English at the University of Minnesota, and the Faculty Scholar for the Archie Givens Sr. Collection of African American Literature & Life. His publications include *A Ralph Ellison Festival* (1980), coedited with poet Michael Harper; *A Stronger Soul within a Finer Frame: Portraying African-Americans in the Black Renaissance* (1990); and the extended essay on African American intellectual life in the multivolume *Encyclopedia of African American History and Culture* (1995). His long-range book project, *The Riddle of Freedom: TransAfrican Explorations in Cultural History and Cosmology*, is nearing completion.

# camera obscura

Since its inception, *Camera Obscura* has devoted itself to providing innovative feminist perspectives on film, television, and visual media. It consistently combines excellence in scholarship with imaginative presentation and a willingness to lead media studies in new directions. The journal has developed a reputation for introducing emerging writers into the field. Its debates, essays, interviews, and summary pieces encompass a spectrum of media practices, including avant-garde, alternative, fringe, international, and mainstream.

*Camera Obscura* continues to redefine its original statement of purpose. While remaining faithful to its feminist focus, the journal also explores feminist work in relation to race studies, postcolonial studies, and queer studies. In addition, its understanding of visual media has expanded to include discussions of newly developing imaging technologies, such as those being used in medicine.

Current special issues include "Marginality and Alterity in New European Cinema" and "Early Women Stars."

Photographs: Paramount and Twentieth Century–Fox

## Hit Me, Fred
Recollections of a Sideman
**FRED WESLEY JR.**
Foreword by Rickey Vincent
344 pages, 57 b&w photos, cloth $29.95

## Sound of Africa!
Making Music Zulu in a South African Studio
**LOUISE MEINTJES**
352 pages, 31 illustrations, 9 in color, paper $21.95

## Disintegrating the Musical
Black Performance and American Musical Film
**ARTHUR KNIGHT**
352 pages, 68 b&w photos, paper $21.95

## Forgotten Readers
Recovering the Lost History of
African American Literary Societies
**ELIZABETH McHENRY**
440 pages, 4 b&w photos, paper $18.95
*New Americanists*
*A John Hope Franklin Center Book*

## Games of Property
Law, Race, Gender, and Faulkner's *Go Down, Moses*
**THADIOUS M. DAVIS**
352 pages, 21 illustrations, paper $21.95

## Black Nationalism in the New World
Reading the African-American
and West Indian Experience
**ROBERT CARR**
384 pages, paper $21.95
*Latin America Otherwise*

# boundary 2

**Benjamin Now:**

**Critical Encounters with The Arcades Project**

Volume 30, Issue 1  March 2003
*Philip Rosen and Kevin McLaughlin, special issue editors*

*The Arcades Project* is the unfinished, final work of the influential cultural theorist, critic, and historian Walter Benjamin. Until 1999, this huge, unruly manuscript, which provides a more complete picture of the diversity of Benjamin's work than formerly available, had not been fully translated into English. "Benjamin Now" is the first collection of essays in English to focus on that text.

While this essential text's title refers to its ostensible subject—the nineteenth century shopping arcades of Paris—*The Arcades Project* is a mass of cultural, political, and social material presented in the form of a vast montage. "Benjamin Now" reconsiders the significance of Benjamin's theories and writings in light of this final project.

*Contributors: T. J. Clark, Howard Eiland, Peter Fenves, Tom Gunning, Michael Jennings, Claudia Brodsky Lacour, Kevin McLaughlin, Philip Rosen, Henry Sussman, Lindsay Waters, Samuel Weber, Peter Wollen*

U.S. $14 for single issues
U.S. $32 for individual subscriptions
U.S. $133 for institutional subscriptions

Outside the U.S. add $16 for postage

Available from Duke University Press
1-888-651-0122 (toll-free in the U.S. and Canada)
or 1-919-687-3602
www.dukeupress.edu